GRACIELA

Graciela

One Woman's Story of War,
Survival, and Perseverance
in the Peruvian Andes

Nicole Coffey Kellett
With Graciela Orihuela Rocha

University of New Mexico Press | Albuquerque

ISBN 978-0-8263-6353-4 (paper)
ISBN 978-0-8263-6354-1 (e-book)

Library of Congress Control Number: 2021953094

Founded in 1889, the University of New Mexico sits on the traditional homelands of the Pueblo of Sandia. The original peoples of New Mexico—Pueblo, Navajo, and Apache—since time immemorial have deep connections to the land and have made significant contributions to the broader community statewide. We honor the land itself and those who remain stewards of this land throughout the generations and also acknowledge our committed relationship to Indigenous peoples. We gratefully recognize our history.

Cover illustration by Felicia Cedillos
Designed by Felicia Cedillos
Composed in Adobe Garamond Pro 10.25/14.25

This book is dedicated to Graciela, her family, and her comuneros.

CONTENTS

ILLUSTRATIONS

ACKNOWLEDGMENTS

The roots of this book extend to my first introduction to the mountains of southcentral Peru and to Graciela; many people have made that journey possible. First, I owe a huge thank you to Brian Bauer for drawing both my husband and I to Andahuaylas. Thank you for inviting Lucas to work on your three-season archaeological field project and generously opening the field house to a nonarchaeologist who contributed absolutely nothing to your research: me. It was through your willingness to shelter me that I was able to make valuable connections for my dissertation research, which ultimately led me to Graciela. Thank you, Brian, for taking a chance on me, for continually supporting my research in Peru, and for your ongoing hospitality. Thank you to the entire archaeology team for your collegiality and patience, particularly Miriam Aráoz Silva and Carlo Socualaya Dávila. I send a heartfelt thank you to Sabine Hyland for your comradery in the field and your ongoing support of my research amid your busy life.

I would like to thank all the individuals at the microfinance organization, SOAR (pseudonym), with whom I collaborated for my initial research in the Andes, including the director, along with many others. Through my engagement with SOAR, I was introduced to the richness of life in and around Andahuaylas. To protect the confidentiality of the organization, I will not name individuals specifically, but I am particularly grateful to those who introduced me to Sacclaya and rural communities surrounding Andahuaylas. My work would not have been possible without each of you. I am forever indebted to what I consider my *comuneros* in Sacclaya who opened their community to my presence and constant inquiries. Specifically, I wish to thank Concepción Pocco Quispe, Claudia Merino Pocco, Donatila Merino Pocco, and Mónica Rojas Merino who housed and fed me for an entire year. I would have been truly lost without your kindness and enduring patience. Thank you to my neighbors in Sacclaya—Pío Pocco Olivares and Flora Rosales Quispe, along with their children, Yanet,

Rolfi, Alex, and Antoni—for making me feel welcome in the community. Thank you to our compadres Miguel Pocco Solano and Teufila Huasco Mallma and their children, Cinthia, Denis, Lizbet, Angel, Noé, and Abraan. Thank you also to our compadres Belisario Quispe Huasco and Maribel Rosales Quispe and their children, Briset and Karen, for your ongoing friendship. I am grateful to Henny Margoth Raygada Lazarte and Percy Barrio de Mendoza for our many conversations and the opportunity to rent your home while in Andahuaylas. Thank you to Nelva de la Cruz for patiently introducing me to the Quechua language, a language I continue to struggle to learn yet will always revere.

I am grateful for the friendships that have long anchored my husband and me in Andahuaylas. Thank you to Martha Luna Salcedo for our extended talks on your patio while drinking maté and eating sweet breads. You will forever be my "Peruvian mom" and I will always cherish the outfit you hand knit, which first clothed both of my children. I am grateful for the extended Luna family, including the late Mariano del Pilar Luna Rozas, Martha Salcedo de Luna, Martha Luna Salcedo, Gaby Luna Salcedo, Mariano Luna Salcedo, Rodrigo Luna Salcedo, Violeta Luna Salcedo, Igor Montoya Molero, and Hiliana Montoya Molero. Your family has supported mine in so many ways throughout the years and I am incredibly grateful our paths crossed. I am thankful for Maximiliana Mallma Medina, Maribel Sofia Mallma Medina, Ana María Mallma Medina, and Juan Elías Chávez Mallma. I am forever indebted to your family members in Lima who literally saved my parents while visiting Peru. Thank you for repeatedly opening your home to me and my family, offering a safe and nurturing base from which to conduct research for this project. I am incredibly appreciative of your friendship and encouragement throughout the years. Thank you to our compadres, godchildren, and their extended family in Pacucha, including Justiñano Arohuillca Oscco, Maria Buitron Junco, Froilan Marciel Arohuillca Buitrón, Rosa Huachohuillca Velasque, Wendy Frineth Arohuillca Huachohuillca, Brenda Sharmely Arohuillca Huachohuillca, Fray Zaniel Arohuillca Huachohuillca, Jaedy Magnori Arohuillca Huachohuillca, and Eder Arohuillca Buitron. My husband and I cherish our visits and are happy we have witnessed the growth of your beautiful family.

I would like to thank the Peruvian scholars who generously shared their time and invaluable insights with me while in Ayacucho, including Jose Coronel,

Ranulfo Cavero, Mariano Arones Palomino, Jefrey Gamarra Carillo, Oscar Fredy Castillo, and Fiorella Vera-Adrianzen. Thank you to Andrea Lombardi and Anael Pilares for your interest in the project. I would also like to thank Nelson Ernesto Pereyra Chavey and Alcides Berrocal Gonzales for putting me in touch with numerous other Andean scholars. It is my hope that we can continue to share experiences, questions, and insights regarding our shared interests in the Andes.

I owe my incredible mentors at the University of New Mexico immense gratitude for guiding me through the deep and complex literature of the Andes and for training in theory and methods of anthropology, but most importantly for ongoing moral and intellectual support. Thank you, Carole Nagengast, Louise Lamphere, and Les Field. Each of you provided the nurturance and pressure necessary to foster my love of anthropology and Peru. I would like to thank those at the University of New Mexico Press for their interest in and dedication to this book. I would like to thank John Byram for your initial enthusiasm for this story, Clark Whitehorn for quickly reviewing material and assuaging my concerns, and Sonia Dickey for supporting the manuscript through its final publication. Thank you to the reviewers for your detailed, insightful, and substantive feedback that guided me toward a much more informed and accessible final product. I would like to thank Max Altamirano Molero for his skillful eye and for allowing me to include his photographs in this book.

I thank the University of Maine at Farmington for financial backing and sabbatical release time, which made research for, and the finalization of, this book possible. I could not ask for better colleagues and friends. I wish to thank Kristen Case for providing vital feedback on drafts of this text, as well as for loving and invigorating writing retreats. I thank Linda Beck for ongoing support of my work and Brad Dearden for serving as interim director of International and Global Studies during my sabbatical release, making this project possible. I wish to thank colleagues and friends who provided keen insight and feedback on the manuscript, including Louise Lamphere and William Mitchell, as well as Emma Ansara, Stephanie Dunn, Lisa Hardy, Mary Schuller, Suzy Kellett, Gwen Kellett, and Dan Coffey. I would also like to thank those who provided key emotional support while in the field, including Jennifer O'Neill, Jodi Frager, Gwen Saul, Christina Getrich, and Shirley Heying, along with many others.

I thank my parents, Dan and Carol Coffey, as well as my sisters, Renee Lysthauge and Michele Lyons, for their unwavering care and support. Thank you to my spouse, Lucas, for making maps for this book and for your ongoing support. Without you, none of this would have begun, let alone come to fruition. You have been my anchor. Through all our trials and tribulations, you are the one I turn to, always, and you still make me laugh. Thank you to my dear daughter, Maya, and beloved son, Mason. Maya, you provided promise and comfort while living in Sacclaya. Mason, you were my post-PhD gift. You both are my . . . everything. Thank you to Graciela's family members who have generously supported this project and to those who shared their own stories, particularly Graciela's husband, brothers, and children, thereby greatly enhancing this book.

Lastly, I thank Graciela. Graciela, you have entrusted me with your story—a rare and precious gift. I thank you, your family, and your paisanos in Oronccoy for trusting me to share a vital, complex, and deeply personal history. Thank you, Graciela, for your friendship and for teaching me the power of love.

Introduction

Graciela, the War, and Memory

"Why must they read this book? I cannot explain it, Nicole. How can I direct them? Surely, it is important, right," Graciela said. I agreed that it is an important story but asked my friend, Graciela, why *she* thought it was significant.

> These violent problems happened . . . suffering, rapes, hunger, thirst, deserted we were sleeping, escaping the military. For fear of dying, we had to escape. Because the military came with their guns, with their knives and killed us. . . . They killed our paisanos [fellow countrymen/women] in this pueblo, our neighbors. There was chaos and we had to retreat, we had to leave our pueblo, our home. We had to retreat because they were killing us. For this, we were afraid. All of this I am telling because some countries, some towns, maybe have not had these problems happen that happened here with me and through reading they must learn.

When asked why people in Peru should read this book, Graciela had a different response:

> To my paisanos, to soothe [them]. All of this happened during these problems, all in different places. . . . We had all of this happen to all our families. Some of their children have survived. Some lost their mothers, their fathers, their brothers, their sisters, their grandparents. All of this they lost. This all happened. Forgetting all of this they must continue working, continue reacting. They must survive. They must triumph.

The violence, the loss, the trauma, and the perseverance that Graciela refers to relate to the actions of Sendero Luminoso, or the Shining Path—a Maoist guerrilla organization that gained currency in Peru in the 1980s and early 1990s—and the violent military backlash. Graciela's community was in the epicenter of a civil war, which caused the death of approximately seventy thousand and displacement of over six hundred thousand people (Comisión de la Verdad y Reconciliación 2003; hereafter CVR). This book provides a deeply personal perspective on the violent history of Peru. A history that people are increasingly forgetting before hundreds of thousands of silenced stories have had a chance to be told, including those of my friend Graciela. Graciela's story underscores not merely the brutality of the war and its undercurrents of racism, sexism, and classism but also the long-term impacts on the physical, mental, and economic health of survivors by fundamentally altering the social fabric of life in the rural Andes.

Graciela

Graciela was born in 1973, she has no formal job, and she has never had the opportunity to learn how to read or write. Her family resides throughout the country of Peru and Argentina, but she is from a small rural community, Oronccoy, in the Peruvian highlands. Oronccoy is in the Department of Ayacucho (La Mar Province) in a region known as the Oreja de Perro (ear of the dog, as it resembles the shape of a dog's ear on a map; see Figure 1). This region represents what the Peruvian Comisión de la Verdad y Reconciliación (CVR) declared to be the most traumatized area in all of Peru throughout its nearly two-decade civil war, which began in the early 1980s (CVR 2003; Jiménez 2009). Of the approximately three hundred families that once existed in Oronccoy, about forty-five remain; of the rest, some are lost to relocation, but many more died. At the age of eleven, Graciela fled her geographically and politically isolated community, ultimately ending up in Andahuaylas, Peru, where we first met.

Presently, Graciela can typically be found on the side of the road huddled on a short wooden stool, below a blue plastic tarp, behind a shiny, yet worn metal cart piled high with stalks of sugarcane to squeeze into sweet juice. She does not dress in what may be considered traditional Andean clothes, but she does not wear pants. She wears a skirt and a T-shirt, occasionally a blouse. She wears a

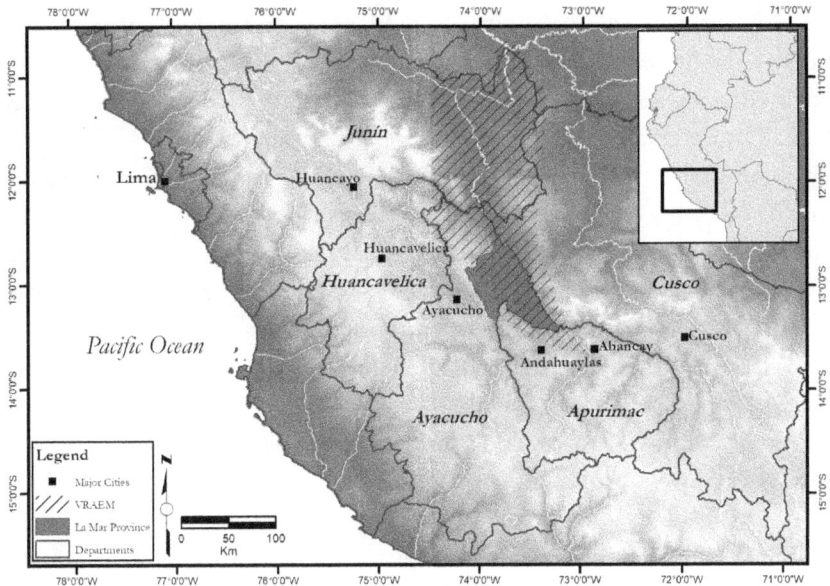

Figure 1. Map of southern Peru indicating departments
and primary cities described in the text. Map created by Lucas C. Kellett.

black-brimmed wool hat to guard against the sun and usually a sweater she knit herself. Graciela is typically carrying a brightly colored manta on her back filled with various goods needed throughout the day. Mantas are handwoven blankets that are typically woven on backstrap looms used to carry children or an assortment of goods (e.g., food, firewood, clothing, and chicha—homegrown maize beer). For shoes, Graciela usually wears *ojotas* (sandals) made of used car tires, identical to those of many others in the rural Andes. To a passerby, Graciela may appear to be a somber woman. When Graciela smiles, she normally covers her mouth to hide the fact that for every pregnancy she has had, six to date, she has lost a tooth.[1] Graciela's eyes appear above the rough, dry, sunbaked hand that covers her mouth. They are marked by a sense of sadness that momentarily escapes in unexpected bouts of laughter, which is one of the many characteristics that make it impossible to forget Graciela.

Typically, one or two of Graciela's children accompany her alongside the cart, as her husband, Juan Pablo, is usually working the fields in their rural community to provide the bulk of food necessary to sustain the family throughout the year. The traffic is always quite heavy in front of the cart because it lies alongside a busy road buzzing with moto-taxis in the city of Andahuaylas, Peru. Moto-taxis are a primary mode of public transportation in Andahuaylas. They consist of a motorcycle outfitted with a small, plastic shell covering a seat that comfortably fits three individuals. Andahuaylas hosts one of the largest open-air markets in Peru, which stretches approximately one mile along the edge of the Chumbao River. So, on market day, *día de la feria*, Graciela's cart sits in a corner on the far side of a colonial bridge to make way for vendors who have traveled to the city from surrounding rural communities to sell the widest range of goods imaginable.

Graciela's life experiences up to the point when we first became acquainted were physically etched onto her body. She embodied not only the traumatic events that had occurred throughout the years of violence but also the unequal relations that define the social fabric of Peruvian society. Graciela's position in life has shaped the way she carries herself, interacts with others in her social environment, and moves through the world. Graciela has long contended with ongoing stomachaches (chronic gastritis), headaches, and back pain. Much of this is likely exacerbated by standing for hours at a time pumping juice for customers or sitting on a small, hard, wooden stool. Yet her physical ailments are also testimony to a lifetime of experiences that have shaped Graciela's person.

It is Graciela's story, which she graciously and patiently shared with me, along with the emotions, the pain, the strength, and the larger context of life in the rural Andes, that we (Graciela and I) strive to share in this book. But why write about Graciela? The accounts of trauma in Peru and elsewhere are widespread, and while unique, they are not novel. What can one story tell us? Graciela's story is just one of hundreds of thousands from the so-called lost generation of Peru. We are writing her history because there are few accounts of women survivors and longitudinal perspectives of the devastating and enduring impacts of the war.

The direct experience of one survivor illustrates the confusion and trauma of a war in which there was not always a clear enemy or direct allies and demonstrates how the impacts of the unrest are long lasting. Graciela is unable to read or write because the violence abruptly ended educational opportunities in her community. Graciela and her family live in a mud brick house lying on a steep vertical cliff on the edge of the city of Andahuaylas, Peru, a region at risk of collapse in the next earthquake or major rainstorm. Yet, due to the devastation of her natal community during the war, she has few other options. In fact, owning a small piece of land and home in an emergency zone represents the greatest sense of stability Graciela has known since childhood.

Graciela's story demonstrates the deep-seated relations of social inequality that contributed to the political upheaval and continue to shape the lives of millions of Peruvians. The gulfs between criollo (ruling "white" class associated with the coast), mestizo (mixed Indigenous and Spanish), and campesino (rural Indigenous/agriculturalists) shaped the violation and salvation of Graciela and her family countless times and continue to influence opportunities and limitations for the hundreds of thousands of this lost generation. Graciela's life history illuminates the intersection of structural inequalities with gender relations, class divisions, ethnic conflict, and racism. Graciela's personal memories relay a compelling story about historical continuity and rupture in which the war disrupted not only individual lives but also communities and altered a fundamental sense of what it means to be human in the rural highlands of Peru.

To begin this introduction, I provide a background on the war, including long-standing racial relations and social dynamics within which the movement emerged, as well as postwar efforts at truth and reconciliation. This brief historical background offers context within which to better understand Graciela's story. I then describe the research and writing process behind this book and close with a discussion of politicized memory, positionality, and truth(s).

Brief Background and Guiding Ideology of Sendero Luminoso

The Shining Path (Sendero Luminoso) was led by Abimael Guzmán Reynoso, who founded the Communist Party of Peru while working as a professor of philosophy at the Universidad Nacional de San Cristóbal de Huamanga (National University of San Cristóbal of Huamanga) in the city of Ayacucho. He belonged to the Communist Party of Peru, Red Flag (Bandera Roja), until 1970 and then led the splinter movement that became Sendero Luminoso

(González 2011). The basic premise of Sendero was to free the oppressed in Peru by overturning the current exploitative system of power in the country.

The contemporary exploitative system of power in Peru could have arguably begun in 1531 when Francisco Pizarro captured the Inca leader Atahualpa, demanded a massive payment of gold and silver for his release, and then brutally executed him. The country's colonial rulers quickly reorganized the system of landholding, concentrating property among small elite.[2] African slaves produced sugarcane along the Pacific coast and fertile valleys in the highlands became large encomiendas and then haciendas, worked by Indigenous communities who also served as forced labor in mines and public works. As a result of the colonial division of resources, Peru had one of the most unequal systems of land distribution in the world (Stepan 1978, 152).[3] Conversely, the Amazon region in the east of Peru remained largely intact due to its inaccessibility (Crabtree and Durand 2017).[4] Peru continues to distinguish ecological zones—the sierra, coast, and lowlands—each characterized by power and racial relationships.[5]

As a result of this colonial division of power and resources, according to the late anthropologist José María Arguedas, the highlands have long been socially divided into two opposing groups: *mistis* (mestizos) and Indians (peasants or campesinos).[6] In racial terms, *mestizo* represents people of mixed blood of Spanish and Indigenous roots who primarily reside in the cities or towns and *Indians* represents Indigenous peoples who primarily live in the countryside (campo).[7] Such distinctions collapse, however, with the Peruvian *chola*: women who bear characteristics of both campesinas and mestizas and who have adapted to urban commerce with wide social networks in the cities (Babb 2012, 42).

The colonists that settled on the coast and largely controlled political power and commerce have been distinguished by a different racial category, the criollo.[8] In general, *criollo* signifies someone who is locally born of Spanish ancestry and it is linked to struggles for independence from a legal system understood to be illegitimate, abusive, and corrupt. With the capital of Peru in the coastal city of Lima, *criollo* has become synonymous with political and economic Hispanic elite separate from the highlands who exert pride in their rich mines and lands, as well as modern cities, while denying any connection to Indigenous people.[9]

It is important to note that racial distinctions in Peru are malleable and opposed to focusing on skin color; racial difference is keyed to access to commodities, education, types of work, social networks, language, residence, and religion, as well as expressions of manners, respectability, and decency (Van Vleet 2019).[10] In addition, Indigeneity is also a part of identity formation that intersects with gender, class, sexuality, and place and is historically situated (García 2008). For instance, race and ethnicity are often written more on the bodies of females than males, thereby making women more Indigenous than men (de la Cadena 1996).[11] Even though racial identities are malleable and various races coexist, the truth is that in Peru "the creole world has always defined itself with its back to the indigenous world," reproducing "stereotypes that prolong colonial subjugation" (Portocarrero and Vich 2012, 147).

Sendero sought to overturn these deep-seated divisions within Peruvian society by attacking powerful entities and creating complete chaos through bloodshed, which would then allow a new form of governance, a utopia of equality, to evolve. Their strategy included gaining control over the countryside to starve the cities through the limitation of access to agricultural productivity, ultimately achieving overall domination in the country (Starn and La Serna 2019).[12] Four themes stood out in Guzmán's thought. First, he emphasized the primacy of class struggle.[13] Second was the need to combat imperialism. Third, he stressed the importance of the vanguard party Guerra Popular (popular war). Lastly, he underscored the Stalinist/Leninist belief that "violence is a universal law . . . and without revolutionary violence one class cannot be substituted for another, and older order cannot be overthrown to create a new one" (Starn 1995a, 409). Sendero also followed Maoist philosophy that argued women are a fundamental pillar of armed revolution, so they actively recruited women and required their unconditional loyalty (Kirk 1993).[14]

By presenting their movement to address long-standing exploitation and inequality, Abimael Guzmán was able to recruit young, impressionable students while teaching at the Universidad Nacional de San Cristóbal de Huamanga in the city of Ayacucho.[15] Many of his students were from poor, rural, highland communities, and he was able to capitalize on their feelings of injustice and acute experiences with inequality.[16] Young cadres would then return to their communities to garner further support for the movement, through *escuelas populares* (schools of political indoctrination), which promised to free men, women, and children from all that oppressed them (González 2011).[17]

While initially support for Sendero ranged from active engagement to passive acceptance, after years of unchecked violence, lack of effective reform, disruption of social structures upon which people depended for their well-being, and increasing demands by Senderistas (Sendero Luminoso guerrillas), support for the revolution began to wane with some communities enacting civil defense patrols to fight against Senderistas. Being unable to comprehend how peasants could resist the People's War, Senderistas reacted by "burning tractors, terrorizing villagers, killing patrol leaders" (Starn and La Serna 2019, 268). According to Starn and La Serna, "their moth-eaten Maoist orthodoxy had always blinded the *senderistas* to rural complexities," which eventually fostered resistance among those Sendero sought to liberate (2019, 268). However, regardless of a community's engagement with Sendero, the military responded with brutal retaliation against any perceived sympathizer. Consequently, individuals were often in a situation where they were unaware of the allegiances of their own family members or neighbors, yet received backlash for suspected treason on the side of Sendero, military forces, and other revolutionary groups, including the Movimiento Revolucionario Túpac Amaru (MRTA, Túpac Amaru Revolutionary Movement), a rebel organization that began in the 1980s, merging the Marxist-Leninist Revolutionary Socialist Party and Revolutionary Left Movement.[18]

As entire communities were ransacked and burned to the ground, hundreds of thousands of individuals from the poorest regions of Peru were forcibly displaced, many seeking refuge in the outskirts of Lima and other major cities, exacerbating poverty (CVR 2003, 6:653).[19] The war continued through three administrations: Fernando Belaúnde (1980–1985), Alan García (1985–1990), and Alberto Fujimori (1990–2000) (CVR 2003). Under the administration of Alberto Fujimori, Abimael Guzmán was eventually captured and, following subsequent arrests of key leaders, the movement eventually ended. Sendero represented a rejection of colonialism and social exclusion that have long dictated racial, gendered, and class relations in Peru that many frustrated agriculturalists initially welcomed; nevertheless, the war ultimately incited racist discourse and exacerbated inequality.

Seeking Truth and Reconciliation Postwar

At the end of the war, the Peruvian government approved the establishment of a truth and reconciliation commission, the Comisión de la Verdad y Reconciliación, in 2000. The CVR was part of Peru's attempt at transitional justice, defined as "a field of postwar inquiry and intervention focused on addressing the legacies of the past human rights violations in the hope that doing so will build a more peaceful future" (Theidon 2013, 6; see also Bickford 2000; Minow 1998).[20]

The CVR's mandate was to investigate assassinations, torture, displacement, disappearances, use of terrorist methods, and other violations attributable to the Sendero Luminoso, the state, and the Túpac Amaru Revolutionary Movement between May 1980 and November 2000 (CVR 2003). The goal of the CVR was to analyze the conditions that fostered the armed conflict and government response, as well as to identify individual and institutional responsibility. The CVR conducted a two-year study that entailed in-depth interviews, focus groups, fourteen public audiences, a review of archives, ethnographic research, and the collection of testimonials from individuals throughout the country.[21] The CVR also identified over 4,600 burial sites and conducted inspections at over 2,200 of them, as well as exhumations in the towns of Chusqui, Lucanamarca, and Totos (CVR 2003, 9:209).[22] Peru's CVR is considered one of the most comprehensive truth commissions in Latin America and has qualified as one of the five "strongest" in history (Hayner 2010).

On August 28, 2003, the commission presented its eight-thousand-page final report to the acting president, Alejandro Toledo, and members of government, including forty-two criminal cases, many of which related to human rights violations (CVR 2003).[23] The nine-volume final report concluded that the war constituted "the most intense, extensive and prolonged episode of violence in the entire history of the Republic" (CVR 2003, 8:315).[24] The war displaced more than 600,000 people and there were 69,280 deaths, double what had been previously cited. The report deemed Sendero responsible for 54 percent of deaths; MRTA for 1.5 percent; and state, military, police, security forces, political parties, and government for the remaining 44.5 percent. Likely, these statistics varied by region of the country and are difficult to track with certainty as the military and Sendero would often leave evidence to make it appear that the opposite party committed the atrocities they committed themselves. Moreover, recent research questions the data gathered by the CVR and argues there were fewer overall killings (48,000), and the state is responsible for a significantly larger share (58.3%) than Sendero (38.3%) or other perpetrators (3.4%) (Rendon 2019). At the conclusion of the CVR's investigation and mandate, the CVR handed forty-seven cases to the prosecutor general to investigate, "of which all but one implicated members of the National Police and Armed Forces" (Milton 2018, 42).[25] The CVR also documented gross violations and abuse of human rights, including torture and inhumane treatment, sexual violence against women, kidnapping and hostage taking, violations of due process, and violations of human rights of children and Indigenous peoples (Amnesty International 2004).[26] The CVR concluded that the judicial system failed to punish actions of subversive groups, protect the rights of detained persons, or end impunity of state agents who committed human rights abuses (Amnesty International 2004).[27]

Of the victims, 79 percent were from rural areas and 75 percent spoke Quechua, while the percentage of Quechua speakers comprises approximately 20 percent of Peru's general population (Lambright 2015, 9). Overall, 40 percent of the victims were from Ayacucho, and taken together with cases from Junín, Huánuco, Huancavelica, Apurímac, and San Martín, they represented 85 percent of the total number of cases recorded by the CVR.[28] Ayacucho, Apurímac, Huancavelica, and Huánuco are four of the five poorest departments in Peru, representing merely 9 percent of the overall income of all Peruvian families. Conversely, less than 10 percent of the people who disappeared or died during the violence came from the wealthier sectors of society (CVR 2003, 1:158–59). The CVR also illustrated that over 75 percent of the victims of the conflict were married men over fifteen years of age. While the Sendero Luminoso targeted local authorities and social leaders, accounting for the disproportionate loss of male lives, women were killed primarily through indiscriminate violence, such as massacres and the devastation of communities (1:164–65).[29] Given the deferential impacts of the violence in Peru, the ways in which Peru continues to remember and curate the past is mired in deeply embedded and continued divisions within society.

Politicized Memory and Curating the Past

In Peru, there are ranges of memory camps with their own experiences of the war that have sought to espouse narratives, with clashes within and between camps. The work of the CVR represent the human rights camp. This approach underscores the entrenched political, social, and economic inequality that led to the violence and continues to go unaddressed. While recognizing that

Sendero instigated the violence, they highlight abuses committed by state actors in fomenting violence and violating human rights. Following the release of the CVR report, this camp centers on supporting symbolic and financial reparations and efforts at enacting justice (Milton 2018). Another memory camp includes the salvation or heroic memory, espoused by neoliberal and conservative actors composed mainly of the armed forces, the national police, *fujimoristas*, American Popular Revolutionary Alliance, conservative elements within the Catholic Church, and associated media outlets (17). The aim of this camp is to disseminate armed state actors' narratives of history and to discredit human rights discourse as frivolous endeavors by leftist human rights groups (see Ulfe, Ríos, and Breña 2016). They also underscore the heroic efforts of state security agents who saved the nation and democracy and are positioned as victims of Sendero's violence. Lastly, they seek to blame the violence solely on Sendero and to make illegitimate the movement and its supporters' aims (27).

Although unable to situate within a camp per se, artists and musicians throughout the country of Peru have offered additional interpretations, narratives, and expressions of the war. Numerous artists, writers, and scholars have engaged with Peru's history in ways that resist consumption, challenge understandings of the conflict, reinterpret and reframe the CVR findings and human rights discourse, and underscore the inability of Peru to overcome collective trauma without addressing dominant cultural paradigms. A full analysis of the myriad ways in which artists have performed and infused memories with emotional force through artistic creations such as poetry, dramatic performances, novels, cinema, and traditional art forms is beyond the scope of this book. Yet a notable example of truth telling includes Edilberto Jiménez Quispe's provocative drawings depicting the violence in his book, *Chungui: Violencia y trazos de memoria* (Jiménez 2009). Artists in Ayacucho also utilize the famous artisan tradition of retablos to depict in graphic 3D form the atrocities that communities underwent at the hands of Sendero and government forces. In addition, performers throughout Peru have infused song and dance with their own memories of the war, contributing alternative narratives of the country's past.[30]

The ways in which memory camps have coexisted and collided is apparent when ingrained into monumentality, or the cultural and political use of public monuments, as well as the censorship of war-related creative works

(Drinot 2009, 19).[31] Memorial museums are often expected to offer "reverent remembrance," as well as "critical interpretation," which can make them "instantly politicized" (Milton 2018, 135). The debate about how and what to include in a museum can illuminate conflicting opinions and interests, which was particularly apparent with the museum Lugar de la Memoria in the upscale Lima neighborhood of Miraflores, as it sparked political and civil divisiveness (see Feldman 2021).[32]

In addition to disagreements over museums and monuments, there have also been attempts to censor various interpretations of Peru's history. In June 2007, the Instituto Nacional de Cultura del Perú, at the behest of the commanding general of the Peruvian Army, Edwin Donayre, removed three drawings from an exhibition by the artist Piero Quijano, one of which "cast doubt on the heroism of the Peruvian armed state actors portrayed" (Milton 2018, 165–66). In 2017, the government of Peru seized the *Tablas de Sarhua*, two textiles from Edwin Sulca, and one retablo made by Nicario Jiménez that illustrate atrocities committed by Sendero and the military.[33] In May of 2018, then congressman Edwin Donayre called for the removal of the film *La Casa Rosada*, which profiles military torture in Ayacucho, from all theaters under the auspices of the defense of terrorism.[34] The following month, pro-Fujimori members of Congress requested that the Ministry of Education review the content in school textbooks related to the "times of terrorism," which the Coordinadora Nacional de Derechos Humanos argues is an attempt to censor information that implicates the military and politicians in serious war crimes.[35] As Olga González states, "The defense of terrorism law supports the reactionary denialism that seeks to conceal the armed forces' systematic violation of human rights in Peru and their impunity" (González 2018).

In examining various interpretations of Peru's past, Cynthia Milton explores the concept of curating. *Curating* means "to care for," "attend to," as well as the process of selecting objects and shaping and ordering them (Milton 2018, 30). A curation of the past makes history meaningful and interpretable so that we may bear witness; however, this process is challenged when myriad social actors contest that past and when that history is difficult and uncomfortable. Efforts at curating may strive to "direct political transformation, such as reconciliation, but they may also silence experiences, contort the past, and contribute to further injustices" (30). As evidenced through overt authoritarian tactics of censorship in Peru, memories of the war could morph into social amnesia, and such acts counter the core principles of transitional justice laid out in the CVR (165). As Peru struggles with how to remember and curate its past and alternative interpretations of its history are silenced, it is clear the country's practice of violence toward Indigenous people is far from over. By sharing her history, Graciela defies such silencing and provides yet another curation of Peru's past.

Research Process

I first met Graciela while conducting fieldwork in the Andahuaylas area of Peru in 2005–2006. Although I conducted fieldwork primarily in a small rural community a couple of hours from Andahuaylas, my spouse and I rented a home on the edge of the city.[36] Graciela lived in the same home, along with her children, working as a caretaker of the surrounding fields and gardens, as well as taking care of multiple dogs. Throughout my time in Peru, I became close with Graciela and her family. I always looked forward to returning to Andahuaylas to share the trials and tribulations of fieldwork and to hear about Graciela and her family. Often, Graciela would tell me stories about her community of Oronccoy as we sat together in the gardens or at the dinner table. As time went on, she shared haunting memories of violence from the war and the hardships of living on the run for years. We also shared positive memories, as my husband and I served as godparents for her daughter's sixth-grade promotion ceremony, we celebrated birthdays together, and we laughed through various daily chores in the patio of our temporary homes. We helped each other out in small and fundamental ways, and throughout that year Graciela and I became more than friends—we grew to depend on one another.

In the years following my fieldwork, I started a family and worked at a research institute, which precluded a return to Peru. I strived to stay in contact with friends from Peru, but of all the people I met during my year of fieldwork, the person I most feared losing touch with was Graciela. But that is exactly what happened. I sent cards for Graciela to the proprietor of the house where we lived together, but I never heard back.[37] Graciela and her family were often on my mind. Once I acquired an academic position with summers open for research, I made plans to return to Peru with the idea of conducting a life history project with Graciela. Since leaving Peru, I had realized that while scholars had written a great deal about the war, I had not yet read a story quite like what I had heard from Graciela, and there were few voices from female survivors, beyond testimonials to the Comisión de la Verdad y Reconciliación. I also recognized how little university students and the public at large in the United States knew about the war in Peru. I wanted people to know not only about the unrest but also about the human, specifically female, experience of survival. I wanted others to see what I saw in Graciela—an embodiment of perseverance and compassion amid brutal violence and tragedy.

I returned to Peru six years, almost to the day, after I finished my fieldwork and left Andahuaylas. After searching for Graciela, I was able to reconnect with her children via social media and planned a return the following summer. Graciela and I reunited during the summer of 2013. Although we were in a different place and we had not seen each other for nearly seven years, it was as if little time had passed. During our first conversation, Graciela repeatedly patted me on the back as we laughed about the growing personalities of all our children and discussed a recent dispute over land Graciela and her husband, Juan Pablo, were having with the municipality of Andahuaylas. During this short visit, I asked Graciela if she would be interested in writing a book with me about her life and she responded, "Of course, anything for you." I worried that this project was something she felt obligated to do and had an extensive conversation with her and her husband about what a project like this would entail.

In the summer of 2014, I traveled to Peru to talk with Graciela.[38] I relished this time with Graciela, as I could focus solely on her experiences and not juggle additional obligations. I wanted this project to be a collaborative effort in which Graciela could decide what she shared and how. I also wanted her to be fully aware of any potential risks, benefits, and other facets of sharing her life story, so we painstakingly discussed all aspects of what we were about to embark on. Throughout my time in Peru during the summer of 2014 and subsequent seasons, I had many conversations with Graciela, her children, her extended family members, and her husband regarding various ethical and technical concerns about writing her life history.[39]

During our first season working together, I found that Graciela was eager to talk. After hours of recounting details of her life, with me continuously asking for clarification to make sure I understood everything correctly, I would suggest a break. She would often ask me to turn the recorder back on after dinner, as she had more to share. Some nights we stayed up late and her husband would join us, recounting stories while working through a small bag of coca, and I would stay overnight.[40] While I would often start the conversation with a question or two, Graciela guided the discussion, which led to deeper and more interesting connections than I could have ever anticipated. When I left Peru a few weeks later, I had over twenty hours of audio recordings, countless pages of typed material, and books of handwritten notes, maps, and drawings. When I returned to the United States, I faced the daunting task of transcribing and translating (Spanish to English) the interviews and sifting through all the data to try to relay a story of nearly incomprehensible (to me) trauma and resilience.

The following two summers, I returned to Peru to review what I had outlined for the book and to inquire if there were other details or components of her life that Graciela wished to share. During these visits, Graciela recalled the same events she had previously narrated, leading me to believe I had found the key experiences to relay in the text, knowing there were still, and likely always would be, gaps with depth beyond my comprehension. I returned during the summer of 2018 to review the manuscript with her in detail. During this summer, I was also able to talk with Graciela's father, her husband, one of her brothers, numerous scholars in the city of Ayacucho, and other individuals, conversations that served to further expand and contextualize Graciela's story.

In describing our research process, it is important to note linguistic challenges. Spanish is a second language for both Graciela and me. We conducted all our interviews in Spanish and while Graciela communicated well in Spanish, Quechua is her mother language. Shared fluency in Quechua would have allowed for a greater depth of overall communication, and there is an undeniable loss in not capturing Graciela's history in her native language. The issue of accuracy in translating personal testimonies is critical yet challenging for even the best translators and made more difficult when working within a second language (Logan 1997). As translator, I take full responsibility for any inaccuracies in reflecting the original spoken word. To minimize translation errors, I often asked for clarification during interviews from both Graciela and her family members. Following interviews, I reviewed field notes and audio recordings and asked for explanations the following day. Upon subsequent visits to Peru, I shared my interpretations and analyses with Graciela to ensure my representation accurately portrayed the story Graciela wished to tell.

Writing Process

In line with Ruth Behar's (2003) theory of collaboration, I see Graciela's involvement in this project as co-storyteller, co-researcher, and co-interpreter. In writing the book, I sought to read a story, or series of stories, that has been told to me "so that I, in turn, can tell them again, transforming myself from a listener into a storyteller" in close collaboration with Graciela (13). Through the role of listener and storyteller, I often found that it was not a simple matter of translating the spoken word. Like Marisol de la Cadena's (2015) work with Peruvian healer Nazario Turpo, a great deal of translation had to occur between our joined, overlapping, yet distinct worlds, a process she refers to as "co-laboring" and that resonates with my experiences working with Graciela.

Graciela and I co-labored through linguistic and conceptual hurdles to understand one another, oftentimes assisted by others. While I could translate Graciela's words, the actions and meanings behind such words oftentimes escaped my knowing. For example, through our co-laboring, I could not quite grasp or adequately describe the conceptual differences in how we each understand and express emotion. I cognitively comprehend Graciela's relationship with what de la Cadena references as "earth beings" and can translate her descriptions via writing to readers. Yet I may never be able to fully transcribe that relationship into my embodied reality. For those realms that defy my own conceptual or experiential translation I cannot, nor do I want to, reduce Graciela's world to mine, or mine to hers, for it was through such differences that our mutual curiosity was fueled and we oftentimes made the most connections.

In addition to co-laboring through conceptual and linguistic differences, a major hurdle we faced was how to present Graciela's history in writing. There was the question of how much of my experience to incorporate into the book, if any. We considered using a novelistic approach recounting Graciela's history, yet in my words. However, we felt such an approach would detract from a more direct communication of her own experiences. We thought of using primarily

Graciela's exact words, direct from the transcripts, creating more of a memoir or *testimonio* (testimony), with my role being merely to organize the content. This approach, however, was difficult due to a lack of seamless prose in which Graciela relayed her life. As is the case for all of us, stories do not line up with a linear timeline, and this is especially true when there are multiple stories of trauma. This approach would also be limited to Graciela's first-person accounts and would not allow the reader insight into the larger context of sociopolitical change, which Graciela knew and lived but often did not include when discussing her personal stories.

Together, we decided to present a third-person omniscient, past-tense manuscript that privileges Graciela's experiences and provides a cultural and political framework to contextualize her personal history. Alisse Waterston's account of her own Jewish father's experiences in World War II, which she calls an "intimate ethnography," served as a model (Waterston 2014, xv). Waterston had a difficult time separating her role as daughter from that of anthropologist in writing her father's history. Although Graciela and I are not biologically related, like Waterston, I had a difficult time separating my own role as anthropologist and friend from the telling of Graciela's story. Therefore, I have tried to tell Graciela's history using her actual words, while conveying the context surrounding and emotions behind such words with my descriptions. I also incorporate the first-person voice of friend-anthropologist, bringing in my own experiences with Graciela, as well as additional historical information and cultural analysis when relevant.

We hope that our audience will not be limited to Latin American and Peruvian scholars per se, as they are aware of this history and its intricacies. We seek to also reach out to lay audiences and students (formal and informal, within Peru and abroad, traditional, and nontraditional) interested in gender and race relations, Latin American and Peruvian history, health, war, anthropology, and related fields. Additionally, we have not couched this story within a particular theoretical framework. Countless ideas stemming from her children, church, the media, and other experiences have influenced how Graciela understands and makes sense of her own life. As a scholar, I have theoretical orientations that affect my research and could provide useful lenses from which to explore the myriad implications of the events that unfolded throughout Graciela's history. However, Graciela and I do not necessarily share the same structures of understanding, and to avoid having certain frames of reference dominate others, we do not limit ourselves to a particular theoretical standpoint from which we analyze Graciela's history. That said, the way in which this book has taken shape is evidence of theoretical influences on both Graciela and me.

Curated Histories, *Testimonio*, and Positionality

In many ways, through Graciela's testimonio, this book is a curation of her history and contemporary life amid continued violence against Indigenous peoples, which is complicated through its various levels of translation. Although this book represents more of a life history than a testimonio per se, in that it is not written solely in first person by the protagonist or witness, it reflects numerous characteristics, concerns, and impacts of testimonial work (see Beverley 2004, 31; Biehl 2013; Crapanzano 1984; Das et al. 2000).

According to Cynthia Milton, testimonials are often associated with seeking redress and prompting action against injustice. The genre tends to focus on giving voice to victims and people typically excluded from communicating via reading, writing, and publishing, giving these individuals an alternative way in which to "speak truth to power and against silence" (Milton 2018, 61).[41] By offering a counterhegemonic interpretation, the genre allows the "non-Western others" voice in recounting their own history but also looks to the future with visions of transformed society (Gugelberger and Kearney 1991, 7, 9).[42] Testimonio is therefore "directed not only toward the memorialization of the past but also to the constitution of more heterogeneous, diverse, egalitarian, and democratic nation-states, as well as forms of community, solidarity, and affinity that extend beyond or between nation-states" (Beverley 2004, 24).

Within Latin America, women have long contributed to testimonial literature. Along with the histories of Domitila Barrios de Chungara (1978), Rigoberta Menchú (1984), Elvia Alvarado (1987), Claribel Alegría (1987), Ana Guadalupe Martínez (1992), and María Teresa Tula (1994), among others, Graciela's story provides a deeply gendered perspective of political and civil unrest.[43] Female testimonials tend to begin with a personal history and roles as daughter, wife, or mother, yet reveal a collective identity, with the goal of documenting an allegory of a whole people, as opposed to an individual account (Gugelberger and Kearney 1991). Contrary to offering an individual perspective, they often provide a uniquely collective vantage point that captures "the reality of multiple identities in ever-changing structural conditions" underscoring aspects of women's roles and empowerment without devaluing structural and institutional barriers (Tula and Stephen 1994, 227). Highlighting a collective orientation, Rigoberta Menchú argues, "I'd like to stress that it's not only my life, it's also the testimony of my people. . . . The important thing is that what has happened to me has happened to many other people too: my story is the story of all poor Guatemalans. My personal experience is the reality of a whole people" (Menchú and Burgos-Debray 1984, 1).[44] Similarly, Graciela's testimonial also focuses on a collective memory of her community, family, and other war survivors and contributes to a long line of female testimonials that provide a collective truth of poor, Indigenous, working-class women who have long been silenced, thereby altering cultural gatekeeping, cultural production, and reconstructing history (Tula and Stephen 1994, 228).

Because testimonios or oral narratives are often told by a speaker from a subaltern to an academic or professional interlocutor who edits and textualizes the account to make it available to national and international literate publics, there is a great deal of possibilities for co-optation or distortion (see Spivak 1988). Yet, as John Beverley argues, the production of testimonio or testimonial life history represents a relationship in which neither of the participants has to cancel their identity. Testimonials can foster a discursive space where "an alliance can be negotiated on both sides without too much angst about otherness or 'othering'" (Beverley 2004, 48). Milton argues that the form of testimonies and those who write them have changed through time and that an interlocutor, such as an anthropologist or historian, is no longer necessary to transcribe and organize another's experiences.[45] In light of concerns regarding the collaborative process involved in life history or testimonial projects, it is important to note the structural conditions of oppression and privilege that necessitated a particular form of collaboration for Graciela and me.

While we worked in partnership to create this book, my process of co-laboring with Graciela was not symmetric or egalitarian. Graciela and I are part of larger relationships of power. I am a white, middle-class scholar working with Graciela, a politically marginalized war survivor in the rural

Andes, to translate her story for audiences beyond Peru. I have access to academic and public audiences, while Graciela is geographically limited to the greater Andahuaylas valley. Given these realities, I am the person tasked with putting words into writing.[46] Within "the hegemony of literacy," I am activating my own position of privilege and utilizing a tool of subjugation to translate Graciela's oral history into writing for international audiences (de la Cadena 2015, 16). People facing day-to-day struggles for survival oftentimes do not have the resources or time to produce their own texts, yet alone purchase or read them. Although testimonials are written to be accessible to a wide range of readers, they are produced for an educated, middle-class audience, oftentimes published first in English (Logan 1997), which is the case for this text. When translated into Spanish, the text then also reaches primarily educated and middle-class readers in Latin America (Tula and Stephen 1994).

In accessing larger audiences via the written word, testimonials are often appealing, as they relay a largely unfamiliar reality to the reader. Consequently, not only is the dynamic between protagonist or witness and interlocutor unequal, "the communication between teller and reader is primarily based on difference" (Tula and Stephen 1994, 232). Nevertheless, although testimonials often replicate power dynamics embedded in production and consumption, they serve as a means of maintaining and developing human rights and solidarity movements, as well as underscoring problems of poverty and oppression "that are not normally visible in dominant forms of representations" (Beverley 2004, 37).[47]

Graciela wants her story to reach audiences beyond her community and Peru. Through the telling of her story, Graciela wants validation. She wants people within and outside of Peru to understand what she and her loved ones suffered and survived. She wants those who know this history to remember it always so that violence does not return. Like Graciela, Lurgio Gavilán Sánchez wrote his autobiography of fighting in Peru's war "in order to retrieve my memory; and also, so nothing like it will happen again in Peru" (Gavilán Sánchez 2015, 1). He emphasizes the importance of transferring his memories into writing, stating, *Verba volant, scripta manent* (Words fly away, what is written remains)" (Gavilán Sánchez 2015, 1), underscoring the power of the written word. By employing the hegemonic hierarchy of literacy via the writing of this book (translated through colonial languages) to be consumed by international readers, Graciela can access audiences that have been entitled to ignore her, due to her own illiteracy and position in society, with the goal of her story serving to build "bridges of solidarity and understanding" (Tula and Stephen 1994, 231).

Exploring Truths

Graciela and I did not complete this project in search of an empirically oriented truth. As Tula and Stephen argue, testimonials are complex and may contain survival strategies that conflict with readers' notions of "the whole truth" (Tula and Stephen 1994, 229).[48] María Teresa Tula lamented journalists who questioned her truth when it exposed macabre crimes and murders committed in El Salvador. She describes how journalists, delegitimate her experience:

> They write, María Teresa Tula "alleged" or "said" that she was tortured. The way they frame my responses makes it sound like there is some doubt about what happened or that I imagined what happened to me. This is very painful for me and anyone who gives testimony about their own torture. (Tula and Stephen 1994, 176)

There are undoubtedly aspects of Graciela's experiences not included in this text, largely due to the complexities of memory, as well as the vast ethical issues to consider in writing a life history of political violence. For example, when does questioning serve to clarify accuracy without interrogating for details that Graciela preferred to remain unspoken? When questioned by a Peruvian colleague about the extent of Sendero Luminoso support in Graciela's community of Oronccoy, I reported what Graciela had told me, which they questioned. I responded that I had asked Graciela about the level of support for the Sendero Luminoso in her community but did not push for further information. I realize Graciela may not have known certain details, did not wish to share them, or viewed them as less relevant to her overall experience. In working with Graciela, I did not seek to unveil secrets or analyze the meaning of silences but rather focused on what Graciela wished to share.[49] Acknowledging that there can be as many memories as social groups in any given society, and that individuals within groups respond differentially to various cultural norms, thereby affecting personal memories (Halbwachs 1992), I work to document what and how Graciela remembers (see González 2011, 9) without questioning her truth.[50]

In addition to inherent omissions, there is the ethical question of including everything that Graciela disclosed and inadvertently contributing to a "pornography of violence," or the use of disturbing stories and images to create an object for consumption by varied audiences not in the spirit in which we together worked to tell these personal stories.[51] Graciela shared some gruesome details of her personal experiences and those of loved ones that she feels are an integral part of her history. It is not up to me to decide what counts as relevant and true in Graciela's history to then edit the story to avoid describing death and suffering that desensitizes the readers and contributes to "the final obliteration of the human subject whose world is already undone by the experience of pain" (Dauphinee 2007, 140). Conversely, war coverage is often sanitized, yet "wars involve bloodshed and slaughter and those involved in them, even indirectly, have a moral and political responsibility to face this simple fact" (Petley 2003, 83). In telling Graciela's history, including the violence and horror, we risk promoting "pornographic metaphor, which conjures a pathological 'other' who is gratified by images of suffering and the ruined body" (Tait 2008, 97). However, it is our hope that through providing context of the situation and Graciela as a person, we allow the reader to bear witness and orient themselves "to the plight of the other," which can enable one to take some burden for what they see (97).[52]

For my part, I would be naive to argue that there are no professional benefits for me in writing this book, and I hope that the royalties from the sale of this book can support Graciela, her family, and her community as they continue to navigate postwar life. That said, my primary motivation in writing this story is to transfer Graciela's oral history into writing so others can learn and remember. I have come to value the true impact of one story. It is not merely a narrative; it is an embodiment of the past on the precipice of the unknown. Some stories provide insight into a present, often hidden, reality that can then transform into a yet-to-be-experienced future. Even if that one story does not fundamentally alter pathways, perhaps it can reveal truths previously sequestered or denied. I feel honored to know Graciela. Through our relationship, I have gained a greater sense of humility and compassion for others. Ultimately, my goal in writing this book is to share Graciela's story so that others may find comradery, connect through differences, and learn from her strength, perseverance, and beauty that bring a sense of humanity and hope to situations of dehumanizing violence.

Organization of the Book

Graciela did not relay her story chronologically. Her account was like real life: haphazard and messy. When describing a particular event, she would jump back to some precipitating issue, which would then remind her of the current situation that she would then discuss in full.[53] I found that Graciela relayed a "sequence of events like the beads of a rosary," selecting particular events that resonated in her memory and describing them in full, but not moving through them in any particular order or in a linear fashion, implying "an active engagement *in* history" (Brand 2020).[54] Therefore, in striving to illuminate the poignant events in Graciela's memories, while also establishing a semblance of order that would be comprehensible to readers, we focused each chapter on formative moments in Graciela's life, ordering them chronologically to aid in the reader's understanding of how historical and social events unfolded and influenced one another.

Upon situating the reader within the context of the war in this introduction, in chapter 1 we move to direct accounts of Graciela's life. Chapter 1 marks the beginning of Graciela's story and describes daily routines in Graciela's home community to provide a window into rural Andean life before the social unrest, including customs and practices that are part of Graciela's earliest memories. This chapter provides a baseline from which to understand the degree to which the war upended a sense of humanity in the rural Andes.

Chapters 2 through 7 are dedicated to chronicling Graciela's experiences with violence and disruption throughout the period of unrest. Chapter 2 describes Graciela's initial encounters with violence, which forced her and the remainder of her community to flee. This chapter examines how Sendero initially set up a base in Oronccoy and the ensuing violence from Sendero and military forces. In chapter 3, we explore the period in which Graciela fled her community and lived on the run for years. Throughout this time, Graciela contended with illness, starvation, and violence while constantly in fear of being detected by either Senderistas or military forces. Chapter 4 centers on the traumatic period in which military forces captured Graciela, as well as when she was reunited with her family. This chapter illuminates the degree to which sexual violence was an integral part of the war and the on-the-ground impact of shifting Peruvian policies. Chapter 5 depicts Graciela's reunion with her family and challenging work experiences in the city of Andahuaylas shaped by discriminatory ethnic, class, and gender relations. Chapter 6 is dedicated to the period in which Graciela adapted to life in the tropical lowlands, gave birth to numerous children, and had to continuously run from Senderistas and other groups inciting violence. In chapter 7, Graciela describes her difficult adjustment to Andahuaylas and her ultimate return to Oronccoy, where she faced tragic memories and illness, yet welcomed more children into her life. This chapter illustrates how the government encouraged survivors of the war to return to their home communities once peace was established yet failed to recognize how the war fundamentally altered life throughout the Andes and Peru more broadly.

The final section of the book moves to a discussion of contemporary challenges in postwar life. Chapter 8 chronicles how Graciela has continued to survive while contending with persistent discrimination, limited opportunities for her family, and challenges in securing promised reparations by the Peruvian state. This chapter also explores potential mining development in Graciela's home community. Such developments underscore the ways in which the exploitation of Indigenous lands and bodies continues largely unabated in Peru. The conclusion analyzes how the war disrupted not only Graciela's childhood but also her community and what it means to be a person in the rural highlands of Peru. This chapter ultimately questions to what degree the war represents a rupture, continuity, or opportunity for fundamental societal shift for the state of Peru and war survivors.

———

As illustrated throughout this brief introduction, Peru is a widely divided country with roots of inequality dating to the Spanish conquest and colonialism continuing through civil war and contemporary life. Capitalizing on feelings of neglect stemming from hundreds of years of exploitation, Sendero Luminoso captured the imaginations of agriculturalists in the southcentral Andes. Following the war's end, Peru as a country has actively sought to construct a national narrative about its violent era with myriad conflicting views, histories, and interests. Graciela and I are not seeking to replace an official memory with another memory that is more inclusive of marginalized groups. Rather we are attempting to layer, interweave, and juggle various narratives, even when they contain contradictory or complex truths (see Milton 2007). By exploring Graciela's life, alongside the history of family members and other survivors, we struggle to establish yet another narrative (or narratives) of Peru's past. We seek, as Cynthia Milton (2007) states, to "broaden the scope of possible alternative historical sources, sites, and artifacts of memory, as well as consequent narratives that form the individual and collective consciousness of the internal conflict" (26).

Graciela's story exposes truths omitted from state-sanctioned accounts and sheds light on the resilience of survivors able to express and represent themselves and their experiences during the violence and in the aftermath of war. It is our hope that through this narrative, readers acquire a shared sense of humanity with Graciela, as well as those living behind untold stories in the Andes, and beyond. Upon providing context of the war, the writing of this book, testimonios, and memory, we turn to the story of Graciela. The following chapter describes Graciela's memories as a young child before the violence began, which underscores the degree to which the war disrupted not only her community but also the entire social fabric of the Peruvian highlands.

Chapter 1

A Time and Place of Tranquility

Peace and Abundance

Graciela's community of Oronccoy lies within the most economically depressed province of one of the poorest departments in the country of Peru, with a poverty rate between 60 and 81.3 percent, yet Graciela recalled it as a place of plenty:[1]

> Before the violence, we had our house. We had maize, wheat, potato, filled to our roof there was ullucu [pink-dotted potato variety], beans, and eggs. We had animals, *ch'arki* [meat preserved with salt]. We had everything. Mantas that my mom and dad made. To sleep, we had beds. To cook everything, we had pots. We had nice pots that they took.

Graciela's community of Oronccoy is in a region referred to as the Oreja de Perro, which was once in the district of Chungui (La Mar Province) but is now its own district within the Department of Ayacucho.[2] This area is considered the "forgotten point on the map" and the Chungui district was "one of the three districts where the Truth and Reconciliation Commission verified the highest number of dead and disappeared" (CVR 2003, 8:33).

This region of Peru is geographically isolated and difficult to access with limited infrastructure. It is located about seven hours by car from the capital city of the Department of Ayacucho, Huamanga. It is easier to access the Chungui district via the city of Andahuaylas (in the Department of Apurímac). You must travel approximately three hours by car from Andahuaylas to the Kutinachaka Bridge over the Pampas River. Once you cross the bridge, you travel on a horse trail about eight hours walking before reaching Graciela's town

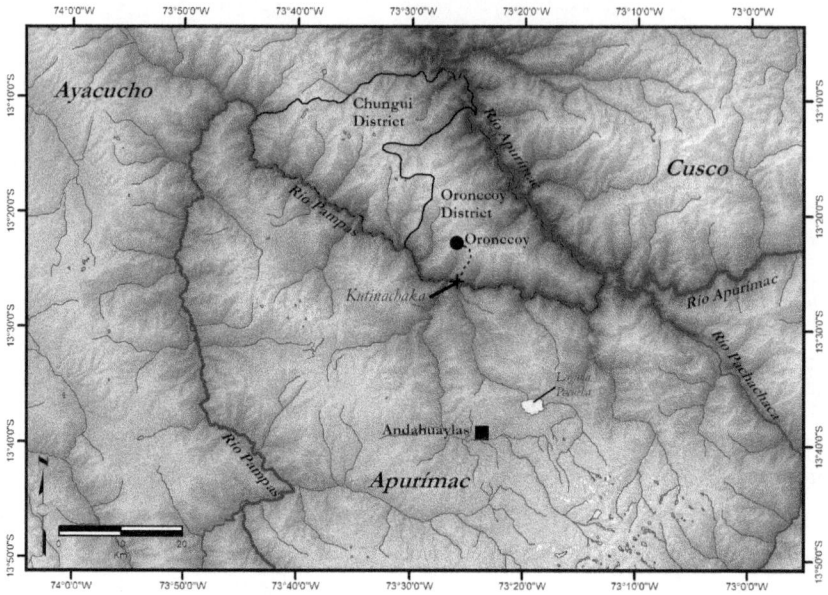

Figure 2. Map of Ayacucho, Cusco, and Apurímac Departments showing the Chungui and Oronccoy Districts that lie in the Oreja de Perro region of Ayacucho. Map created by Lucas C. Kellett.

of Oronccoy. There are no cars or paved roads between the village of Oronccoy and the community of Chungui, making it a three-day journey by foot (CVR 2003, vol. 5). The Chungui region also straddles three ecological zones: the Pampas valley, the Andean highlands, and the Apurímac jungle (CVR 2003, 4:88).

Oronccoy is in a prime location of 12,221 feet altitude, perched on the top a steep incline offering an abundance of products from its drastic elevation relief. While cardinal directions are recognized, Graciela designated space by up and down in altitude from the present location. About a two-hour walk up from Oronccoy is the Pampas, oftentimes known as the Puna, where there are no large trees but rather ichu grass, which the cows eat. Community members pasture their cows in this area, leaving them unattended for weeks at a time, where they lick the *sal rojo* or red salt. "The salt is like sugar to the cows, so they eat the salt, then drink water, and sleep really well in the Pampas happy." Native

Figure 3. A panoramic view of the community of Oronccoy.
Photo by Max Altamirano Molero.

potatoes and *mashua* (an Andean tuber, *Tropaeolum tuberosum*) are grown at this altitude and chuño (freeze-dried potatoes) is produced.[3] "When I was young, my father grew huge potatoes called *papa nacimiento* (large white potatoes), but this potato is no more. It was lost in the violence. It does not grow anymore. Before the war, there was plenty of *papa cancha* for soup, *papa nativa*, papa nacimiento, and *utu paruntu* to make chuño."

If one walked up and over the mountain ridge to the north of Oronccoy, they would descend to the *sachapunku* ("door of the forest" in Quechua), which demarcates the area between the sierra (highlands) and the selva (jungle)—in other words, the door to the jungle. The sachapunku is where white maize is produced, as well as yellow maize for the hens. Further down the mountainside, you begin to reach the jungle, where avocado, sugarcane, peanuts, gourds, yucca, plantains, oranges, and coca are grown. "The quebrada [mountain gorge] is very pretty. When you go below to this part in this mountain, there are big trees and beautiful little hummingbirds and doves. It is the jungle. It is very pretty." There are numerous white rivers and all the water in and around Oronccoy is so clean you can drink it directly, still today.

During Graciela's childhood, in Oronccoy, school typically began at eight o'clock in the morning and ended around four in the afternoon. While some children attended school, others worked in the fields with their parents. Graciela began pasturing sheep with her mother at the age of four and recounted happy memories of playing for hours with her peers while the adults worked in the fields or while they were keeping an eye on the livestock.

> When I was a girl, I was happy pasturing my sheep, playing with my friends when they were also pasturing their animals. We would pass our time just playing. There in Oronccoy in the Pampas, we would pasture cows and we had horses. The calves would run happily. When they were young, like a month old, they would dance happily. They would walk freely, happy, and peaceful. However, when I turned twelve or thirteen it all changed. . . . When we were kids, at times in the night in the moon, when it was lit brightly, the neighbors would come out and the children. Now my friends are dead. Only a few are still living.

A primary task of young children was to protect ripening maize from pesky parrots.

> When we would harvest maize, a quantity of parrots would come. Therefore, when I was the size of my Nayely [Graciela's daughter, about nine or ten years old], we would guard against the parrots in the field so they would not eat the maize. So many would come—100 or 150 parrots—and they would quickly eat the maize, the *choclo* [a specific variety of Andean maize with extra-large kernels]. So, at four in the morning, all the people from my community, the children, all would guard against the parrots, in each field we would play, and we would eat. At five [in the afternoon], we would return to the community. When the children return from the school, we would return to our houses from the fields. Before then [the violence], my mom, my dad, all of us, lived peacefully. Before, we just watched out for the parrots, but now my community members are in Lima, Cusco, and Arequipa. Those who are still living, those who survived, are living in other places, but the rest were killed.

Given how Graciela recounted her early childhood, it is apparent that her current realities punctuated her memories of peace and tranquility because of the war.

Communal Labor Exchange

One of Graciela's primary jobs as a child was to bring lunch to the workers in the fields, or *pampachacra* ("plain or flat farm" in Quechua). She would often carry large pots of chicha (homegrown maize beer) on her back for her father and other male workers to drink during their breaks.

> Much before the violence, I had happy memories. When I lived in my house with my parents, with my mom and my siblings with my little brothers, happily caring for the animals, my father working. At times, I would carry lunch in my manta to where they were planting maize. For example, when we were planting maize below in the Pampas called pampachacra, in there when my father was planting maize, my mother and I would bring lunch to my father. I would bring chicha for my father to drink, happily. . . . In the time of planting, all the people are planting. Various people, our neighbors also, and the children carry the lunch to them.

People did not work for wages but rather worked in *ayni, minka*, and *faena*, long-standing practices in the Andes of labor exchange.

Ayni is a mutual exchange of labor between two people; minka is labor exchange on a group level; and faena is labor exchange on a community level to construct irrigation canals, roads, or other public works. "Ayni you work with me with these potatoes and another day I return the favor. This is ayni. In minka, also one day we pass through three fields or four fields of four people. In their fields, the people work singing." Graciela sang a song in Quechua that they often recounted when working in minka with the central message that "if one stays and others are working, you have to come help too. So that all come together to be equal. When someone stays, then others may want to stay, and so you have to say yes, you must come help, so that all come." Currently, some people will work for wages in Oronccoy, but ayni remains the primary labor-exchange practice. "When there is money, we pay, but when there is no money, we work in ayni." Graciela's younger brother Alex also discussed the continuation of shared labor-exchange practices postwar:

> We do ayni and minka more than anything, because this is how we culti-vate products. This is what our ancestors, the Incas did, and we continue this. It is more practical ayni and minka. And there is not an institution that works for money there [in Oronccoy], so we work in ayni and minka. This is also the time of planting in August and September and during cul-tivating, which is October and November. . . . Because without access to a road, machines cannot arrive like a tractor, so we practice minka, ayni, and there is a tool there we call *chaki taklla*.

The chaki taklla is a foot-powered plow that predates oxen power, which people have utilized throughout the Andes for thousands of years (Graves 2001). Graciela also described continued use of the chaki taklla:

> In papa minka in my community, we plant with chaki taklla. We kick it out with chaki taklla and with our hands, too. This is how we work. . . . In my pueblo, we do not work with cows [to pull plows]. Here [in Andahuaylas] they plant maize with everything, right. With cows and with shovels, but in my pueblo the cows do not work, only us with chaki taklla with the maize and potatoes.[4]

Without trying to foster an essentialized image of Andean people as insusceptible to the passage of time and untouched by modernity (what Orin Starn [1992] referred to as "Andeanism"), it is notable that these communal labor-exchange practices have existed in the Andean region for hundreds of years and may date as far back as 900 BC (Brush 1977, 41). They served as key means to organize the rise of numerous societies, including the Inca (Isbell 1997).[5] The way that communal labor-exchange practices play out today are undoubtedly different than in prior generations or centuries. However, their continuation remains a testament to the perseverance of such practices through immense social and political change.

Graciela described how important it is that everyone harvests collectively at the same time so that the animals do not eat the produce. Typically in the

Figure 4. A man in the agricultural sector of Ccanccahua in Oronccoy using a chaki taklla to plant potatoes. Photo by Max Altamirano Molero.

Andean highlands, the timing of planting is staggered within approximately three months, as planting first occurs at higher altitudes, then middle altitudes, and finally at lower regions. Harvesting is later completed collectively (Mitchell 1976). Everyone trades working in one another's fields to finish the work in about a month, clearing out fields for animals to graze. For particularly large harvests, they make *pachamanka* (earth/pot) in the fields. Pachamanka is a traditional Peruvian dish and style of cooking that dates at least as far back as the Inca. To make pachamanka, you heat stones in a fire and place them in an earthen oven, known as a *huatia* (earth oven).[6] Then you wrap various meats—including lamb, mutton, chicken, pork, and guinea pig, all marinated in spices—in banana leaves and place them in the oven. People also cook other regional produce in the huatia, including potatoes, habas (green lima beans), and sweet potatoes and sometimes cassava, maize, and chili.

People often accompanied work in the fields with music.

We work with chaki taklla, and when we work, we are singing! Women too are singing and men with their quena [traditional Andean flute] planting potatoes. Like a faena, we plant the potatoes. We all drink liquor or other things like chicha and *caña* [sugarcane alcohol]. . . . We carry the lunch on horses. When there are various people when we plant the potato with chaki taklla, we bring the lunch on horse. Working with their quena and their chaki taklla singing.

While working, they would often sing a song, or in a style of music particular to the La Mar Province of Ayacucho, called Llaqta Maqta with a charango, a small Andean stringed instrument of the lute family, which is sometimes made of an armadillo shell.[7] According to Graciela's brother Alex, "Llaqta Maqta really is a music that we play that is native to Oronccoy. We practice this in whatever festival, anniversaries, birthdays, whatever fiesta, this is Llaqta Maqta."[8] They would often tell a *watuchi*, or in Spanish a *cuento*, while working, which is kind of like a joke or a story. After Graciela told me a watuchi about a tree by the name of Pati that grows in the quebradas (mountain gorge or valley bottom), she sang me a song in Quechua that she regularly heard as a child. She quickly became emotional and began to cry. I insisted she did not need to continue singing, but she carried on to the end of the song. The song described life in her community long before the violence.

Centrality of Animals in Daily Life

A major challenge when planting and harvesting fields was managing the cows. In Oronccoy, people plant potato using a *camayuc*, an individual voted in by the community and tasked with managing rogue cows.[9]

So, the cows, some are good, and some are robbers, right? Some want to eat the *pasto* [grass], but then others want to eat the potatoes and everything. They see where we are working, so they come to rob. When everyone leaves, they come and eat these potatoes of the community. They can crush them. Therefore, the camayuc guards it.

Normally in Graciela's community, cows roam free for weeks at a time; people do not pasture them daily like in many other Andean villages. With the cows roaming freely, if the owner wants them to come, they will leave out salt to attract the cows. However, during planting and harvesting "the cows are walking around crazy." So people put the cows into a circular corral made of rocks called a *puzo*. The camayuc must look after the cows and make sure they do not escape and wreak havoc on the fields. "The camayuc does not plant, he protects, and he guards the planters. He has to get up early and go to bed late to protect this side from the animals. . . . So I [as a camayuc] might say to someone, 'Your cow is a thief!' They will get mad when I say this." I laughed with Graciela when asking if this was like a jail for cows, and she explained that it is very much like a cow jail that people also use for horses and mules. When a person's cow escapes and is found guilty of theft, the owner must pay a fine of ten to fifteen soles (three to five US dollars). It is very exhausting for the camayuc, and they may not eat for two days as they constantly guard the cattle.

In addition to the cow jail, people also manage the cattle by marking them. In Oronccoy, people celebrate a festival called *errancia de vaca* or *vacahueri* (festival of the cow). For this event, people mark cows for identification by applying heat to steel branding irons. Neighbors from surrounding communities come to help decorate the cows with colorful ribbons and everyone drinks lots of chicha and *trago* (120-proof alcohol cut with water). With all the surrounding communities helping brand the animals, everyone knows which cows belong to whom in case an animal is lost, stolen, or determined to be a robber. "With their ribbons, they know [which animal is theirs]. Many cows come together, and every person knows their animals. The neighbors say that they saw our cows or did not see our cows at times when we are looking for our animals. They will say, 'They are over there or over there.'"

While the cows pose a risk to the fields, they also face dangers themselves from wild animals such as hawks, foxes, and condors. People must watch pregnant cows closely as newborn calves are at risk. According to Graciela, when it is cloudy, the condors do not come, but when it is clear, they must guard the animals against the condors. Graciela explained that while they try to prevent condors from taking their animals, "They [condors] are animals too and so once a year maybe God gives them a gift." In addition to the cows, the horses also roam free, but people regularly pasture sheep, goats, and pigs, otherwise "if we leave them alone, the foxes will take them." Another threat to livestock is disease, which can easily become fatal, given the limited access to veterinary

Figure 5. Mules in front of homes in the community of Wayrapata (Chungui District).
Photo by Max Altamirano Molero.

medicine. A particular insect creates a sort of plague, *hoja tayllarapi*, which destroys animals' livers. When an animal becomes sick with this illness, people consider them a loss.

A loss of an animal brings great sadness.

> We cry for our animal. Because sometimes us in the campo, for example, we only work with the animals using the sheep's wool to make clothes and blankets. When you raise an animal and a fox takes it, you have much pain. In rain and in sun we eat *canchita* [roasted maize] with cheese while we are walking behind our animals.

Throughout the rural Andes at dawn and dusk, it is a common sight to see women walking behind a herd of mixed animals such as sheep, cows, goats, pigs, and a dog or two and, in some areas, llamas and alpacas. Women will typically be spinning wool with a *puscha* or throwing rocks at the animals with a *huaraca* to keep them moving in the correct direction. A puscha is an Andean

Figure 6. Women and girls from Huancas, Andarapa, pasturing their animals on the way to Mollebamba. Many of the people who live on the southern side of the Pampas River were displaced from Oronccoy during the violent period. Photo by Max Altamirano Molero.

hand spindle that is used throughout the Andes to make thread from raw wool. A huaraca is a sling made from alpaca wool that dates far before Inca expansion and was likely used to hunt pumas and foxes, as well as protect llama herds.[10]

In addition to being connected to animals from spending so much time together and using their wool for blankets and clothing, animals are also valued as an investment and for the milk they provide that is also made into cheese. "Therefore, the cow gives us her milk, so when it dies, we have pain, and we cry. For this, I have pain. . . . When the animal grows, you can sell it for money. For example, if a cow has a baby, it is male, and it grows up, I can sell it for a lot of money, but when a condor eats it, I cannot sell it. I sell nothing, so for this we cry." Animals are like a bank investment.

When you have an investment in the bank, it is equal to the cows when they have babies. However, many wait three or four years to sell them. But those businesspeople pay 400 or 500 soles and sell them for 1,500 or 1,600 soles, they say. For a bull, they earn double! For us, we get a little. We suffer in the campo.

From Oronccoy, people must take their animals all the way down to a town across the Kutinachaka Bridge, a roughly eight-hour trip by foot, to sell them in the market. Buyers will argue that the animal is skinny from its long journey to the market and refuse to pay a fair price yet take them to the coast to fatten and sell them at a much higher rate. "They [buyers] take them to Lima and fatten them up quickly to then earn more money, but some with a conscience pay well, others do not."

Given the financial value of animals, people butcher animals only for special occasions, and always in a manner that minimizes suffering. When Graciela was young, her father butchered the animals for her family.

When my father kills a pig, it does not cry. He kills it very quickly with a rope. He ties it around the neck of the pig. When it is around the neck it does not cry, but with a knife, it is stronger. He also takes off the pig's testicles. He cuts them off. When the pigs are male, he cuts off their testicles and they get fatter. . . . He takes them off beautifully, my father. . . . With testicles, they sell for nothing, one hundred soles or so, but when you take off their testicles, the big pigs sell for four hundred or more soles.

As Graciela described, animals were respected, cherished, and carefully cared for, and their loss was mourned deeply.

Cyclical Festivals

While Graciela makes use of the Gregorian calendar, in relaying her earliest memories, Graciela reflected a cyclical sense of time, which Catherine J. Allen (2002) describes as "a world full of circulating currents. . . . Time moves ahead like a river to drop from view into a subterranean interior that contains both past and future. Future time does not lie ahead of us, but comes up at our backs" (194–95).[11] The passage of time in Graciela's early life was indeed recurrent, centering on the interrelationships between the seasons, animal life cycles, and community festivals. For example, since the maize- and milk-based dish *mazamorra* is a major part of the festival Todos los Santos (All Souls Day), it must occur when the cows are lactating, which only happens when there is enough pasto (grasses) during the rainy season.[12]

When the winter [dry season] ends and the rains begin [October/November], there is pasture, so the cows give milk for Todos los Santos. At the time of Todos los Santos, the cows start to find their partners, so at this time it [milk] comes. . . . For Todos los Santos, we have a festival equal to carnival, but we give offerings and big masses with prepared food with fried egg, mazamorra, and milk.[13] In each house, we mostly make food. We kill a cow, we kill a pig, and I kill my sheep. My neighbor maybe kills their pigs or their cow so then we can exchange sheep meat for cow meat for pig meat. Moreover, when we have money, we make an offering of other food; soda, all the food in the store, apples, squash, all. . . . We visit the cemeteries just like in carnival. We make a festival with our quena [flute] with cascabel [bell instrument]. With food, we drink. More people produce tuna [prickly pear cactus] so we invite people to eat tuna. We carry it all on horseback because there are no cars. . . . They say in the middle of the day they bring it for the saints, the angels that have died, so for these we bring offerings and have mass. We bring meat, fruit, bread, potatoes, and mazamorra. This is an offering. In the middle of the day, they eat the offerings to punish the souls of the dead brothers of my father. "They come, their angels. For this we leave the offerings," said my grandparents. Then flies would come, and grandmother would say, "They've come—the souls were crying." I would not believe, and I would be hungry. "Do not eat food for the souls!" they would tell me. Until now, we put it [food out] in Todos los Santos.

Other festivals anchored Graciela's early memories in Oronccoy, particularly that of Pascua, or Easter.

We had many beautiful festivals. We would have festivals for saints, bringing out the saints. This was our custom for Easter. . . . We would bring the cross during these festivals, these *raymis* [parties]. We would bring it to a hill to protect us during Easter. We would wrap red flowers around the cross. We would have a *hira* flower called *herain*. It grows in the forest and is a purple color. The following day, we would change the flowers, then we would return it to the hill. We would dance. We would laugh. We would sing. We would kill a cow to eat. . . . Every Easter we kill a cow. The people kill the cow for the community. We would prepare pachamanka and all the meat. The children, all the people, would help. Not one person would be left out. Everyone would eat. One person would prepare apple juice. We would not buy anything from the store. People also managed the animals for the festivities. There are large corrals like those that you see in Machu Picchu, made of rocks. With large rocks in the afternoon, we would go to separate the mom [cows] from the babies. We would separate them in the corrals. The following day, we would take the milk in large buckets. We would take the milk to make mazamorra for Easter day in the house. We would make milk mazamorra. We would make apple mazamorra. We would bring the apples from the fields. Horses would carry them; two or three cargas [loads]. We would take these to make mazamorra—it was delicious. We would eat it all in the community and then the following day it would end. This is our custom of Easter. We would all eat little plates of mazamorra, white maize, and sugarcane chicha. My grandfather would bring them in large buckets so we would also have just straight caña, this liquor that is all natural. We would take this, and my uncle would make caña and trago. It is very strong.

Graciela's discussion of the communal sharing of food during festivals highlights the importance of food, particularly meat, in the rural Andes, as it is often a primary source from which to forge and fortify reciprocal social relations.[14] Time is marked by seasonal festivals, compadrazgo (Godparent) events, and other life-cycle processes in which the exchange and consumption of meat is a central focus that allows individuals to express generosity and respect for one another. People often tie animals to communal obligations such as *cargos*. For example, most festivals entail the identification of a mayordomo, or an individual who has the cargo (responsibility) of supporting the event through providing food and drinks for the community, oftentimes sacrificing some of their own animals for the event. Through such cargos, one can gain prestige in the community. Those who partake in cargos are considered *buena gente* (good people) and can secure labor in times of scarcity (Mitchell 1991). The cargos also serve as a form of social leveling in which those deemed to have greater resources are tasked with redistributing their wealth with the community.[15] Therefore, small and large livestock not only represent financial security through their market value but also provide social capital or collateral by serving as a means to build relationships, secure needed labor, and engage in community events.

The ways in which people tie animals and food to communal obligations and social relations is readily apparent in Graciela's description of locating bulls for the Easter celebration. Easter coincides with the mating season wherein people bring bulls into the community to impregnate the cows. The community typically charges someone with finding the most aggressive bulls in the community to partake in the games.

> So, if I have a crazy cow, but you do not have one [and are charged with finding one] you have to bring me trago, beer, or maybe you have to cook me your guinea pig, rooster and bring it to me. "Lend me your crazy cow to bring to the stadium," you would say. Yes talking, chewing coca, and drinking you would then accept it, right?

Graciela then described how during the games to soften the bulls' aggression, people feed them chicha.

> During this time of Easter, we would also have huge ollas [large ceramic pots] filled with chicha in the middle of the corral, and we would feed the chicha to the bulls. The crazy cow would enter [the corral], scratching the ground, the crazy cow. And in the olla is fermented chicha and they would drink it like water, getting drunk. I do not know why, but they drink it, these crazy cows. When they finish, then the toreros [bullfighters] enter with their capes. But my dad would enter not with a cape but with a manta and *chumpi* (handwoven belt). My father is very adventurous.[16]

Once the bulls were tired, people would tie colorful *cintas* (ribbons) in their ears and put a cover on the bull like a manta called *engalme*. "The engalme that we would put on their backs, it is beautiful with beautiful embroidery. A cloth appears a little delicate. We put this on their back with ribbons. It is beautiful. The ribbons are long on both sides and hang from their ears."[17]

Graciela described carnival, another festival in Oronccoy that is supported through the cargo system and is readily practiced throughout Latin America. At each carnival celebration, people perform a *yunsa* (*sacha kuchuy* in Quechua) in which they tie hanging prizes such as fruit, bread, cookies, plastic buckets, and even roosters, from trees. These are prized possessions not typically consumed or used during daily life. Every year the community chooses an individual to chop down the trees, leading to a frenzy of delight as people run to acquire as many goods as possible, not entirely unlike a piñata. The person selected to cut the tree is marked as the mayordomo who will then host the celebrations the following year, providing food, alcohol, and goods for the festival. Throughout carnival celebrations, people join hands in large circles around the trees dancing, singing, and drinking for hours.[18]

The entire carnival celebration lasts one week, and each community has a particular day that they host the festival. This provides an opportunity for individuals from different communities to visit one another and for young people to meet potential suitors. Each host community is obligated to feed their guests. For example, those who come to Oronccoy can enter someone's house and the hosts will feed them. Then those hosts could in turn be guests at another community. Each household offers what they have available. Some houses may offer maize and cheese, while others may have potatoes, meat, or other vegetables. Typically, the hosts place the food on a manta as an offer to the guests.[19]

Communities spend months preparing for carnival celebrations, as it is typically the one time of year that women and men acquire a new set of clothing to show off during the festival. For this reason, during the months leading up to carnival you will find men and women set up on backstrap looms behind their houses weaving new mantas and chumpis with elaborate and detailed figures. Before in Oronccoy, according to Graciela, men and women made all their own clothing from wool, but currently they only make socks, sweaters, mantas, and chumpis by hand and shop the feria (market) for a new pollera (large skirt), ojotas, and *lliklli*, while men will often buy new hats, jeans, and shoes for carnival. A lliklli is a rectangular-shaped Andean shawl worn over the shoulders. Beginning in pre-Inca times, a lliklli was held together in front of women's chests with a *tulpi* (prehistoric Andean ornament), which has been generally replaced with a large, metal safety pin.[20] Moreover, in previous generations, people dyed wool using traditional plants, including the nogal tree (*Juglans neotropica*) to create brown.[21] "Before our old people made things with lamb's wool and they would clean it to make the brown color. They wash the wool and then dye it with this nogal for the ponchos." According to Graciela, traditional dyes are no longer widely utilized in Oronccoy.

Death is another event that entails ritual practices. When an adult dies, older women will sing in a particular fashion called *qarawi*.[22] Jeffrey Gamarra describes qarawi as an "Andean song of welcoming that can only be sung with the voice of a woman" (Gamarra 2000, 277). It is custom for close family members to wear black clothing for a year following the death of their loved one. To mark the completion of a year, the community has a celebration during which the family members change back into colorful clothing. When a young child dies, however, there is no expectation to wear black clothing. Graciela explained, "However, when it is a baby, you do not wear black clothes. Always here you wear black when the older people die, but not with the babies." Moreover, women do not sing qarawi, but people sing, dance, and drink alcohol (chicha and caña) above the ground where they bury the child. "There is a festival when a child dies. You dance. You dance on top of the ground. You make the burial with music singing." When I asked Graciela, her husband, and her brother Alex why the practice surrounding the loss of a child is so different from that of an adult, they said that "always the father and mother are sad when their baby dies, but others dance. It is just custom."

Graciela's explanation of children's funeral rites may be reflective of how in many cultures, children's, in particular infants', funeral ceremonies are less elaborate and marginal, as an early death can carry connotation of indifference or stigma (e.g., Einarsdóttir 2004; LeVine 1982; Oliver 1955).[23] Yet, her explanation could also reflect merely the funeral rites that are open to the community, as well as regional differences. In the Andes, the loss of a child, while not uncommon, can be devastating to a parent, and they strive to make provisions to ensure the well-being of the child's soul in the afterlife (e.g., van Kessel 2001) with a belief that their child's spirit will join *pachamama* (Mother Earth) and return as a newborn (Bolin 2006). According to Aláez García (2001), like adult funerals, children's funerals can take several weeks or months as the remains are dressed in special garments, wrapped in a blanket, and buried in a bundle. Over the following eight days, the family members wash and burn the deceased's belongings and offer coca leaves and drink on a small household alter. Then they return to the cemetery with food and drink (Bolin 2006, 60; Onofre Mamani 2001; van Kessel 2001). Perhaps Graciela was referencing the final process of funeral practices for children, the collective sharing of drink and food at the cemetery in honor of the deceased child.

Health and Healing

A key component of Graciela's childhood was learning about natural remedies, which she continues to prefer over Western medicine. Much of what she learned came from her grandmother, and she credits non-Western medicine for her grandmother's impressive longevity.

> My grandmother lived to be over one hundred years old, but my grandmother almost never was sick. . . . See, at the end she was walking with a cane before she died. . . . She was in the bed for no more than one month before she died, and she only used herbs. Until now, she never used medicine, injections, nothing, all natural. She also cured her horses with ants, and she cured with fruits and with herbs. . . . When she had a cough, she would use herbs, only just herbs. She lived in Oronccoy all her life. At the end, she lived with my uncle an hour below Oronccoy. She only used natural remedies her whole life.

Graciela's mother was also very knowledgeable of natural ways of healing. Graciela explained that one day when she was a girl; a young woman fell and broke her upper arm. Graciela's mother bathed the arm in matico (*Piper aduncum*) then wrapped it in a splint made of *chuchau* (a plant that resembles carrizo, an Andean reed) and sheep's wool, and it quickly healed. Another time, Graciela's mom healed a man who broke his leg.

> When they were playing [soccer], this person broke their leg. The bone was sticking out like this [motioned as if bone was sticking straight out from

shin] so my mom pulled it like this [roughly pulled on my arm]. They were screaming, but it went back into place, so then she wrapped it with chuchau, and it healed. He never went to the hospital.

Graciela and her family utilized a wide array of natural herbs to maintain their health. To prevent hemorrhage, especially during a woman's menstrual cycle, they used an herb called *cuchu cuchu* and *ortiga*. Ortiga is also good for *nervios*. Nervios is a syndrome that is indigenous to Latin American and Caribbean populations. The term is sometimes used interchangeably with *nervousness* or *anxiety* but varies from the Eurocentric definition of anxiety disorders found in the *Diagnostic and Statistical Manual of Mental Disorders* utilized by the American Psychiatric Association. Instead, nervios can explain an illness, a symptom, or a cause of another illness (Baer et al. 2003).[24] "For hemorrhage, you just boil the roots of cuchu cuchu and ortiga, but for nervios, you boil the leaves too. Ortiga is a fruit to help with nervios. However, this ortiga is very hot, but for the nervios, this is good. All over the body, you put the fruit. For your head when it hurts." Graciela said they also use the herb *balediana* for bronchitis and that *chicmu* helps to soothe cough and colds.

When you have bronchitis, you take this *balediana* and *chicmu*. You toast the *balediana* with a candle and boil it. Then later, you cut a lemon in half, toast half of it, but not the other half. Throw it in the glass and add salt of the rock, that the cows like, this black salt. Put a little of this in the glass and then drink it hot. This is good. I have given this to my daughter for her cough.

Graciela favored natural remedies and used the herb *marqarinqa* to manage her chronic gastritis. "Right now, I am taking this for my gastritis. The doctor in Curahuasi that did my operation gave me drops for my gastritis, but I do not take them, I only take my herbs." Graciela claimed the drops the doctors gave her at the hospital made her stomach swell: "They did not do anything for me. The marqarinqa is more effective for my gastritis. With this, I have calmed down a little." Marqarinqa grows by the *lambras* tree (*Alnus acuminate*), which has wide leaves effective in treating inflammation. "When you have a scar or a cut, you take the red from this tree and you put it on the cut." Graciela's son,

Hermenegildo, and husband, Juan Pablo, often look for marqarinqa and bring it to Graciela. "With water, only I drink it with my breakfast. I do not eat anything until I drink it in the morning, but it is very bitter." Graciela also consumes the juice from the prickly pear cactus, called tuna, to soothe her gastritis. One day she cut a piece of the cactus growing outside her house to show me the sticky substance inside, which she consumed daily and credited to drastic improvements in her symptoms. In addition to not liking how pharmaceuticals made her feel, Graciela also discussed their associated financial costs. "You need lots of money in the hospital when you are sick, but us poor use our herbs."[25]

———

Graciela's stories of her early life, although perhaps somewhat rose-colored through the prism of memory, can elucidate myriad ways in which the introduction of violence terrorized communities throughout the rural Andes. Sendero Luminoso, while seeking to liberate campesinos, largely ignored, and in many cases directly countered, the primary foci of life in the rural highlands of Peru intimately described throughout this chapter—namely, communal labor exchange and leadership; cyclical ritual celebrations marking the seasons, death, and other life processes; regional market economy; and reliance on the natural environment. First infiltrated by Sendero and then faced with violent military backlash, Oronccoy represented the area of Peru most acutely affected by La Violencia. The entire structure, orientation, and makeup of Graciela's community was forever altered by outside forces that sought its liberation yet ultimately fostered fear, distrust, trauma, displacement, and death. For Graciela, Oronccoy shifted from a land of plenty and peace to a site of tragedy and horror, literally overnight.

Chapter 2

Infiltration and Violence

Initial Presence of Violence in Oronccoy

Graciela's initial experience with violence in Oronccoy occurred when she was roughly eleven years old. One evening, Graciela was suddenly startled awake by ten masked men throwing open the wooden door of her house.

> So, when I was young and went out there [to the kitchen] there was no gas, we cooked with firewood. Therefore, I was sitting in the doorway of my kitchen to light the candle. I was tired, with *sueño* [sleepiness]. At six in the morning when I was a girl. . . . They appeared in my door like this with guns. I had never seen a police officer or anything. I did not know anything when I was a girl. "What is this?" I asked. . . . With masks, they came, "Where is your mother? Where is your father?" they said. Like this, I was sitting, and my mom and dad were in their rooms sleeping with my siblings. "There they are," I said, "sleeping."

The men entered the house and demanded that Graciela and her family tell them where they kept all their money and belongings. Her father tried to explain that they did not have money or belongings, only animals.

> They said, "Where is your money? Where are your things?" . . . "We have nothing," my father said. "We have nothing, only animals. We do not have money." "No! Bring it to me! Give me the money," they said. Therefore, we almost died. "I am going to kill your father," they said. I was crying. I could not believe this in my heart, what was happening. It appeared as if my father was going to die when they cut him. They held his throat in the same

manner you hold a sheep for slaughter. They cut him just a little, a little cut on his throat, so he now has a scar there. "What can I give you? We have no money," my father said. . . . So, they said, "Your brother. Where is he?" "He is below in the house," my father said. For sure, they were looking for my uncle to kill him. "Bring us there!" they said, cutting my father a little more in the throat. They were cutting him a little bit. They said, "Take me to where your brother is." They were yelling. These people came with guns. "Take me to your brother. Bring me to his house!" I was watching with fear.

The men then ransacked Graciela's house in search of money and other goods. At this time, her family had many hens and eggs that they kept in a gourd called *poto*.

In this poto, we held many eggs. So, all of them were looking on the second floor of our house looking for money, these people. We were watching and keeping quiet, and they took the eggs. "To the kitchen!" they said to my mom, so with fear my mom went to the kitchen. We had ch'arki from sheep, so they also took this ch'arki. They took the eggs, all the things from our kitchen in the night. But thankfully, they did not kill my father. I was thinking for sure, when they cut my father, they were going to kill him. I do not know everything that happened to my father, but thanks to God until today, my father is alive!

After ransacking the house, the strange men with guns took Graciela's father in search of his brother, Graciela's uncle. "However, my uncle was not there. I do not know where my uncle was. Because he was not in the house, they beat my father." Graciela of course did not see this at the time because she had stayed in the house with her mother and siblings. Graciela's father later told her what had happened.

My uncle, they did not find him in the house. They only found a woman in the house with her children. My uncle was older at this time, and they asked, "Where is your husband? We are going to beat him," they said. My aunt was trembling, and my father too was afraid. There was no one there; there was nothing, so they all beat my father and my aunt. They were beating her and saying, "Where did your husband go in the night? We will look for his tracks, his trail, to bring him here. We will look all through the community. We will grab him and cut his throat."

Graciela did not know why these men were searching for her uncle but relayed that he had served in the military. "My uncle was military. When he was young in Lima, he served for the military. He had learned how to fall out of helicopters they said. . . . I do not know why they were looking for him. I do not know. To kill him or what I do not know."

Graciela's brother Alex also recounted memories of this fateful evening:

For the first time when I was five years old, five or six years old, when I was entering kindergarten to study one night, in the middle of the night a car came to Oronccoy, but further below there we were sleeping and entered masked men, black masks. There my father was sleeping and further below was my uncle who had a house five minutes by walking. They came and as a child, I was sleeping, but I woke up and they took my dad to kill them, and they beat them up severely and threatened to kill them.

At this point in the discussion, Graciela's father interjected. Pointing to his neck he stated, "They cut my throat with a knife, with a knife." According to Alex, this event represented the beginning of continued and increased levels of violence in Oronccoy. "This is when they first came, but little by little they came more, more came, terrorists came, military came." Graciela and Alex both claimed the men that came that evening were from the neighboring community of Mollebamba but were not military. As Graciela declared, "For sure lazy people had come to rob us. Then later people returned with the military."

Neglect and Unrest in the Oreja de Perro: Setting the Stage

The violence Graciela described stems back to a longer history of unrest, revolt, and neglect in this region of Peru. Throughout Peru, beginning in the 1930s and through the 1960s, agriculturalists contested the long-standing hacienda system that contributed to one of the least equitable land distributions in the world (Stepan 1978, 152). For instance, in 1961, 0.1 percent of landholders possessed eleven million hectares of haciendas and the Cerro Corporation and sixteen families owned 93 percent of available arable land and pasture in the central highlands (Crabtree and Durand 2017). Rebellions took place, and by the early 1960s, Peru was experiencing "unquestionably one of the largest peasant movements in Latin American history" (Handelman 1975, 12). Under the presidency of Fernando Belaúnde Terry, agriculturalists throughout the highlands joined peasant unions and federations to recuperate hacienda land. Between 1963 and 1964, an estimated three hundred thousand agriculturalists seized nearly four hundred haciendas. Belaúnde disapproved of their extralegal mobilization and authorized repressive action against invading campesinos. By the time the Agrarian Reform bill finally passed Congress in 1969, over three hundred farmers had been killed (Heilman 2010, 123–24).

The Agrarian Reform of 1969 is considered "the second most sweeping [land reform] in Latin America after that of Cuba" (McClintock 1984, 49; see also Crabtree and Durand 2017). While the reform expropriated land from the hacendados and transferred into worker-managed cooperatives (Sociedades Agrarias de Interés Social), it curiously idealized the Indian past while striving to incorporate Indigenous peoples into the national structure and educate (i.e., Westernize) them (Mallon 1992).[1] In fact, President Velasco abolished the word *indio* (Indian) from the official vocabulary and replaced it with *campesino* (farmer or peasant), stressing class relations over ethnic identity (de la Cadena 1998).[2] The term *comunidad indígena* (Indigenous community) was officially changed to *comunidad campesina* (peasant community) because the term *indígena* was understood as derogatory (González 2011, 26). Nevertheless, categorizing individuals as "peasants" also serves to marginalize and ostracize people from society (Huayhua 2019, 420).[3]

By focusing on class relations and disregarding Indigenous identities, the government enacted land reform policies with little comprehension of actual, existing Indigenous social/political organization or labor practices (Skar 1982). Consequently, the emerging leadership in the cooperative replaced the traditional civil-religious hierarchy system, *varayocc*.[4] The cooperatives also disrupted the careful balance of power structured in the moiety system. Moieties represent a form of Inca-imposed social organization in which smaller ayllus were embedded in larger ayllus, forming moieties.[5] In areas that were not of high priority, such as Andahuaylas, years passed without substantive change in land tenure.[6] Moreover, the land reform coincided with an overall economic recession. In the early 1980s, potato production in the southern Andes fell by 40 to 50 percent, wages dropped, inflation rates rose, and 60 percent or more of Peru's industrial capacity was idled, leaving few if any opportunities for agriculturalists to work as urban wage laborers.

Amid frustrations with the Agrarian Reform and overall economic decline, Sendero emerged. Sendero Luminoso first organized in the regions most neglected by the Agrarian Reform, historically exploited by the state, and most acutely affected by the country's economic crisis—primarily the departments of Ayacucho, Huancavelica, and Apurímac. These departments, while diverse, had experienced centuries of insurgencies and rebellions (Heilman 2010; Stern 1982), are the most economically impoverished departments in Peru, are largely rural, and primarily speak Quechua.[7]

Initial Presence of Sendero Luminoso in the Oreja de Perro

Graciela's community was once largely controlled by the Hacienda La Chapi, which was owned by the Carillo brothers and was one of the largest haciendas in the region. During the era of land rebellions, agriculturalists seized the Hacienda La Chapi. The hacendados were assassinated and the Civil Guard responded by demanding food as well as reprimanding, torturing, and assassinating campesinos (CVR 2003, 5:87).[8] This event was engrained in the memories of agriculturalists, and Sendero capitalized on feelings of injustice. Given the history of neglect, unrest, and persistent poverty, many in this region initially welcomed Sendero's message of equality. According to a Peruvian anthropologist, Luis, who worked on the Comisión de la Verdad y Reconciliación, "So they [Sendero] went to this area to radicalize the population. Initially they [campesinos] accepted the narrative" (Luis, pers. comm., August 10, 2018).

As early as 1978–1980, Sendero began working in the towns of Andarapa, Ongoy, and Ocobamba seeking to indoctrinate the communities of Oronccoy, Pallqa, and others in the Chungui district.[9] They focused on secondary schools (high schools) where many kids from the Oreja de Perro studied, particularly from Tastabamba, Oronccoy, Putucunay, Socco, Santa Carmen, and Mollebamba (CVR 2003, vol. 5). The Comisión de la Verdad y Reconciliación

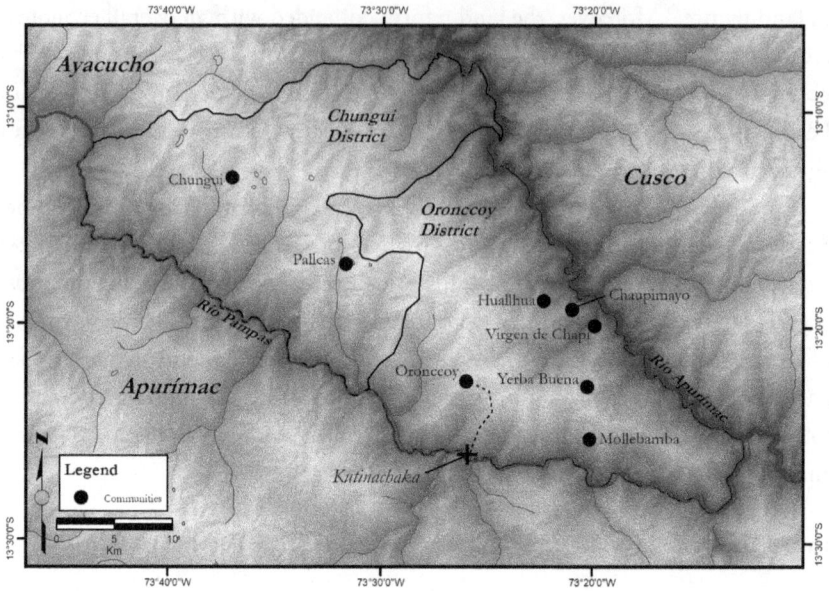

Figure 7. Map of the Chungui and Oronccoy Districts showing
some of the communities mentioned in the text. Map created by Lucas C. Kellett.

states that Sendero "educated the *comuneros* in the *Oreja de Perro* zone, especially Oronccoy, which was then the starting point of *Sendero* presence in the Chungui district" (CVR 2003, 4:107). One student from Oronccoy described meeting Abimael Guzmán while studying in Ongoy. Guzmán would come to the school to give *charlas* (workshops) about the problems agriculturalists faced, stressing the negative results of the Agrarian Reform and the failure of previous revolutions due to not setting up bases of support in campesino communities (CVR 2003, vol. 5). Some of these students continued their studies at the university in the city of Huamanga (Ayacucho) and then returned to their rural communities to foster support for the revolution.

Given the region's isolation, rich resources, and strategic location, Sendero set up bases of support in this area (CVR 2003, vol. 5). A Peruvian anthropologist, Carlo, described the isolation and consequential lack of state presence in the region making it attractive to Sendero, "It is a forgotten zone. There is no presence of the state. To have state presence it would be very difficult. The army cannot get there. There are no schools, no health center. It is an abandoned area, so this is the place for Sendero to establish themselves" (Carlo, pers. comm., August 11, 2018). Another Peruvian anthropologist, Luis, further argued:

> Sendero wanted to set up a base in Oreja because they could set up communications between Ayacucho and Apurímac. In addition, it straddles the highlands and jungle. From Chungui a few hours to Chapi, it is jungle. It is in the middle of Apurímac and Ayacucho and there are no roads. They wanted to establish a base of support, political control. (Luis, pers. comm., August 10, 2018)

After the war, the Comisión de la Verdad y Reconciliación report held Sendero responsible for the "forcible transfer of people" from the Oreja de Perro region as they forced the population to move solely to be able to have a captive group of people available to work to meet its logistic needs (CVR 2003, 6:632, 654).

Sendero Luminoso: Garnering Initial Support

Graciela said Sendero's ideologies began to circulate in Oronccoy through teachers from Huamanga for about two years before they felt any violence in the community.

> There was a high school functioning before [in Oronccoy]. One year, or, yeah, two years, they were with these dirty politics. They were studying with the children. One called himself a Senderista. This politician was teaching our young people in the school. There were more complications, but our young people did not know anything, but the professors were teaching this. They said they were from Ayacucho from the Universidad de Huamanga. In reality, the parents did not know.

When Sendero first arrived, people were unclear of its aims, and sympathy resided with its notions of economic justice where the core value is reciprocity and resentment against individuals amassing wealth. From the beginning, they made their coercive capabilities apparent to the peasantry and often took advantage of local conflicts to be heralded as "just" (Degregori 1998; see also La Serna 2012).

For example, Sendero often targeted and killed cattle thieves and the political elite in various highland towns and cities, portraying their victims as cut off from others socially because they "don't speak Quechua and act like *mistis* [mestizos]" (Berg 1992, 96) to gain rural men and women's support. Support also came from those most disadvantaged by the Agrarian Reform because Sendero specifically targeted the cooperatives. Moreover, they ended up sweeping out the state's repressive apparatus and police forces, which peasants resented and feared because they acted "more cruelly and arbitrarily than the guerrillas" (98). In José Carlos Agüero's reflections on being a son of the Shining Path he does not see agriculturalists as easily manipulated puppets but claims his "parents did intrude in their lives decisively. They were like activators: they tapped people whose skin was already sensitive to the touch. And what they brought with them was bad: death in the worst cases. . . . Incarceration or uprooting from home in other cases" (Agüero 2021, 56).

Carlos Iván Degregori (1998) notes that the rural youth helped Sendero garner support among the peasantry, and this effort was most successful where there was a significant generational gap in educational levels.[10] The young people were the "ones with the eyes" (*nawiyoq*) who saw things their "ignorant" parents had not noticed. Therefore, even when parents disagreed with the actions of Sendero, their reaction was ambiguous due to the cultural ties that bind the generations together. Moreover, unlike the 1965 guerrillas involved in the land reform, "the 1980 combatants were not alienated from the rural world, where they were born, had relatives and learned Quechua," and so they successfully recruited peasants into their movements, although they also resorted to forced recruitment (Flores Galindo 2010, 225).

Some peasants believed pachamama refused to tolerate more earthly suffering and the world had to change, with entire towns unfurling the red flag in support of Sendero (Flores Galindo 2010, 225). Ronald Berg (1992) conducted fieldwork in the community of Pacucha in the province of Andahuaylas, which is in route to Graciela's community of Oronccoy. He asserted that in some cases peasants' acceptance was pragmatic—it provided concrete gains on a personal, familial, or communal level—and in other instances, people expressed passive support, a "willingness to tolerate the presence of the guerrillas, but a disinclination to take any action against them, including informing to the police" (186). In other cases, people accepted Sendero out of fear. Jaymie Patricia Heilman describes the situation in Carhuanca, where most people who remained in the district accepted Sendero because "they were too frightened to object" (Heilman 2010, 189). While some regions were peripheral to the movement, leading to various levels of engagement on the part of the community, other areas, such as Graciela's community of Oronccoy, represented an epicenter of Sendero presence.

According to Graciela, the presence of Senderistas in her community made other people from outside of the region assume that everyone in Oronccoy supported Sendero and were therefore terrorists. "Therefore, they [the military] thought all of us were terrorists. The military said we were all terrorists. It was complicated. . . . However, we were not terrorists. We had not done anything. We were innocents. How could you say a baby that was born was a terrorist? The old people?" Graciela said that a few members of the community initially supported Sendero: "There were maybe five [people] who were involved in this violence, in this terrorism. Maybe, maybe, but we did not know who they were, but for the fault of them, all of us were guilty, the children, the elderly."

Sendero Luminoso Makes National Headlines

Sendero's first public action occurred on May 18, 1980, when Senderistas seized and burned unused ballots for the national election in the town of Chuschi (Cangallo Province, Department of Ayacucho). By September of the same year, Sendero began its "moralization campaign" in Chuschi and the Sinchis (counterinsurgency police) responded by arresting and torturing four schoolteachers for burning the ballots (González 2011, 42). Sendero continued to carry out actions in five provinces of Ayacucho, and by the end of 1981 Sendero controlled at least nine communities in the Pampas River region (42). In 1982, Sendero decided it was time to "hammer the countryside" (Degregori 1998, 136). To do so, it was necessary to "dislocate the power of the bosses [*gamonales*], disarrange the power of the authorities, and hit the live forces of the enemy . . . clean out the zone, leave an empty plain [*dejar pampa*]" (Degregori 1998, 136). Like the Agrarian Reform, Sendero replaced the varayocc (staff holders) with "popular committees," thereby disregarding Andean conventions (Poole and Rénique 1992, 62). Degregori (1998) argues that the replacement of authorities chosen through the vara system by young Senderista cadres not only was an insult in the most "traditional" zones but also contrasted with the community's entire political and social structure (134). Trusting young, inexperienced cadres to govern the towns also resulted in them assuming attitudes of vengeance, which ended up causing large-scale massacres.

Sendero soon moved from targeting individuals to more emboldened acts.

In 1982, 150 Senderistas charged two police stations before assaulting the prison in the city of Huamanga (Ayacucho), releasing 255 inmates, killing 16 individuals (including two guards), and wounding 12 (*Sarasota Herald Tribune* 1982; see also Gorriti 1999). Nevertheless, in 1982, the government still viewed Sendero as a threat limited to a largely neglected, remote corner of the Andes (Bourque and Warren 1989). The precipitating event that put Sendero's emergence on the national political scene occurred on December 31, 1982, when the capital city of Lima suffered a massive blackout, with the only light radiating from a hammer and sickle blazing on San Agustín hill, which overlooks the city.[11] The following day, President Belaúnde sent the armed forces into Ayacucho and declared a state of emergency.[12] On January 26, 1983, a community of agriculturalists killed eight journalists who were reporting on a brigade of Sendero guerrillas that had been slayed. A few months later, on April 3, 1983, Senderistas killed sixty-nine campesinos in Lucanamarca (Huanca Sancos Province, Department of Ayacucho) (CVR 2003).

The assassinations reinforced public perceptions of the *serranos* (highlanders) as instigating irrational and unchecked violence. According to Susan C. Bourque and Kay B. Warren (1989), "fears of the indigenous population have long been a factor in the calculations of political leaders," and such fears have inspired military solutions and repression on more than one occasion (15). Even the Peruvian military depicted the insurgency in racist terms, "stereotyping perpetrators as untrustworthy racial half-castes and the masses they led as violent, uncivilized Indians from the backward Andean region" (Wilson 2009, 56). The Belaúnde administration and political right did not care to understand the guerrillas or their motivation, only to eliminate them as they represented "terrorists," a soulless new species that spread like a plague throughout the world, inspired by "Marxist" and "totalitarian" ideologies (Flores Galindo 2010, 222). Such prevailing perceptions appear to have instigated the military response and an escalation in violence, as illustrated by the dramatic increase in the number of deaths since January 1983. According to the Comisión de la Verdad y Reconciliación final report, the number of deaths in the Department of Ayacucho nearly doubled in one year, with 2,232 deaths recorded for 1983 and 4,453 deaths in 1984.[13]

Military Presence in Oronccoy

Sometime after the masked men entered Graciela's house, she faced her first direct encounter with the military, which occurred at "the time the frost falls to make chuño [freeze-dried potatoes]." Her father was suffering "pain in his stomach" so he was not working much in the fields and her mother was experiencing "pain in her head." Due to her parents' ailments, Graciela oversaw all aspects of running the household. There was no electricity in Graciela's community (there is still no electricity), and Graciela would typically light a candle when she first woke to start the day's work.

One morning just as Graciela was about to light a candle, a silhouette of a man's head appeared in the entrance of their small door. Within moments, this stranger was standing in the middle of her mud brick house, holding a gun.

> We did not know who these people were with guns. I was scared. From my back they said, "Go, go to the plaza!" Then my mom and dad were in the bed and said, "Get up out of the bed. Let us go." My father had pain and could not walk, but they said, "Hurry up! Let's go!" to all of us. With fear, we walked. My mom too, we walked out the door. They were all over the place. They would say to get together. They brought two horses, *palos*, and *picos* [sticks and hoes used for agriculture] what you use to harvest with. There was a young man with them named Valerio. He studied in this high school. They said he was a terrorist. They grabbed this young man. They were carrying a book about the size of this photo [6 x 9 inches]. They grabbed him with both arms. "*Agachinse*" [bow, crouch down], they would say. They kicked him and threw him down on the ground. . . . There were a lot of us in the plaza flattened on the ground on top of the frost still. It was cold like in Huancabamba [a community south of Andahuaylas at an altitude of about 11,942 feet]. The young people and the babies were crying. Their moms were holding them like this [Graciela demonstrated holding a baby close to her chest, guarding them from others]. Other people were running from the military. We were afraid that we were going to die.

There was utter confusion as Graciela, her family, and community members had never seen individuals that looked like these men; their height, their dress, and their weapons were all foreign, yet Graciela claimed many of them were military personnel and civilians from Mollebamba who were working together.

We were scared, as they had come from Mollebamba, the military and the

civilians. . . . The community of Oronccoy was down on the ground, but
the militaries and civilians from Mollebamba, people from Mollebamba,
came with the military. . . . So they took us all out of our houses and
brought us to the plaza. Other men were punishing us. Scared, we were on
the ground, yes. They brought from Mollebamba pico, palo, and horses so
they could kill us and bury us. . . . They killed a young person who they
said was studying these terrorist politics. They grabbed a young person
named Valerio.

Graciela explained that they shot Valerio on a hill below Oronccoy called
Chuñuña. "Yes, in the beginning, this happened when we were living there. The
killing began with this young person. We were still living at this time in our
houses when they returned to kill this young person when they returned from
Mollebamba."

The Comisión de la Verdad y Reconciliación reported that there was a police
base in Illahuasi de Andarapa and individuals from the base entered Mollebamba
and took seven comuneros. With this action, they began to expel the Senderistas
from Mollebamba and form a system of lookouts. Together with the police,
individuals from Mollebamba began incursions into the Oreja de Perro area to
prevent an alignment with Sendero. In 1982 they traveled to Oronccoy,
considered a support base for Sendero, and brought all the community to the
plaza and assassinated Valerio Flores, accused of being a leader of the local
subversive group. The CVR report describes the event in detail:

In 1982 *los ronderos de Mollebamba* entered Oronccoy, considered a base of
support of the subversives, captured Valerio, a local command of *Sendero*,
brought all the population to the plaza, in front of all he was tortured by
taking off his legs and cutting off his tongue, his tongue was finally hung
from a school post. Later they obligated the population to organize a *rondas
campesinas*. (CVR 2003, 5:92)

Graciela explained how people from Mollebamba became embroiled in the
violence. "In Mollebamba, the people were peaceful, but they began this
terrorism and then brought it here, so they organized the people from
Mollebamba, so from Mollebamba they came to kill us. I saw all of them

carrying picos, palos; with horses, they came for this, they were a part of it all." I asked if the people from Mollebamba supported Sendero or the military and Graciela responded, "They were from the beginning from Sendero and then the military came. First, they were terrorists and then the military came, and with the military they came for us." Women from Oronccoy participated in a focus group with the Comisión de la Verdad y Reconciliación and reflected on the shifting alliances that Graciela mentioned. The women claimed, "The first people who labeled us as terrorists were the *comuneros* from Mollebamba" (CVR 2003, 5:90). The women described how the people from Mollebamba supported the military: "But these same people were the first to come in favor of the terrorists before. We could not recognize which one of them was what and we were afraid . . . the community members of Mollebamba started to kill us and the same with *comuneros* from Chungui and Pallqas" (5:90).

At this point in explaining what had happened, Graciela took hold of my notebook and sketched a map showing the location of Oronccoy, along with numerous other communities. She described how later she learned that military soldiers terrorized other villages on their way to Oronccoy. "From here they came, our neighbors no more. From there they came, our neighbors, to kill us." In describing "our neighbors no more," Graciela was referencing how military soldiers were making their way to Oronccoy from a military base in Chapi, wiping out entire communities in their path. Graciela explained that the military "wanted to live in this pueblo. There is land for animals. There is rainforest close. There is all. The military knew this. . . . There is more than in other communities, so they came to kill us with bullets, daily, daily the military came. They came until everyone was dead. They came to kill everyone."

Support for Sendero Luminoso Begins to Wane

Initial support for Sendero came from its ability to get rid of enemies (primarily the mestizos, who appeared to be gaining all the power); however, when Sendero countered political and kinship structures vital to economic production and societal reproduction, agriculturalists began to realize that they were not participating in the revolutionary movement. Once they recognized that "the committees imposed by *Sendero* gave them less voice in deciding their own destiny than the governing structures imposed by the departmental and state bureaucracies, they began to retreat from *Sendero Luminoso's* programs" (Isbell 1992, 72).[14] As agriculturalists expressed more resistance to Sendero, Senderistas reacted through increased violence toward them, as well as further activity in the cities.

As Sendero Luminoso continued to enact its strategy for revolution and overall support for the movement began to wane, they soon shifted from targeting deviants and those with power to killing people simply because they did not share their political ideology (La Serna 2012, 195). Sendero sought to maintain an iron grip on territories it strived to liberate and tolerated no dissent, publicly trying, whipping, and executing offenders (Flores Galindo 2010). According to Degregori (1998), the deaths soon surpassed a tolerable limit, not simply because the agriculturalists have a "culture of life" but because one had to take care of the labor force, and to kill, or eliminate, a link in a family/labor network had repercussions beyond the nuclear family. A Peruvian anthropologist, Raul, described the enduring impacts of killing an individual within extended family networks in the rural highlands:

> When they killed a person in the [rural] zones, they did not just kill the nuclear family, they *choque* [collided, crashed] with all the extended family, with all of the community. In contrast to the city with a focus on the nuclear family, [in the campo] there are political consequences that affect the community. The community festivals are important, community and religious cargos, making houses, and faenas. All the collective activities in the community are important. In the city, each person lives their individual lives, but in campesino communities reciprocity, mutual help, and solidarity dominate and it is important to be very open and wide. (Raul, pers. comm., August 10, 2018)

Another Peruvian anthropologist, Fidel, claimed people also began to lose trust in Sendero when they started to target community authorities and exacerbate divisions within the communities:

> They began to kill them [community leaders], so then people went against them [Sendero]. They would go after the authorities. Then, for example,

in Oronccoy, if there were a family with a lot of land or many animals, they would go after them. In addition, if people had an argument about a festival or something, then Sendero would take advantage of this conflict and kill them. . . . So this really differed from their original message. (Fidel, pers. comm., August 12, 2018)

Additionally, Sendero countered Andean ethics through expressing a lack of respect for life or death. Sendero did not strive to control excessive violence, as the revolution "carries with it weeping, pain, suffering and death" and followed the logic that the old must be destroyed for the new (Flores Galindo 2010, 227). Sendero killed mercilessly and refused to bury their victims, the universal rite of mourning.[15] Kimberly Theidon (2013, 54) describes how dehumanizing this time of violence, or *sasachakuy tiempo*, was for campesinos. According to survivors, "The *Senderistas* killed people in ways we do not even butcher our animals" (438). Moreover, because people were not allowed to bury their dead, dogs and pigs were found gorging themselves on cadavers (54).[16]

Figure 8. A cemetery (campo santo) in the community of Oronccoy.
Photo by Max Altamirano Molero.

Sendero sought to prevent the weekly markets from functioning to restrict supplies to the city and prohibited fiestas and drinking, which local communities objected to (Isbell 1992, 66–67). Another fissure of Sendero was a discrepancy between traditional strategies of Andean domination and the strategy of "people's war." According to Maoist guerrilla groups, "when the enemy advances, we retreat" (Degregori 1998, 141). When Sendero followed this idea and retreated to protect its own cadres, they clashed with the ideology of the traditional Andean *patrón* who protects his or her clients (141). Furthermore, the rebels continued to anger villagers with forced recruitment, demands for food, and executions of informers. The youth thus became torn between the party's ideology, on one hand, and their familial ties (and common sense), on the other.[17]

Increased Military Backlash

As local resistance to Sendero grew, so did the military's response to the unrest. During the administration of Alan García (1985–1990), the initial intention to respect human rights and hold accountable those who violated them was overshadowed by the scorched-earth and no-prisoners policy advocated by General Clemente Noel in 1984 (see Poole and Rénique 1992; González 2011). Consequently, violence escalated exponentially in the emergency zone.[18] Beginning in 1982, "red zones" appeared where the Sendero Luminoso sought shelter and protection, which the military later targeted (Flores Galindo 2010). Sendero Luminoso guerrillas hid among peasants in rural communities, and it was impossible for a Peruvian military officer to distinguish between peasant and subversive, so "the military had to poison the water and render [it] intolerable as a refuge" (233).

The military soon realized that the Andean world was far from homogenous, with multiple internal conflicts, old land disputes, and interethnic rivalries. So the military strategy included recruiting peasants, promising to protect them and satisfy some basic needs, and then throw them back against Sendero, calling them *montoneros* (Flores Galindo 2010). The military also conducted a counterguerrilla campaign, in which the military strove to set all groups against each other and tolerated no neutrality. To survive, a community had to demonstrate loyalty by arming itself and apprehending Senderistas and offering proof, which the community of Huaychao did by hanging seven supposed Sendero Luminoso boys (between ten and fifteen years old, according to photos) (234). The military also began a psychological war that depicted Abimael Guzmán and Senderistas "as vampires, *pishtacos* whom peasants must kill without compassion to prevent the evil from spreading" (237).[19]

Like the military, Sendero also did not accept neutrality and responded not against the military, who were often barricaded in their garrisons, but against those who by choice, or force, fought on the front lines. The Comisión de la Verdad y Reconciliación claimed that in Ayacucho "the entry of the armed forces initially caused the reaction of the PCP-SL [Partido Comunista del Perú-Sendero Luminoso] to increase intolerance and violence with the murder of snitches" (CVR 2003, 1:108).[20] In 1983, Senderistas massacred sixty-nine people in the Ayacuchan town of Lucanamarca. Some were shot in the chest or head, while guerrillas poured boiling water over others before slitting their throats with rusty knives and machetes, including eight elders, pregnant women, eighteen children, and a six-month-old baby (La Serna 2019). Rural populations were soon at the mercy of both Sendero and the military, as they were vulnerable to suspicion and reprisals from both sides. Agriculturalists realized that "survival might well depend on showing one face to the soldiers and another to the guerillas" (Theidon 2013, 15). In effect, people lived separate public and private lives, hiding their conflicted allegiances, creating a sense that people were "two-faced" (*iskay uyukuna*) and leading to distrust, as "one could never know which way anyone might turn" (15). Consequently, the dividing line was not rich against poor or white against Indian but rather community against community, comunero against comunero (Flores Galindo 2010).

Living amid the Epicenter of Violence

Due to Sendero initially setting up a refuge in the Oreja de Perro region, the state targeted this zone, and the military backlash was particularly brutal. According to Peruvian anthropologist Fidel, the Oreja de Perro region faced reprisals from all sides:

> This zone of Oreja de Perro was known as liberated by Sendero and supporting Sendero, so when the army came, they saw them all as terrorists

and killed them. So then Sendero started to demand support, food, all, and then the military came and killed everyone. There was a lot of killing and raping. In this time, the people of the campo, the women, did not know who these people were. At times, Sendero would kill, and at times, the military would kill. It was difficult. (Fidel, pers. comm., August 12, 2018)

Graciela relayed the overall sense of confusion and fear living in the epicenter of violence during this time:

We did not know if this was part of the communists or part of the military. We did not know. We just knew the people came with guns. We were just children; we did not know. We did not have television or anything. When we were children, we just had our eyes on our animals; our sheep to take care of things with the house is all. We did not know people with guns. . . . They would kill without compassion. Everyone would hide, but they would still come, pull people out of their homes, and kill them. It did not matter if it was women, children, pregnant women, men. They killed everyone. They used guns, bullets.

Graciela's brother Alex also discussed living in the middle of the violence:

The terrorists came and they killed us equally. The military came and they killed us equally. They came because I think they were confused. Therefore, Senderistas would come and say we were with the military. "You are supporting the military," [they would say] and kill us. The military would come and say, "You are terrorists. You are convening. You are talking with the terrorists. You are a boss of this," and equally kill us. The people were confused. There was a confusion. Here we support and they kill us. Here we ask for asylum. We ask for asylum to the military and equally they kill us. We ask for asylum from Sendero and equally they kill us. . . . My sister, my parents, and all the family and more, all of my *poblanos*, were tortured and rights were violated, women, children eight, nine, ten years old, adolescents were raped by the military, by the soldiers that came at this time, the Sinchis that came from another site to the poor people that did not have knowledge of anything. We did not know how to read or write. We were illiterate and were mistaken as terrorists and killed, raped, and tortured with knives; they killed with guns. Others, they cut their throats like a sheep, as whatever animal, and it did not matter the age, and this is what we suffered. . . . The people who committed the most violence came mostly from the military that at the time was called Los Sinchis. They are the ones that killed the people, the people that did not know anything.[21]

Although the CVR recognizes Chungui as one of the hardest hit districts in Ayacucho during the war, the counterinsurgency police known as Los Sinchis particularly brutalized the southern area of the district, the Oreja de Perro. As the CVR notes, "Unlike the northern part of Chungui, the *Oreja de Perro* area [where Oronccoy is located] had suffered the incursion of the *Sinchis* of Andarapa," which entered the area to supervise the watchdog system and functioned out of Mollebamba (CVR 2003, 4:95). The military installed a base in Mollebamba in 1985, following the installation of a base in Chungui in 1984.[22] The installation of these bases militarized daily life, restricting individuals' movements and at first forcing individuals to sleep at the base. The CVR reports that almost immediately after setting up military bases, the military tried to organize civil defense committees (*ronderos*) "getting some former *Senderistas* on the side of the military, as happened in Mollebamba" (CVR 2003, 4:96–97). While the formation of *rondas campesinas* signaled a primary move away from Sendero support, as illustrated in Mollebamba they were also often forced by military troops.[23] The formation of increasing numbers of rondas, or "committees of Civil Autodefense," ultimately resulted in a warfare between Sendero and the peasants (Degregori 1998, 145–46).[24]

Graciela's husband, Juan Pablo, described how the entire community was caught between the Senderistas, the military, and ronderos:

Also, the military came and killed. The military killed more. They killed without compassion. It was the same with the *Gente Civil* that formed the ronderos, they also killed like that. They killed with knives, not with bullets. With machete and with knives they killed. Grabbing the people. They killed, they cut throats, and they raped all the young women. To the women, they grabbed the women and raped them, whatever they wanted to do. We would try to escape, but then maybe meet with the military, and then

Figure 9. A cemetery (campo santo) in the community of Mollebamba.
Photo by Max Altamirano Molero.

the Senderistas would kill us for supporting them. They were the same. . . .
It was a trauma, a total trauma. We did not think of living. We thought we
would die. "What day will I die?" we would say. This is all we would think,
"What day will I die?" Children, elders, young people.

The number of deaths and disappeared in the Chungui district rose
substantially following the establishment of the military bases and rondas,
making the period between 1984 and 1988 the most cruel and bloody state of
the war in the Oreja de Perro region (CVR 2003, 4:2003).[25] The Comisión de la
Verdad y Reconciliación described the multiple levels of devastation in this
region:

The massacres and the devastation of the towns in the entire Apurímac River Valley and in some districts such as Chungui, there is almost no community or annex that has not suffered some combined incursion of the military
and self-defense committee, with its aftermath theft of goods and animals,

executions and burning of houses. In the area of the *Oreja de Perro*, there was a special degree of violence with the *ronderos* assassinating the alleged *Senderistas* who they found in the mountains. (CVR 2003, 7:791)

The practice of comuneros killing comuneros in the Oreja de Perro region underscores how the war in Peru was less an "internal war" or "political internal conflict" with binary distinctions between perpetrator and victim, terrorist versus hero, and more of a *guerra fraticida*, a fratricidal war: a war between brothers.[26]

While Graciela recognized her own suffering, she always situated it in relation to that of others, and she recounted the impact of the widespread violence on people from neighboring communities. According to Graciela, "Other paisanos [peasants] maybe had worse things happen." She described how in a community not far from Oronccoy, Yerbabuena, a man had his hand shot off by the military. "There were many communities in Oreja de Perro, many paisanos affected, many things that passed. Some cut off ears after killing them to count [have proof] of how many people they had killed." Graciela described how the military would enter different communities, round up people, and bring them to the town of Mollebamba. If people ran off trying to escape, the military would shoot them. Soldiers would also "torture people—cut fingers, ears, and tongues. They would ask, 'Where are the rest? Where are the terrorists? You know!' They thought we knew terrorists, but we did not. They killed people from babies to elders." Graciela's brother Alex also discussed how people were tortured: "Other people were killed with knives, who were tortured, whose fingers were cut, their tongues, they took off their ears. They cut off their ears, all tremendous suffering that we experienced." A taxi driver from Cusco I met in 2018 echoed Alex's and Graciela's narratives. The driver had served in the military for nine years, primarily in the Departments of Ayacucho and Apurímac. While driving between Cusco and Abancay, he told me that when they found a suspected Senderista who refused to talk, they would cut off a finger or an ear. He also reported that they shot animals merely to assure that Senderistas did not eat better than they did.

As the taxi driver relayed, the military and Senderistas not only threatened Graciela's community with violence but also stole their livelihoods. Graciela described how the military would seize their animals and crops:

We would harvest our potato, our maize. We would mound it up. They would watch us. The military would appear and watch us harvesting. When we would go hide, they would then take it all. It was the same with our cows and our horses. With bullets, they would kill them. With their guns, they would kill our animals. When we would leave them in a place for a while, we would return and see that they had killed our animals with their guns. They would not leave them for us to eat them. For them they would kill them. They would eat them. They would take them. We harvested potato and maize to eat to live and they took it all. They came and took all of it.

When I asked if Senderistas or the military did most of the theft, Graciela responded:

It was complicated. Yes, but mostly it was the military that came with the people. This community mostly was taken by the military. From here, from this community, first they said we were terrorists that we understood like terrorists. . . . Yes it was of both, we had to be careful. Mostly, the military took our animals. Why we had fear because they had guns, but we had nothing to defend ourselves.

Living in fear and with little to nothing to support themselves, Graciela and her community soon realized that escape was the only option for survival.[27] Graciela and entire population centers throughout the district of Chungui fled their communities at this time, taking refuge in the hills and jungle (CVR 2003, 4:94).

The infiltration of a particular ideology into Graciela's community upended her entire life. Prior to any national declaration of revolution, Sendero Luminoso had long began their campaign of support in the Oreja de Perro region, particularly with Graciela's community. Following centuries of neglect and exploitation, the initial message of Sendero gained credence in the Oreja region. Yet, any initial support soon waned upon further exploitation, demands, and countering of Andean conceptions and ways of life. Nevertheless, the region had been marked as a terrorist holdout, leading to unprecedented military backlash. Consequently, all residents of the region were subjected to suspicion and reprisals from various sides of the conflict, leading to destruction of communities, death, and mass exodus. At a young age, Graciela was largely unaware of the larger forces at play that upended her life and that of her comuneros as she found herself fleeing the only home she had ever known and fighting for her life on the run for years to come.

Chapter 3

Living like Deer

Surviving on the Run

Initial Escape

At a certain point, the violence and loss of livelihood made it impossible for anyone to remain in the community of Oronccoy. Virtually everyone who could walk escaped and Graciela's brother Alex explained that not just those from Oronccoy left. "We escaped to the mountains. All the people. It was not just us who escaped, the entire pueblo escaped. Various pueblos escaped. We all left and hid in caves, deserted." Graciela described having to leave with nothing:

> More violence came with the military. They killed us people from the community, so we were afraid, and we escaped to the forests, to the caves. We were hiding, sleeping in the caves with the clothes on our backs. We did not have any clothes to change. With fear, we left our houses, so people carried what they could. . . . With our lives, we escaped; our lives, nothing more. Nothing else was important, not our clothes, nothing, no animals.

Everyone who fled left their dogs behind, tying them up by their homes so they would not follow those who were escaping and be a liability. "When we had escaped to the forests, to the mountains, the dogs in the houses were crying. Our animals, three of them were crying. They were so sad." At this point, Graciela made a howling sound imitating the dogs' cries and her eyes became wet with tears. "We had to leave them in the house. The dogs were crying so much. It was so sad." Respect and compassion for all wild and domestic animals is a well-documented aspect of Andean ethics; however, the significance of dogs has been cited for "their role in the soul's journey through the afterlife"

(Lambright 2015, 146). Yet another form of torture, during the war, people were often required to not only abandon but also torture and kill their own dogs, and in some cases even consume their flesh (146). Graciela gravely described how people had to leave all their highly valued animals behind when they fled their communities. Some people in Graciela's community had hundreds of animals that they had to abandon, and "the military killed all of them. No one was there to support our pueblo. No one stayed. All was forgotten. We escaped to the mountains. We were looking for Chaupimayo. We left all our herds, all our animals—our roosters, horses, our sheep, goats, our pigs."

As previously described in chapter 1, animals represent a key means of solidifying social and community relations, as well as providing fundamental dietary and financial resources. Moreover, animals, along with landscapes and plants, represent a constellation of other-than-human sentient beings that make up an integral part of life in the Andes (de la Cadena 2010, 341). According to de la Cadena, the mutual nurturing of all world beings is called *uyway* and it "colors all of Andean life" (354). Therefore, the indiscriminate killing and abandonment of animals not only caused a material loss but also was a means of tearing apart the fabric of Andean social life and well-being.[1]

In the wake of their departure, the military burned all their houses to the ground. "They burned our houses also. Some people were caught there inside their houses, living in there as if we are here. When they came upon them, they would shut the door and burn them inside. . . . Equally, we were escaping our deaths. We had such fear of being killed." Graciela described the pain of having to leave the elderly behind when they escaped, knowing that they would be burned alive, including her neighbor Donita. "Donita was in the bed, and she could not escape, so they found her and they burned the house, shutting the door. What courage she had, right?" Graciela's brother Alex also described the burning of houses. "[The military] burned their houses, closing [the door] and covering all with gasoline. In this time, kerosene existed and with all of this and other weapons." Alex explained that they had fled Oronccoy at one point and sought to return, but "they continued to burn our houses. There was nowhere to return. Where would we return to the pueblo because our houses were burned? Yeah, it no longer existed." In the end, Graciela fled with "my father, my mother, my neighbors, my comuneros, all of the community. Therefore, the rest of them they killed. They killed them."

Figure 10. View of the Apurímac River and part of the territories of
the communities of Huallhua, Vaca Wasi, and Belén Chapi from the road to
Amaybamba (Oreja de Perro region). Photo by Max Altamirano Molero.

As a result, according to Alex, "in the mountains, for four or five years we lived. Some were escaping for five years, some for eight or ten years."

Living on the Run

Given the escalated violence from multiple parties, hundreds of thousands of rural inhabitants fled and often headed to the cities, creating a massive urban migration.[2] Between 1982 and 1987, "communities of Oronccoy, Santa Carmen, Tastabamba, Putucunay and the rest of the annexes in the region dispersed in groups towards the jungle and quebrada" (CVR 2003, 4:90). The district of Chungui, for example, lost half its population overall between 1983 and 1991, going from a population of 8,257 to 4,338—a greater level of population loss than any other district in the Department of Ayacucho (CVR 2003, vol. 4). The emptying of areas such as Ayacucho created a new dependency on the cities, yet Sendero continued to attempt to cut off the metropolises. Over half of all terrorist acts by 1985 occurred outside of the Ayacucho region, breaking ties of reciprocity that linked rural and urban populations, leading to a further deterioration in peasants' standard of living (Bourque and Warren 1989, 18).[3]

The community of Oronccoy escaped together; however, they quickly realized that they were leaving too much of a *rastro* (trail). Consequently, they separated into groups of twenty to thirty people, each with a community authority member, to prevent leaving a traceable mark. "We separated into other groups because when the military looked for us, the tracks, the trail there, was a lot, so with this trail they would find us, so when we were small groups, we did not leave a trail, only a little. To prevent us from being caught, we separated ourselves."

Juan Pablo described how challenging it was to find food to eat while on the run:

At times, we just had to eat the mountain herbs and calabaza [pumpkin, gourd], nothing else. The calabaza maintained us. All the people without salt, without sugar. There was not salt either. Where could we buy salt? How could we salt things? From where? We would eat calabaza, calabaza soup, calabaza with potato that we would dig up. At times, we would eat maize too. At times raw maize. We could not let there be smoke. In the day, we could not make smoke because someone would see it, and so we had to make it in the night, or they might surprise us, so we had to be careful. So, we ate raw maize. Raw maize, whatever things like this. . . . Without salt! Without salt, without salt. There was not sugar or salt.

At another time, Graciela's brother Alex also discussed the lack of food and salt: "We did not eat food. We did not have salt. We did not have food to eat. There was no food. We ate herbs, mushrooms. All we ate just to survive. There were places that did not have water, so we ate a cactus that we peeled, the *pincas de tuna*, called *chuna* in Quechua." Graciela's father interjected at this point stating, "There was no salt! We did not have salt!"[4] According to the CVR, without salt, clothes, or shoes those who had escaped the violence began to die of typhoid and malaria (CVR 2003, vol. 5).

Graciela and Juan Pablo described how while they were on the run, they would forage for other herbs such as *chilitos* and mushrooms to prepare *tallarin laurel* and would sometimes hunt small animals, but they hardly ever ate meat or drank milk, also widely viewed as luxury food items. Soap is another rare consumer item in the rural Andes, and Graciela noted its absence while they were in hiding:

> At times, there was *quylluchumpa*. With this, we would wash our hair. We would wash our clothes with ashes. We would put water in an olla with ashes to wash our chumpis. The water would be white, and with this, we would clean our clothes. We only used herbs, nothing more. There was also an herb called *jaboncilla*. We washed our clothes with this also. There was nothing. No soap. Where would we get soap? There was not anything.

Graciela and Juan Pablo both described efforts to maintain some semblance of humanity by striving to stay somewhat clean, yet it was often a futile effort. Anything they used was foraged and temporary, as they had to remain on the move to avoid detection. As Graciela and her family soon discovered, however, there were obstacles to continued flight.

Fearing Detection

In this region of Peru, there are numerous bridges made from ropes and cement built precariously over roaring rivers. Senderistas commonly cut or dynamited them during the conflict to keep people from fleeing to other regions. Most agriculturalists were unable to swim, and geographic barriers trapped them. Graciela explained, "There were bridges to pass, but they cut all of them. They cut all of them, totally." According to Alex, "They cut the bridges. To access or cross the Cortina River there were bridges, but they cut them, dynamited them. There was not a place to cross." Graciela added, "Like us who live in the campo, we do not know how to swim." Confined to territories, people were in constant fear of detection.

> We were out in the rain, not in a house. We were living like deer, escaping for our lives. This happened daily that we were escaping in the night as well from the military. For example, there was a hill, as if on that road there would appear to be people, so we would escape carrying our babies. When

Figure 11. The Kutinachaka Bridge over the Pampas River that separates the Ayacucho and Apurímac Departments. This photo illustrates the high water during the rainy season making it particularly difficult to cross. Photo by Max Altamirano Molero.

Figure 12. Oroya (waru, a cable traverse) of Yauyaku over the Apurímac River that connects part of the population of Oronccoy with the Valley of Inkawasi. It is the only means in the area to cross the river and exchange products with the other side. Photo by Max Altamirano Molero.

we would hear them, we would hide when we were in the mountains. When there were young people, babies from the community, sometimes they would be crying because there was no milk.

The children were unable to nurse because mothers were malnourished and unable to produce breast milk.

> There would be nothing to eat. For years, we lived like this. South of Chaupi. By the Champas River. Do you know the Champas River? That is where we would be, below Chaupi. In this river, there was a lot of water, and in there we would escape from the military. Someone would bring us water. It was salty. This is where we would escape from our pueblo of Oronccoy. In here, we would talk to the people that know. The older people like my father . . . During the day, they would be looking, searching for the military. When they would see us, they would come. They would come and kill us. For this in the night or early morning, not much smoke passes, but in the afternoon when there is humidity, the smoke passes, so we all had to be careful in the night too. For example, in the night we saw from afar the light from the candles, so when the candles were lit, they could see us quickly.

Being malnourished and crying of hunger, children soon came to represent a threat of detection. According to the CVR, various groups of Senderistas striving to avoid detection by military forces viewed children crying of hunger as a liability.

> In various camps of *Oreja de Perro* [*la fuerza local*] obligated the mothers to kill their own children, some chocked in the chest, but when the mother did not want to obey the camp's political command, he grabbed the little children by the feet and struck their heads against a rock. Others gathered them and tied a rope around their necks and hung them. The argument for murdering these children was that their cries gave them away in front of military patrols. (CVR 2003, 5:106)

It became increasingly difficult for Graciela and others to remain hidden, especially with the proliferation of "helicopters and bombs falling exploding." Graciela described her level of fear when she would see helicopters above looking for them, as they hid in the *paja* and in the *shamu* (straw and trees):

> Before [the violence], we did not know helicopters. In this time, in the violence, a helicopter came like doves searching for us, and we would hide in the straw inside the shamu, the *samos*. The trees called shamus, inside these we would hide the children and ourselves too. They [children] did not understand helicopters and they had a very strong sound. . . . At times, they would drop bombs and that would make us jump. Sometimes it would be from far away, but the ground would be shaking, and smoke would rise. . . . Those helicopters came, planes, bombs that were exploding on all sides so we could not cook. We cook just with firewood and when you cook with firewood there is always smoke, so the military would be looking for us in the mountains and they would throw bombs, so we could not [cook]. So, we would have to cover the light from the candle. At night when there would be smoke, the military would come, and then if there was no smoke, but there was light from a lantern or a candle, this they would see. They would say, "There they are!" and come or throw a bomb or a grenade.

Graciela's memories echoed those of the previously mentioned taxi driver who served in the military. He described searching for lights or smoke in the hillsides. When they detected people, they would throw bombs in the general direction, then watch women, men, and children tumble down the hill, dead. When reporting this, he shook his head side to side while looking down saying, "It was horrible, just horrible." With ever-growing surveillance and the presence of military personnel, it became increasingly difficult to evade detection, and death became a constant presence for Graciela and others living on the run.

Omnipresence and Threat of Death

Graciela recalled the consistent presence of death all around her.[5] "Yes, and there were always dead people when the military arrived. There were always dead people." Substantiating such experiences, the CVR reports that in 1984 close to Huallhua in the quebrada of Chakiqmayo, military forces from

Andahuaylas and ronderos from Mollebamba brutally murdered a group of thirteen people displaced from Tastabamba, Huallhua, and Oronccoy (CVR 2003, vol. 5). In 1986, military troops from Pallqas killed thirty-one refugees from Oronccoy and Chillihua in Chaupimayo (vol. 5). Juan Pablo explained how he would find dead bodies when looking for his paisanos:

> The military would run after them—those who had escaped—and find them and [there were] tons of dead bodies. In Yanacocha, they lined up twenty young people, including children, and shot them and threw them in the ground. They would torture people, cut their fingers off. There would be ten groups, the military would arrive, kill one, and others would run with fear. All the communities—Yerbabuena, Liampata, Santa Carmen, Oronccoy, Tastabamba, Huallhua, Occoro, Totora, Putucunay, Chillhua, Chupón, Pallcca, Pantu, Vacahuasi, Chapi—it was all the same in the other communities. People have holes in their bodies from where they have gunshot wounds. Violence in all these villages. . . . One day there was rain, it was the rainy season. We would leave tracks in the mud, so it was very dangerous. There was a woman who left tracks and they found her. They cut her throat, covered her face with her hat, and the men raped her dead body. They killed her baby. There were military tracks sixty-five feet up from this where we found the dead woman's body.

In referencing how they knew the military committed this atrocity, Graciela and Juan Pablo described the tracks. They talked about how, to assess where different groups were located, they became proficient in recognizing footprints, with military boots being particularly distinct.[6] With regard to necrophilia, according to Jelke Boesten, groups of soldiers watched each other rape dead women in many cases. One solider recounted how his colleagues raped women:

> I'll tell you. So, I said to Gilbert: let's cut her up and throw her out. We managed to throw her into the river. When we arrived to where the troops were bathing, they were raping her. She was dead. You know why? Because she was tall, *gringa*, good looking. But she was no good anymore, she couldn't satisfy anymore. The troops were raping her. She was decapitated, of course. They had her on the table, and covered her upper body and were

raping her. They were many, twelve or fourteen. With a stick, I threw them out: "Savages! She is dead!" "She is nice and warm, *mi tecnico*," they said. (Boesten 2014, 32)

Boesten describes how such acts were clearly not committed for political reasons or as an act of war and were permitted by authorities with the explanation of satisfying men's needs, accentuating dominant regimes of male power and race relations (32).[7]

After about two years of surviving on the run, outsiders captured Graciela's eldest brother.

I was there with my brothers when other people came in the night wearing ties, five or seven of them in the night. They were saying, "We are going to kill him." . . . Seven people then took him. They all had new clothes on and only spoke Spanish. They had guns. I did not understand that they were saying they were going to kill him. I did not understand a word of Spanish. They were insulting my brother in Spanish. I wondered why they wanted my brother. I had never seen these people before. Where did they come from? They said, "Come with us now." The oldest said, "Come with me," and my brother said, "Yes." From this date, my brother never returned. He was only seventeen or eighteen years old. I was with my mom and dad crying. I was crying and had swollen eyes. I was wondering when he would return.

Soon after the men left, Graciela's family searched everywhere for her brother. "My brother had not returned and so we looked for him." When recounting this experience, Alex and Graciela discussed how long they searched for his body. After consulting with their father, they all determined that they had searched for his body for three days before locating it.

My father found him far high up in the hill. He did not know at first who it was. There was blood everywhere. We found him dead with a white shirt. He had a bullet on the left side of his head, and it left out of the right side of his head. His eyeball was hanging down. Blood covered all over his body and the ground.

Alex also described finding his brother's body: "When we were where they killed my brother, there was a hole, a little hole that would only fit me doubled over. They left him there. When they killed my brother, they left him on his side." Graciela interjected, "We saw him on his side, but where did they kill him, we did not know. We cried a lot. Now my brother does not wake up. He did not return in the afternoon or in the night. Where did they kill him?"

Perceived Protection

While fear, death, and trauma dominated Graciela's time in hiding, it also contained a sort of miracle. Throughout this period, Graciela and others slept on the ground or hid in caves, yet they never encountered dangerous animals.

> In the mountains, along the rivers, we would escape. During all this time, there were no spiders, no snakes, nothing in the selva [rainforest]. However, in Chaupimayo in my pueblo at this time when there were cows by the house, pumas, tigers, and lions would eat the cows and horses.[8] During these problems, no tiger arrived to eat us. Pumas, lions did not arrive, nor spiders. Nothing, nothing bit us. Nothing killed us. The only thing that was our enemy that wanted to kill us was the military and more the terrorism. We were not terrorists. It was complicated. This mostly was our enemy, but there were not poisonous animals, spiders, snakes, tigers, pumas, nothing was there. However, before the violence, pumas and lions would eat our cows. Before the violence, we would never enter caves. But [while on the run] we would enter and nothing bit us, nothing. Peaceful. For this God was guarding us, we would say. . . . Now I think why they did not bite us. For sure, we had nothing. The military would kill us with shovels, with everything. For this reason, the animals did not bite us, not bother us. They did not do anything to us. For this, the Señor [God] guarded us.

According to Graciela, the fact that animals did not attack them the entire time they were living in such dangerous circumstances was a true sign that God was looking out for them.

Outside of enemies, the other primary threat while living on the run was illness, yet this also represented a sort of wonder for Graciela. Graciela described how she had a fever for almost a week while escaping in the mountains:

> I was hungry and thirsty. With the fever, I was less hungry, but was thirsty and there was not water, far, far away. I was dying of thirst. I was crying. I was crying tears of hunger also during this violence. This we suffered a lot, from hunger. I cried, but I could not die. Some men who were much stronger caught this fever. All caught this fever. A man from here fell to his knees. Fell from the fever. The man was from here. My mom also became sick. My father also became sick. I have my younger sister. At that time, she was three years old. She also almost died from this fever, this sickness. We made a carrier from the trees to carry her. . . . Various died, but not many, maybe five or so. The children more than anything. Those who were three, four, or five years old. More they died of hunger with the fever, of hunger, of thirst. . . . So, a child when they are beginning to crawl, they can hardly crawl, they have no strength to get up. This is how they would crawl with the fever in the forest, but when we were hiding with this sickness, the military did not come to this place.

Graciela described one man who lost his toes and another man who lost his entire foot from the knee down due to fever, or what she called lepra (leprosy; *Mycobacterium leprae*). "Lepra they say this sickness, this fever. He had such a bad fever. There were not doctors, there were not pills, nothing, and there was no communication. During this time, there were no cellular phones, nothing. We could not communicate, there was not anything."[9] They treated the fever with different herbs such as yerba buena, *horiganitas*, and *sachacoles*, which they knew about from generations of curing illness with natural remedies. According to Graciela, surviving illness with the help of natural plants was another sort of miracle and a sign that God was on the side of the campesinos.

End of the Line

Graciela's family "lived like deer" on the run for more than three years. "We hid in the caves because if the military found us, they would kill us. For three years, we lived like this. My brothers were skinny. We were starving." Graciela explained that her siblings were little and hungry:

They sometimes cried of hunger when my mother did not have milk. They were four years old and my mom fed them milk from her breast. Therefore, my mom was not eating much, so did not have milk, so she cried. She would cry and say, "They are hungry, and I am hungry, I want milk." When you do not eat enough, you cannot give milk. So, my little brother would cry.

While the older children could walk, adults carried the younger children, especially when they had to flee quickly. Graciela's father consistently carried her brother Alex. As Alex described, "All my life, since I was little, I was glued to my dad. Always I was together with him." Graciela interjected, "When the military came with the bombs [she made a *boom boom boom* sound] when we were hiding with my mom, with my father, my father was escaping carrying my brother. He was never left behind. He was always with my father, but the rest were with my mom." Whereas Alex stayed closed to his father and the other siblings remained tied to their mother, Graciela soon separated from her family.

Because Graciela was the oldest child in her group, the authorities determined that she would join another party from Oronccoy separate from that of her family. "I had separated into another group. They said, 'You are older,' so they separated me out into another group from my mom." According to Graciela, the leaders in each group would sometimes separate people into different groups according to age, but "I had pain for my mom, but I had been separated." Not long after Graciela separated from her family, the military captured them.

The year was around 1988 and Graciela's family was hiding near the community of Pantu. The group was vigilantly watching any foot traffic below from what they thought was an adequate hiding space; however, the military sighted them from uphill. "Those that were coming from below, they were watching, but they did not know that there were also people coming from above, and so from above they could see them. . . . From above like a hawk looking at a chicken, they [military] came from above, and they [family members] were trapped." Graciela described how the military came with guns and her father surrendered: "'Take us or kill all of us. Kill my wife, kill my children, and kill all of us together. . . . It is better than dying of hunger, of thirst, of everything,' he said. 'We cannot bear it. We cannot endure it. It is better that they kill all of my children, my wife, and me.' Fortunately, the military did not kill them." Graciela provided an explanation of why the military spared her family:

My mom is *blancuna* [white]; well, she is half white. When my mom was young, when I was about sixteen or seventeen years old, my mother was a beautiful *gringita*, blancuna [light-skinned person], tall. Therefore, they grabbed and took my mom to this pueblo. It is a community called Molle-bamba. They took my mom, my father, my little brothers, Alipeo, Alex, and Edolo, the three kids they took with them there. They did not kill them, luckily, but the rest they killed, because they were escaping.

To understand why Graciela referred to her mother as a "gringita" and "blancuna," it is necessary to explore Graciela's family history.

Graciela's grandmother worked for the Hacienda La Chapi, and while there, the landowner, or the hacendado, impregnated her. As Graciela stated, "in there, someone from another country came to my widow grandmother and impregnated her—one of the workers, the hacendado." Although Graciela could not be certain if this was a consensual relationship, her understanding was that it was not, and no lasting union or relationship developed between Graciela's grandmother and the hacendado. "He left like a seed in my grandmother, but we do not know him. Until now, my mom does not know her father. Her father does not know her. Who is he?" Almost instantly, a somberness came over Graciela as she described the situation further:

My mother is not a Vilmos [pseudonym for last name]. My mother is blancuna [white]. She was much more beautiful when she was young. But where is my mother's father from? Was he from Lima? From other countries, he came to work in the hacienda, La Chapi, the hacienda that lies farther below my pueblo. In there, people died in La Chapi. In there, people said my mother's father was white and tall. They said he was a gringo.

Graciela said that numerous people from the community believed that Graciela's maternal grandfather was from Belgium, but she would never know for sure.

When Graciela's mother was about three years old, her mother (Graciela's grandmother) became a widow. Graciela explained that others felt she needed to remarry. "A man said you are a widow, so they looked for a stepfather for my mother." Unfortunately, this stepfather was extremely abusive. Graciela described how the stepfather often drank liquor and became violent: "This stepfather hit my mother a lot when she was a baby just three years old. Therefore, my grandmother also hit my mother a lot. Much mistreatment my grandmother also endured from the stepfather, from her husband." The sister of Graciela's mother, Paulina, who was about eighteen years old at the time, asked that Graciela's mother go live with her in a community below Oronccoy to escape the abuse. Graciela's grandmother agreed to let her daughter live with Paulina, while she remained in the home with her abusive husband.[10]

A particularly poignant moment in Graciela's history occurred when the man who impregnated Graciela's grandmother came searching for his child (Graciela's mother) and Paulina hid her in a large pot.

> When she was with my aunt, they came to capture the daughter—to capture my mom to bring her to Lima when my mom was little. When the father came to look for my mother, there are the things you put chicha in, ollas. That you make with the *tierra urpu* [very large earthen jar]. There were two in there. They said this is the father and we are looking for her. Therefore, my aunt hid her in the urpu, put the cover on to hide her so that they could not take her with her father.

Upon failing to locate his daughter, the man reportedly left and never returned to search for this child. Graciela's mother often reflected on this fateful moment with mixed emotions, particularly during the time of violence, and sometimes blamed her sister for hiding her, claiming, "If I had gone with my father, maybe I would have studied in Lima."

Graciela's assumption that the military did not kill her mother and the rest of her family when captured due to her mother's light skin (a direct result of her Indigenous grandmother likely having been raped by a supposedly white hacendado) underscores the power of racial relations in Peruvian society. A focus group of women from Oronccoy described the level of violence and enactment of rape at the Hacienda La Chapi to the Comisión de la Verdad y Reconciliación:

> Also, my grandfather died working, vomiting blood and many times when the people died working in the haciendas, they left the women alive. This *hacendado*, when the widows would go to the hacienda, many times would

be raped. One of the victims also was my mother's mother. They had to go to the haciendas to work, leaving their children. We were born when the situation was the same, this was from the time of my parents and my grandparents. They also provided services to the hacienda, when I had more or less two or three children this problem came to an end, and it is for this reason that recently we care about the education of our children. Because the children of the former generation were still ignorant, both men and women, we are all ignorant. (CVR 2003, 5:91)

As illustrated in Graciela's family history and manifestations to the Comisión de la Verdad y Reconciliación, the light-skinned hacendado exercised free rein over dark-skinned Indigenous labor and women's bodies. Dark skin served as a liability and light skin allowed situational privilege in the 1960s, as well as the 1980s, continuing to the present day.

———

Upon surviving terror and violence within the community, Graciela and her comuneros fled, leaving their livelihoods, land, animals, homes, and loved ones behind. Surviving on the run with merely the clothes on their backs, Graciela and her family "lived like deer" for years. In constant fear of detection, they struggled to find food to eat and stave off illness. The omnipresence of death and violence all around them served as a constant reminder of what would become of them if caught. Yet due perhaps to dominant racial hierarchies and shifting political policies, Graciela's family was spared their lives upon capture. After separating from her family, Graciela continued to live on the run for several years. While on the run alone without her family, Graciela met the man who would one day become her husband, Juan Pablo. As Graciela stated, "With my mom gone, I was alone, an orphan crying. This is when I met Juan Pablo."

Chapter 4

Courtship and Capture

Courting

The man that would become Graciela's husband, Juan Pablo, lost his family during the war. Juan Pablo explained how the military killed his first wife and children:

> My wife from before was captured by the people from Mollebamba. Together with the military, they killed her in Chaupimayo. She was killed in Chaupimayo. Various women were captured with my wife, various. They were killed and then buried just in one hole. . . . They took my wife and killed her, along with two of my children. Two children; with my niece, three. They completely killed three children with bullets. They did it with bullets. One child was five years old, another was three years old, and the baby was only two months old. They all died.

Juan Pablo had one five-year-old son who survived. Once his wife and two children died, he continued living on the run with his surviving son until the military captured his son. "I just continued with my one son. I was continuing together with my son and my son was captured, so it was just me who stayed. Another person took him and gave him a name, the name of this person. He was adopted." At the time, Juan Pablo did not know where they took his son. "I did not know where [they took him]. I could not leave, so I did not know anything of my son." Both the military and Sendero stole young children during the war. Sometimes guerrillas and military personnel would take and train young children as soldiers. Other times they took children and forced them to work as domestic servants or adopted them into their families.[1]

Without any immediate surviving family members, Juan Pablo soon united with Graciela's small group of paisanos from Oronccoy living on the run. He began to express interest in Graciela, which she did not reciprocate. Graciela described their initial encounters:

> He united with the group I was in. When groups were killed off, those who escaped found other groups to unite with. He started to fall for me. He always talked with me, but I had no interest in him. . . . At times, he would talk to me, but I did not give it any importance. So, we continued walking [staying on the move in hiding] for much time. One day when we were sleeping, he put his hand on me when I was sleeping. I did not like it. "Take away your hand!" I told him. Another time he held my hand. I did not want this. I did not want it. So, another time we saw two military men and [our group leaders] said to get down so [the military men] would not see us. They were saying be careful because if the military sees us, they will kill us. So, we stayed there the two of us, me and Juan Pablo. However, I was not thinking anything of him, so I was just thinking simply of respect because he is older than I am. In there he said, "I want to be with you," but I did not accept it.

Although Graciela did not want to have an intimate relationship with Juan Pablo, their group authority members thought otherwise.

> There were always authorities in each group. There always existed in each group the authorities to help us keep quiet, to give us what we lacked, [to say] where we all are going to eat. Therefore, there was an elder, and Juan Pablo had talked to him. [The elder] said to me, "He is older, and he is alone. Why don't you want to live [with him]?"

While Graciela did not want to be with Juan Pablo, she felt she had no choice, given her predicament.

> I told this authority Juan Pablo was bothering me. He said, "Why not be together because you are both alone? He is alone and you are alone, so you should just be together." However, I totally did not want that. I am still not

in love with him. I had no choice. I did not like him at all. My mom was not there, and the leader was in agreement with Juan Pablo. I did not want to live with him.

Feeling trapped in a relationship with Juan Pablo, Graciela began to resent his presence strongly.

So no, I did not have the decision of whether to live with him or not. In the beginning, Juan Pablo would say to me, "I want to live with you. I love you." I was being courted and I thought, "I hate you." I was saying these words in my heart. I hated it. I did not want it. "Why don't you live with him?" [The authorities] would say, "Yeah, he is older, but this is not important," but with these words, I was mistreated. "How are you going to live?" [Juan Pablo] would say. However, it was not just him. All the authorities were bothering me about this. This leader agreed with Juan Pablo. I could not say anything. "You need to live. You are alone. He is also alone," [the authorities] said. I did not want to live. I did not want to live. So, at night he would put his hand on my back, but I did not want it. At times I would ask God that the military come and kill him. I would say this in my heart. I did not live with my own choice. I would ask this, but God permitted it. However, little by little, I became accustomed. . . . He was nice and would care for me, but I did not want him for a year or more. I did not have cold feelings nor warm feelings for him, nothing for two years. I got used to him, but I never loved him. . . . Until now with my children, with Rous [Graciela's daughter], I say I am not in love. Your father loves me, but I do not know. I do not feel cold nor heat, I say.

Graciela rejected the idea of being with Juan Pablo at this time and felt an intimate relationship with him would put her own life in danger.

Yes, for one year or two years, I suffered. Our relationship got worse. I did not want to make a relationship with him. One day he said, "Do you want to have a relationship?" and I said, "No!" I did not want it. Do you know why I did not want it? When I saw other women carrying their stomachs when they were pregnant, it was difficult to escape in the mountains when their bellies were full. So, I was thinking for sure, when I have a sexual relationship with him, I would get pregnant, and how would I escape? There were various girls during this time who became pregnant. Two girls were killed. Another cousin who was full and about to give birth was killed. Escaping, escaping, but for sure became tired from walking, and so they killed her. They cut her throat. I saw two pregnant women have their throats slit, because they could not run. I was thinking if I am with him, I will get pregnant and will not be able to escape. A third [woman] we found in the forest who had been killed. Her baby was in her stomach. It was also dead. This is what was in my thoughts. For sure, I would be like the others if I became pregnant when I am with a man. It is better to not. When I have a husband, it is better to be healthy to be able to escape freely. This is what I was thinking. For this, I did not want to have sex. One day Juan Pablo grabbed me to have sex with force. Therefore, with another form, I was afraid, but I did not have anyone on my side for advice. I did not have my mom. She was not there. So, I was guarding in my heart is all because it would be worse if I had sex and I was furious with Juan Pablo. I hated him. . . . I had great anger toward him. I had rage. I said to leave me alone. I explained that I would not be able to escape if I was pregnant, and if I died who will care for you. I did not want to be with him, but I got used to it. Now I do not love him—never have. He loves me. He knows I do not love him.

Not only was Graciela pressured to be with Juan Pablo, soon she would find herself further trapped alongside him without her fellow paisanos.

Capture

Graciela and Juan Pablo continued living on the run with this small group for over a year. One night Graciela and Juan Pablo went down to the edge of the Pampas River to gather sachacoles, an herb to make pachamanka. They stayed the night in a cave, and then at six in the morning they made their way up from the river to join the community that was harvesting potatoes and making pachamanka. "So, we were getting this [sachacoles] to help make pachamanka. When we were by the river, we heard a bullet and we hit the ground. The ground was also shaking. Therefore, we were afraid and escaped." Graciela and

Juan Pablo did now know where the bullet came from or in what direction to escape. They quickly walked toward the village, and when they reached the top of a hill they saw military boot tracks spread out in all directions. Graciela and Juan Pablo ran toward their group of paisanos to tell them that the military was surrounding them. "We then saw tracks from the military, their trail. 'The military is here,' we were saying. We went to hide . . . but we could not escape. It was five or six in the morning at this time, when the sun was coming up. 'We need to return to the Pampas River,' they said. We were saying, 'Where are we going to pass? There is nowhere to pass.'" Soon they heard another gunshot and chaos ensued.

> We heard a shot and so everyone escaped, and no one stayed in this community. Everyone fled. When people heard the shot, they were afraid, and everyone ran with fear. . . . From here mostly this community, this group, escaped, but we could not escape too. They were assaulting us with bullets, the ground was moving, and there was smoke from the bullets. . . . The military were yelling to return and that they would not kill us. However, with fear no one had a voice to respond. They appeared drunk and were yelling at us saying, "Do not escape. We will not kill you." But my neighbors, everyone escaped. Everything, even the ground, was moving. . . . All escaped up the mountains, but there were helicopters. We were flattened to the ground, and the helicopter was flying above, so there was nowhere to escape. To return, where would we go? Where could we pass? Where could the cousins go? We could not swim. We could not pass the river swimming.

Feeling completely trapped and surrounded, a truck then approached Graciela and Juan Pablo.

> Then we saw a truck coming, crawling here. They grabbed us, the military . . . They came with guns, and they were so tall! I could not talk or anything, nor could Juan Pablo. We were looking in all directions, they were so tall, and there was nothing we could do. We stayed and just sat there. They said, "Call your family. Call them!" so I yelled to my cousin Anita, she was like the size of Nayely [nine or ten years old], "Hiliana! Hiliana!" I was yelling, but they could not answer, they were going up the

quebrada. They were not dead, but the air was smoky and there were all kinds of noise. Bullets were passing! Choo choo choo! [Bullet sounds] The bullets were falling, and I heard this and was shaking with fear. . . . Someone was going to die for sure with these bullets. For sure someone in the quebrada, my family, my cousins, my uncles.

Immediately everyone escaped the village except Graciela and Juan Pablo.

> Most of this group was escaping. Only two did not escape; Juan Pablo and I were the two they grabbed. They took my manta that I weaved. They asked, "What is in your *qipi*?" and looked all through it. They looked at Juan Pablo too, but we had nothing. We said to them, "There is nothing, sir." For what would I carry in my manta? We had nothing, not even clothes. When they took this from us, we had nothing. We had nothing to change into. I said to them, "I have nothing," and they looked in my qipi, in my manta, and there was nothing. They also looked at Juan Pablo's manta and it was empty. "You have nothing," they said. We had only vegetables to eat for the pachamanka.

Not having anything of value, the military men opted to tie up Graciela and Juan Pablo.

> We did not have anything, not even anything to eat. They said, "They do not have anything. Do not kill them." They said, "Carry it!" So I grabbed my *mantita*. They grabbed me with their rope. They also grabbed Juan Pablo with the rope with lots of pressure. They grabbed us and said, "Tie them up so they do not escape." They grabbed us and took us below Oronccoy. We could not walk when they were grabbing us like that.

The military men led Graciela and Juan Pablo to the place where the group had been making pachamanka.

> So, they said to us, "Is she yours? Is she your wife?" "Certainly, yes," Juan Pablo said. From here, they brought us to where they were cooking pachamanka and there was a mule. "Come here to look for the others," they

said. They asked that Juan Pablo go finish making the pachamanka that the community had started, and they wanted to eat. They untied Juan Pablo's hands to cook the pachamanka and then the others left with a mule, saying, "Let's go look for the others." So, they went. They were liars when they said this. Juan Pablo stayed, and they took the mule and me and they raped me.

Collisions and Lies

As Graciela continued to recount what transpired once she left Juan Pablo's side, her eyes filled with tears. Graciela pointed to where the military had taken her and Juan Pablo on her hand-drawn map. One group returned to Oronccoy and another group remained in the fields where they were making pachamanka, near an apu (sacred mountain) called Llamayoq. They took Graciela to the latter location, where there were fields used to pasture animals, referred to as *llachuq*. "Llamayoq they call it, which was down here. This hill is there. There lived the beautiful Incas. They made houses with rocks.[2] So here are corrals, here is where they took me. In this llachuq, they grabbed me. It was about ten in the morning, early, when they took me." At this point in relaying the details of that fateful day, Graciela was vigorously crying. I wrapped my arms around Graciela, assuring her that she did not have to continue, but she said, "When they were raping me, I was thinking, 'I am going [to die].' I did not know anything." I held Graciela while she wiped her eyes and nose with a cloth she had beautifully embroidered with colorful flowers and hummingbirds, and she continued to describe what happened next:[3]

> Then they returned after they raped me. They went back to where they were cooking pachamanka and said to cook for them. It was worse after they raped me. I could not eat anything, potato, nothing. "Peel it or they will kill us," Juan Pablo said. "Do not cry. You cannot. Eat," he said, but I could not eat anything. . . . "We have to escape," I was saying to Juan Pablo. I wanted to escape. "It would have been better if they killed me," I was saying. "They mistreated me," I was saying. I told Juan Pablo that they raped me. . . . He did not do anything, and they raped me. I did not want to stay to be mistreated.

Once they had cooked all the pachamanka, the military tied Graciela's and Juan Pablo's hands once again and walked them back to Oronccoy. "Then we arrived here to Oronccoy at six in the night. It was almost dark."

When Graciela and Juan Pablo arrived in the community of Oronccoy, they found that most of the houses had been burned to the ground; only the walls remained, surrounded by eucalyptus trees. "There were many military, like fifty military people there. A quantity kept arriving. At times, there were thirty or forty that came from here and there. They came from here and captured people. We rested when they brought us here." Graciela explained that many of the military had come from Lima and other coastal areas. They were not used to the cold climate and high altitude. "Therefore, there were many, many from the military who were fainting when they arrived at our community. They were carrying many things, then they fainted in this community. When they came here, a military man fainted, and they put him on the ground. The other military went to collect firewood."

When they entered the village, the soldiers untied Juan Pablo's hands and demanded that he help them collect firewood from the surrounding eucalyptus trees. "There was a huge pile of firewood, so they started it on fire to heat up the person [who fainted]. Here they left us. When he was not reviving, they said to us, 'If this man does not wake up, we will kill you. If he dies, we will kill you.'" Graciela explained that the military were so incensed that this man fainted and apparently blamed Graciela and Juan Pablo for his condition. Therefore, if the man died, they declared retribution on Graciela and Juan Pablo.

> When he was warming up in front of the fire, he revived. With the heat of this fire, he woke up! Therefore, they did not kill us. Rare thing, right? All the military turned white. *Acuchao el clima* [the strong climate] caused this. When he felt the heat, he reacted, so we slept in this community. Because he was sick, they were staying there until the following day, but we had been walking all day and were dying of hunger.

The term *acuchao el clima* or *choque el clima* (to crash or collide with the climate) is a common statement in the Andahuaylas region. It speaks to the cold, harsh climate but is more than a descriptive term. *Acuchao el clima* rather affords the weather a certain level of malevolent agency and peoples' varying abilities, or knowledge of how, to interact with the weather. It reflects a living relationship that people have with the environment and natural forces. For instance, in Andean cosmology when people reference an apu, they are not claiming that mountains are Gods or that those mountains have Gods in them. Rather, mountains, as well as fields and other natural entities, can cause harm or bring prosperity to humans. For that reason, people must consistently honor natural entities with pagos (payments) and other ceremonies to foment a positive reciprocal relationship, not entirely different from give-and-take connections established through festivals and compadrazgo relations. Highland Indigenous residents have the experience and knowledge of how to conduct pagos and interact with the environment. Those who do not have such a background collide with the weather and suffer.[4]

As the military man, likely from the coast, was reviving from the acuchao el clima, they presented Graciela a plethora of food. "Other military were bringing bread, *canchas* [roasted maize], habas, all of these meats, and I was receiving it all in my skirt. 'Eat it! Eat it!' they said, but I could not eat because I was filled with fear." Graciela pointed to her mouth and motioned down through the bottom of her throat, explaining that she could not swallow food.

> I lost all my hunger with fear. . . . The food would not enter, as I was afraid for sure they would kill me. Juan Pablo was eating quickly and thought for sure they were going to kill us. He said, "Don't cry. Eat. They brought food for us to eat." But I could not eat. Potatoes, all they gave us in the evening. They had canchas, ch'arki, *azucars* [sweets], *caramelos* [candies], and gave all of it to us; gave it to me. . . . I thought for sure they would kill me. Maybe they will not kill me. Two things were running through my mind: I will die, or I will live. I thought, look at all this food. For sure, they will not kill me. How is this, I thought. This is what I was thinking. This happened at six or seven at night.

The forced eating reminded me of a story recounted to me by the taxi driver who served in the military. He stated that the military so feared being poisoned they would force campesinos to first eat the food and wait a half hour to an hour to assure it had not been tainted.

Graciela relayed subsequent events that occurred once the sun set that evening:

Then began the sleeping. All the military went to sleep in the pampa. Here we slept with Juan Pablo, we slept. My hands were tied still to sleep. Juan Pablo's hands were also tied up to sleep, so the civilian said to me, who was twenty-six years old or so, young. He said to me, "I will untie you if you do not escape." . . . So he untied me, and we were going to sleep peacefully. Then at nine at night, three military men came and said to me, "Come to the boss to give your declaration." They commanded me to do this, three soldiers. Three militaries called me at nine in the night to give my declaration. My manifestation. Do you understand, Nicole?

I asked for clarification on the manifestation (declaration), so Graciela explained that the military would ask her: "'Why did you escape? Why are you escaping like a deer? You are a terrorist or not?' they were asking." Giving one's manifestation basically meant providing a declaration that one was not involved with Sendero. Before going to give her manifestation, the young man who untied her hands tried to warn Graciela.

So, this young man [sleeping at my side] said to me, "Do not get up. Do not give your case." When the three soldiers said to get up to give my manifestation, the boss was the one yelling, the young man that was sleeping at my side said, "Do not go. Do not go." I asked why. He said, "They will rape you. They will rape you, do not go." I did not listen. I thought it was better to give my case to the military because I was afraid. For sure, I should go to give my manifestation. I will go and present myself to the boss, but the boss that was sleeping there did not arrive. These military did not bring this boss. Because they brought me to rape me. All of this happened, Nicole.

I clarified that three men called Graciela to give her manifestation and then all of them proceeded to rape her.

Yes. This pain I have in my heart. When I remember, I have pain, Nicole. Why did I allow the violence, I ask God? I must not speak the name of God, but why did God allow this? However, thanks to God, I am living. God brings the day and the night, right? I thank the Señor. Nevertheless, this young man, now I do not know if he is good or what happened to him, because many people mistreated me. All of this happened, Nicole.

Graciela questioned why the young man who was sleeping next to her and Juan Pablo tried to protect her. Then she continued to portray the remainder of the evening:

At eleven at night, another military arrived. They called me, "Come to give your declaration." I did not know what to make of the situation. Are they going to kill me? Are they going to rape me? It is better not to go. They came to rape me. They did not come for my manifestation. With lies, they called me . . . They said, "Hurry, you need to give your manifestation." They called me three times. Three times, they called me. Each time to rape and abuse me. There was nothing I could do for my case. They took advantage of me.

I asked if anyone responded when this happened, if anyone did anything at all.

Nothing. At my side, Juan Pablo was sleeping. When I returned, I told my husband. I said they all mistreated me. He also was sleeping with fear. There was no one there to help us. There was no one there to support us. We were with fear. . . . Therefore, my husband knows all that happened to me. All this that happened, he knows, but he understands. When we lived in peace until now, I cry about all that happened. This pain I have. My husband says, "Yeah, do not remember all of this. Right now, we are peaceful, and all this that happened in the violence has passed. It is better that now we are peaceful. We are in peace."

With tears running down her face, Graciela continued:

They were calling me just to rape me, Nicole. This was the suffering. I would have preferred to just die at that moment, but I did not die. They did not kill me either. For this, Juan Pablo said to me when we woke up, "It would have been better if we escaped and they could not have raped you." "No, we cannot escape. It is better that they do not kill us. We have to just be peaceful," I said. "But if we escape, they cannot rape you," he said. "No," I said.

Graciela's voice began to tremble as she expressed how Juan Pablo continued to hold on to feelings of anger, regret, and resentment from his inability to protect her.

> Sometimes my husband says he hates the people who raped me. With the military, they took me. How could he have responded? He left me, Nicole. He was afraid they would kill me. . . . And for my husband, when there were three people, how could he have defended me? My husband, how could he have defended me, my Juan Pablo? They had guns, knives. He was crying when he saw me.

Sexual Violence during the Conflict

Although the CVR was exceptional in capturing the experiences of female survivors, according to Kimberly Theidon the abuses suffered by women during the war, particularly rape and sexual assault, were grossly underreported (Theidon 2013; see also Ulfe and Romero 2021)).[5] People rarely discussed rape in the first person, especially among men, out of shame and stigma. For men to admit rape, they confessed either to being a perpetrator or bystander, or to being unable to protect their women.[6] Women also remained silent out of fear or the stigma associated with sexual assault, even though women often endured rape to protect their daughters and other loved ones (Theidon 2013).[7] Even with inherent limitations, the Comisión de la Verdad y Reconciliación determined that rape was widespread during the violence.

According to Jelke Boesten, "Rape was mostly perpetuated by the army and police forces as part of a systematic war strategy, Shining Path and even civil patrol forces (organized by the military) were also found guilty of rape and sexual abuse" (Boesten 2010b, 312). Of the testimonies given to the Comisión de la Verdad y Reconciliación, 64 percent were from women, and of the 538 reported cases of rape, "83 percent were attributable to armed agents of the state" (CVR 2003 quoted in Theidon 2013, 107). Survivors of massacres and incursions, notably those from Putis, Chungui, and Accomarca, testified that rape was a part of these assaults and that it was common for women and girls to be raped before being shot and buried (Boesten 2014, 23).

Jelke Boesten (2017) argues that conceptualizing violence against women as a continuum unveils the violence that is hidden, normalized, and institutionalized in daily life, during both peacetime and wartime in private and public realms.[8] Available data suggest that Peru has one of the highest rates of domestic violence in the world (Boesten 2006) and throughout the war, the boundary between public and private violence became blurred as combatants abused their wives and gender regimes were (re)established in the aftermath of war (Boesten 2010a, 114).[9] While previously existing gender dynamics exacerbated violence against women during the war and the war further instigated gender-based violence, there were specific expressions of wartime gender violence. CVR investigators Henriquez and Mantilla "suggest that rape and other forms of sexual violence was indeed a war strategy against suspected terrorists—that is, the whole rural population—and a form of torture, imposed from above and out of control at the bottom" (Boesten 2008, 209).[10] If young recruits failed to rape women, they themselves would be subject to sexual assault. Kimberly Theidon describes a conversation she had with a man who served in La Marina in Ayacucho in the early 1980s about the consequences of refusing to rape women: "The rest of the men would take him aside and rape him. All of them would rape him, with the poor guy screaming. They said they were 'changing his voice'—with so much screaming, his voice would lower and wouldn't be a woman anymore" (Theidon 2013, 135). Graciela's brother Alex relayed his own memories of watching young girls—ages ten, eleven, or twelve—each with a line of ten to fifteen military men waiting their turn to rape them.

While rape was clearly used as a weapon of war, many expressions of wartime sexual violence did not fit a clear-cut definition of two opposing warring camps and included "opportunistic rape, sexual exploitation and 'entertainment,' rape by neighbors or even family members and rape in the aftermath of war" (Boesten 2010a, 111). Rape also fortified deep-seated gendered and racialized hierarchies throughout Peru by confirming a "racial and social hierarchy of 'rape-ability' of women" (Boesten 2010b, 312). A clear hierarchy existed within the ranks of the military as lighter-skinned women "were reserved for the officials; the *cholas* and 'Indians' were turned over to the troops" and an ethnically and racially stratified rank determined a man's place in line (Theidon 2013, 134).[11]

According to Graciela, rape was widespread during this violent period.

> For me, I was raped only two times [although multiple instances and by multiple men each time], but others in my community were killed from being raped. The violence not only affected me. There are others like me, women, like me, young girls, until they were dead, they were raped, killed. It was more difficult.

Graciela described how Juan Pablo's cousin, Marta, and another girl escaped from Oronccoy and went to the community of Santa Carmen. "Therefore, when they finished killing others from the communities, these two girls escaped from Oronccoy to Santa Carmen." The soldiers captured Marta—"she was a beautiful, blond-haired person and nice"—and the other girl and took them to an abandoned house. "All of the tiles from the house were gone, and so inside this place with no roof they took them, the soldiers, and these girls. In here, they raped them. Raped them in a house. They then killed Juan Pablo's cousin."

In the intervening years since the war ended, people continued to elaborate on how exactly Juan Pablo's cousin, Marta, who was pregnant at the time, died:

> They cut her throat, our Marta. They then took a knife and cut out her baby. Alive, they cut out her baby. It was crying and they took it out by its feet and then threw it and hit its head with a rock. They killed the baby. This vein in the head came out and its head was completely crushed. This woman told me this just recently, this story. Such anger. She was abandoned and the military came from the base. All of this happened in the problems. We all have *pena* [grief, anxiety, pain, embarrassment] and we all were afraid, what if they kill us like Marta? They could take out our babies with knives.

While it is impossible to know to what degree people altered the story of Marta's fate, if at all, through its retelling by various parties, the story clearly served to instill fear, hopelessness, and confusion, as well as to shape enduring memories.

Why did they kill her? Why did they not have compassion? So many people came, and they killed in my pueblo and in Tastabamba. They took over this part. From this part, another group was taken. They came to punish us. They came and tied us up with rope, but metal rope like goats. They tied up the men and so they had no defense.

I asked how many people Graciela knew who had been raped during the war and Graciela responded:

That had been raped? Many! I had been raped two times and others had been raped like dogs, killed. Incredible. Always there are people walking with the military to inform the authorities, always getting information about the military, and passing it to the communities, always passing the word about who is dead, who killed them, what they did, when they killed them, all of this, and how many were raped. Thanks to God, they raped me, but I am still living. I am healthy.

As illustrated by Graciela's experiences, sexual violence was rampant and readily discussed during the years of conflict, underscoring the injustice in its continual oversight in postwar reconciliation efforts.

Pacification and Incarceration

For Graciela, the violence began and was extremely rampant under the Alan García presidency between 1985 and 1990 yet shifted slightly under the administration of Alberto Fujimori. The rise in violence and inability of the government to contain Sendero fostered a desire for new leadership, and Alberto Fujimori, of Japanese descent, rose in popularity as a populist candidate defeating conservative candidate and novelist Mario Vargas Llosa for the presidential seat in 1990.[12] Within weeks of taking office, Fujimori instigated austerity measures he had previously criticized, known as "Fujishock." While he managed to reduce drastically the country's inflation, the privatization of state companies, closure of state-run institutions, and removal of price controls on fuel and basic goods caused a rise in poverty.[13] His leadership also proved heavy-handed and corrupt, with implications for the rising violence in Peru.[14]

According to Graciela, when Fujimori took office, in 1990, the violence was "slightly pacified and there was a little more compassion for the people." Graciela explained that the violence began to wane as the government had signed a peace agreement.

> The military killed MANY for this with fear we escaped to the mountains. However, the last years when we were deserted, there was a little declaration by the government of pacification, I believe. With this, they took us. Without this pacification, they would have continued to kill us. These last years the government said, "Do not kill. Grab them. Capture and bring them." Because of this, they did not kill us. There was a reclamation for this, they did not kill us. Much before there was more violence and orders for the military to kill us.

As the government policy reportedly shifted from kill to capture suspected terrorists, the military incarcerated Graciela and Juan Pablo.

The following morning as the sun was rising, the military personnel led Graciela and Juan Pablo out of Oronccoy toward a jail cell. Graciela pointed out on her hand-drawn map how they walked from below Oronccoy to the community of Mollebamba.

> From my community in Oronccoy they captured various groups. The soldiers took them to the community of Mollebamba. In Mollebamba, there was a soldier cartel. When they brought people from the communities of Oronccoy, Santa Carmen, Liampata, the communities that live around Mollebamba, they put them in here [the cartel].

Unlike the numerous deserted communities Graciela and Juan Pablo passed on their way from Oronccoy, people filled the town of Mollebamba. Soldiers brought Graciela and Juan Pablo to the military base in Mollebamba and put them in a cell together with a door that looked out onto a road heading toward Andahuaylas. Much to their surprise, in addition to abuse from military personnel and Senderistas, community members also mistreated Graciela and Juan Pablo.

> When we arrived, it was not the military that insulted us, it was the

community that insulted us. "Carajo Terrocos [fucking terrorists]!" They said we stole their cows and animals to insult us. In my conscience, I know I did not steal their animals. This was in my conscience and I cried. People always passed the cell insulting us. We suffered a lot. . . . So here we are civilians, women, men, all of us they insulted, calling us terrorists, but in reality, not one of us was a terrorist. We were deserted in the mountains escaping and living like deer. . . . Now at times I say, "Why did they insult me?" I did not do anything.

Graciela continued to describe confusion over the discrimination faced by other campesinos and town residents:

The people that lived in Mollebamba do not respect us. They do not have compassion for us. There was no one to rescue these people. There was no one. They respected us like animals, like trash, they looked at us. . . . However, it is not very far, they are our neighbors, this pueblo Mollebamba. There we were in jail and there they lived with the military, and they were stronger, more powerful. They were just our paisanos. For this, until now, my husband is angry at times.

The military officers told Graciela and Juan Pablo that they would kill them if they tried to escape, and they kept them in one cell together. "There was no one to complain to, and I was afraid looking at their guns, pistols, walking. 'Surely they will kill me,' I would say." Graciela described how the military treated them while incarcerated:

In there they gave us, the soldiers' boss, brought us food in a metal bowl that was all mixed like you would give a pig. In this bucket, they gave us our lunch, our dinner, our breakfast like mazamorra. I could not eat this mixture. I could not eat it. They would shout at us, "Eat it already! Eat it quickly or we will kill you terrorists!"[15] They called me a terrorist and Juan Pablo a terrorist, but I was only seventeen years old and I did not know why they were treating us like that. I did not know how to explain it to myself. I was here in the jail a week. I was in the small, small, closed cell for one week and I was cold. They did not give us a mattress and a blanket to keep us warm inside.

One day a military man came and told Juan Pablo he had to help peel potatoes, so they removed him from the cell to work in the kitchen. Once Juan Pablo left, Graciela experienced further threats.

> When they took him, a military man came inside the jail cell. With force, he grabbed me to start raping me. With force, he came inside and threw me on the ground. He had a gun. . . . He said that they were going to rape me. I did not know anything, and I did not have any sentiment other than hatred. I thought it would have been better if they killed me. He said, "We are going to rape you. We are going to rape you numerous times." He told me they [the military men] were saying this among themselves.

At this point in recounting the event, Graciela began laughing. I thought perhaps I had misunderstood the context of her story, but then she replied: "At times when I remember things I laugh. At times, I have pain. At times, I cry. Now I am not crying. Yesterday I cried."

Then Graciela continued to explain what happened next and I better understood what prompted her laughter. "He grabbed me and knocked me down on the ground by swiping my feet." Graciela stood up and demonstrated how the man tried to knock her down by sweeping his legs under her feet.

> I started crying and screaming when he grabbed me, but I won! I did not have strength, but I won against this military man. I pushed him so he did not rape me. However, I was afraid. I thought for sure he would now kill me. I cried and cried. When I won, the military man left. He did not rape me. I did not speak a word of Spanish at this time. No one spoke Spanish in my pueblo, only Quechua, but I won from force. What did he say to me in Spanish? Many insults when he left! However, he did not rape me. I won!

Graciela continued to describe how she was so full of fear that the military man would return to kill her, but then a military official soon came to her cell.

> He asked, "How are you, Graciela?" with kindness. This military did not enter the cell but talked through the window. "How are you, Graciela? How do you feel?" He asked why I was crying. "Why are you crying? You are

good. You are happy, peaceful. You are just a minor." I said that a military man came and tried to abuse me, tried to rape me. "It is better that you kill me," I said. With much pain, with much pena, I spoke with much force. "Just kill me. It is better than mistreating me," I said. The military said to me, "Who came in here?" "A military came to rape me. Also, in Oronccoy military men raped me." I said all of this in Quechua. This military man spoke Quechua.

The military official left in search of the perpetrator.

He was looking at them wondering which one said he was going to do this. So then, he found an officer and he stood in the doorway all night and castigated him. He then went and talked to the man and said, "How could you do this to her? She is a minor. How can you abuse her? How can you rape her?" So, all night this military was reprimanded with much embarrassment.

According to Jelke Boesten, there are reported cases in which soldiers were reprimanded for raping women, nevertheless, according to one colonel, rape and abuse were considered "minor errors" that did not really warrant punishment and were a result of men unable to control their natural sex drive around the "temptation of women" (Boesten 2010a, 121).

In his memoir fighting first for Sendero, then with the military, before joining the priesthood and eventually pursuing a PhD in anthropology, Lurgio Gavilán Sánchez expresses disgust at how the military treated women. Gavilán Sánchez describes how the military would bring women ages seventeen to twenty-three to where the military men slept and "they bedded down with the recruits. The sergeants took turns first, and then the rest of the soldiers until they wore them out" (Gavilán Sánchez 2015, 50).[16] While the abuse of women was widespread, the military apparently sought to conceal it. In 1985 in preparing for a military inspection, they decided to kill the women they had taken prisoner. Gavilán Sánchez explains:

They brought the women to where we slept, and all the soldiers had their way with them. The women cried, "Don't kill us." I was frightened too.

Around twelve that night they took the women out to the parade ground where we always lined up. All of us had to witness their execution. The grave was already dug. Two shots sounded in unison and the women fell over, dead. Now it was not because they had committed any error, but because the inspection was coming, and it was better to make them disappear. (51)

Unlike the women Gavilán Sánchez profiled, fortunately, Graciela survived her encounter with the military and was about to be released.

Family Reunification

After reprimanding the man who tried to rape Graciela, the military official returned to the cell and asked Graciela about her family.

He said to me, "Do not cry, do not worry. I have talked with your mom and dad. You are not going to die. Who is your mother? What is her name? Your mother lives in Andahuaylas. Your father also lives in Andahuaylas." "My mom is Magdalena Supa Puyucahua. My father is Justiñano Merino Amaru," I said. "You do not look like a Supa Puyucahua," he said. "You look like another, but your father is Justiñano. Do not worry, he is coming. Do not cry. We are not going to kill you. You can have your freedom. You are a minor. You need to study. You have to have a future," he said to me.

While Graciela was in jail, someone recognized her and told her *padrino* (godfather), who had performed her first hair-cutting ceremony and baptism when she was ten years old, that she was in the jail. Her padrino then located Graciela's father in Andahuaylas to let him know her whereabouts. "At three in the afternoon, my father came to the jail! 'Your Godfather told me you were here,' he said. I cried . . . "

When Graciela's father arrived at the jail, the military personnel said, "'She is not your daughter. She is blancuna [light-skinned]. You are *tragano* [dark-skinned].'" Graciela explained that her father "is half *moreno*" and he kept insisting that Graciela was indeed his daughter. "'No Señor, this is my daughter,' my father said." While Graciela's mother was "half white" from her hacendado father, Graciela's father was dark skinned and therefore identified as tragano, once again underscoring how skin color dictates social positioning in the Andes.

The military personnel eventually conceded, saying, "'Take her, she should study. She should have her liberty.'"

Although Graciela was technically free to leave, she and her father remained in the jail for one more week. Graciela had been sick with bronchitis and her father had a terrible case of bronchitis pneumonia causing him to cough up blood.

> I said, "My father is sick." I told the official. This soldier spoke Quechua to understand both Spanish and Quechua. I said, "My father is sick. He is spitting up blood. He has bronchopneumonia." He told the official in Spanish and he returned to the jail and gave my father an injection. My father improved the following day. He was not spitting up blood and was feeling better.

The officials allowed Graciela and her father to stay in the jail until they fully recuperated, but they did not have enough food to regain their strength. "We had nothing to eat. Not a dish, nothing. I could not make a meal or anything. At this time, I had no money. I did not know how to buy anything. I only knew natural things. My father had always bought the cows. How much he had bought when I was young, but I did not know anything." Then a woman came to the jail asking Graciela about her father and offered to let Graciela work to be able to feed her father.

> Then a señora came. "How is your father?" she asked. "My father is sick," I said. "So, go and get maize, haba, quinoa," she was saying. "Yes, daughter, go," she said. My dad was in the bed sick, so I went with the señora. She helped me cook maize. Therefore, from the cell when I helped, she paid me one sack of maize each day. I was helping for one week.

There were many houses in the community that Graciela would pass when she walked to the market to buy food to prepare for her father. Graciela described the living situation of a particular woman who lived just down the road from the jail:

> There was a woman, Saywa, who lived there in this part below. She did not have a husband. She was about forty years old. They [military] came every night and raped the señora. For sure, the señora did not tell anyone. She

was afraid. Like horses, the soldiers ran. At eight in the night, they would go there, many of them. This woman Saywa was from the community Santa Carmen. She was an older señora. She had a husband, but the military killed him. She had a son about nine or ten years old, her first son. They would come in the night, every night running from the jail.

In describing the men coming to Saywa's house every night, Graciela made a "bok bok bok" sound on the wooden table to imitate the loud echoes of military boots on the ground. "How many times the military raped her every night. Like horses, they would go to the house, raping her . . . This señora Saywa was raped a lot. When the moon came up and there was not light, many men would enter, like five or six each night. How did this señora continue?" I asked if she was living in the house alone. "Yes, with her son, alone with her son."

After about a week of rest, Graciela's and her father's health restored and they were free to leave the jail. With the clothes on their backs, Graciela and her father walked to the city of Andahuaylas. After approximately five years, foraging for food to survive, under constant threat of capture and death, hiding in bushes and caves and eventual incarceration, Graciela headed toward an unknown city to reunite with her remaining family members.

———

Following a nonconsensual courtship, numerous rapes, and incarceration, at last Graciela reunited with her father and the military gave her liberty to pass freely. In recounting her departure from the jail, Graciela began laughing: "I walked by the officials with their guns. 'Here is your certificate to pass freely. You are young, a minor of only seventeen years. You have a future. You need to study,' they explained to my father." Graciela felt a moment of peace as the military man advised Graciela to take care of her father and to study. The fact that all their schools had been destroyed, their homes had been burned to the ground, and fellow paisanos had been killed or displaced, however, overshadowed any feelings of hope. While Graciela was thrilled for her freedom and anxious to see her family, she found herself traveling to a strange city, and Juan Pablo had gone missing.

Chapter 5

Exploited Displacement

Life in the City

The year was 1990 and Graciela was seventeen years old when she and her father traveled from Mollebamba to the city of Andahuaylas. They went to the house in which her father, mother, and other siblings had been living in the community of Kichkapata (neighborhood of Andahuaylas) since their capture roughly two years prior. When Graciela and her father first arrived at the house, her mother was not there as she was working, but later in the day, as the sun was about to set, her mother returned. "My mother arrived home late crying, 'My daughter!' It was very painful." Graciela's siblings were young, and she demonstrated their various heights with her hands, saying, "My siblings were like a stairway," as they were close in age. Graciela's brothers Alex, Juaqin, and Edolo were living at home and working as laborers in a woman's field and Graciela's sister, Mia, was helping her mom in the house. Graciela's brother Alipeo, however, was not living with the family. After the military captured and briefly incarcerated Graciela's family, a military man came to the jail and took Alipeo to care for his cows, and the family could not object. "He was little when the military took him, [roughly ten years old] when they took him, my brother Alipeo. A señor took him, took my brother to help him care for his animals." Like Juan Pablo when military personnel took his son, Graciela's family had no contact with Alipeo since his capture and did not know if he was still alive.

From living on the run for so many years, everything in the city was foreign to Graciela. At first, she wanted to socialize, but her parents would not let her. "At times, I wanted to go to festivals, but my mom said I could not go because for sure, there would be police there and they would kill me. I thought they would kill me." Transportation was also new for Graciela.

Also coming from the highlands, I did not know what a car was either. There the buses would come. When I would climb onto the bus, I was so afraid I would fall. I was afraid looking at the floor. When you never know anything like that . . . I had such fear. They would say, "Sube, sube!" [Get on, get on] to my mom to go to Talavera [a town adjacent to Andahuaylas] to work from the corner of the plaza, but I did not want to get on the bus. I was seventeen years old and was afraid! Never had I known anything like that. My stomach would just turn looking at it.

Graciela's family worked harvesting maize for the *dueña* (owner) of the house in which they were living. "This was tough work for them, and they were so little cultivating maize. Mia was only four years old, so she was still just with my mom, but my siblings worked hard, and my father worked hard. They would work in the dueña's field, but she would not pay them. They were like slaves." Graciela's brother Alex described how they all began working at a young age in Andahuaylas merely to survive:

At eight, nine, ten years old, I worked in the night irrigating the fields for the bull to come and then working the next day carrying the water. We just sacrificed. They would just pay us in maize from working all night. The next day we would make *mote* from the maize to eat. Working like this, a tremendous sacrifice. We could not continue our studies. Maybe we could return [to school], but my parents would have had to establish stability, like secure work in the fields, a secure place to live to then study. However, in this time, no, because we had to work daily, but to go to school you go until one in the afternoon, and to work from nine in the morning to nine or ten in the night [it was impossible]. We had to work with firewood, cut firewood, or in the field cultivating maize, cultivating potato, or irrigating the fields in the night. We did not lead a normal life. We did not live a childhood when we were children. All that happened, we lived a life of an adult. In our childhood we never really played, we did not know games like with cars, almost nothing. We did not play. It was all family labor, my mother, my father, all my siblings, we had to all sacrifice to maintain the house and to provide what my younger siblings needed.

In describing his childhood before having the opportunity to pursue an education, Alex reported to me that he had no joyful memories. "I have no memories of feeling happy." He described how all he remembers is feeling scared Sendero or the military would catch and kill him and his family. "From five to ten years old, all I remember is fear, hunger, and thirst."

Juan Pablo's Disappearance

While Graciela was adapting to life in the city, she constantly worried about Juan Pablo. Although she originally had hateful feelings for Juan Pablo, their relationship did not begin consensually, and she maintains she does not love him, Graciela had begun to rely on him for survival. Moreover, while it was common for men to discard women who had been raped by military forces, Juan Pablo continued to support and honor Graciela through her traumatic experiences and ongoing dark memories. Consequently, her feelings for Juan Pablo were complicated. She did not know what had happened to him since the officers took him to peel potatoes in the jail and he effectively disappeared. "Many months, three months, I was in Andahuaylas. When I was in jail, Juan Pablo said, 'If the military does not kill me in ten or twenty years, then I will come look for you and marry you.'" At this point Graciela did not know if Juan Pablo really would return for her, or if he was even still alive.

Although Graciela did not know it at the time, when the military took Juan Pablo out of the cell, they moved him to the temporary military base in Chapi to work for three months. Juan Pablo explained what had happened:

I was captured in Oronccoy, and from Oronccoy the military took me to Mollebamba. From there, Graciela stayed in Mollebamba at that base. She was a woman and so she stayed there with the official and they took me to Chapi, to the base there, the military base. Therefore, I was there in Chapi, they told me to speak to my family, and so I asked why.

The military officers advised Juan Pablo to speak with his compadre who was the president of the civil defense. Juan Pablo's compadre was planning to charge the base and free the incarcerated. To prevent a violent clash, they advised Juan Pablo to sign an *acta de capitalización* (certificate that promised he would not join the Senderistas) and released him.[1] Once released from the military base in Chapi, Juan Pablo set forth to find Graciela.

Juan Pablo traveled to Andahuaylas and found where Graciela was living with her family. Graciela described her parents' reception of Juan Pablo:

> He arrived at my mom and dad and talked with them, but they did not want him. They said, "Our daughter is a minor and you are like this. You cannot." Always I had in my heart missing Juan Pablo. My mom said, "You cannot live with this old man. You are young. He is a widower." When my mom said she did not want me to live with Juan Pablo, he left alone.

After Graciela's parents rejected Juan Pablo, he went to the jungle. He had left on bad terms, as he expressed grave jealousy toward Graciela.

> Juan Pablo was very jealous. . . . He thought I was with other boys. However, I was not thinking of being with other men. I still do not know about being in love. I did not know. Therefore, this is what he was thinking, but I was not. He was very jealous of me, so he went to the jungle. He did not want to leave me, because he always wanted to watch me. Because he was so jealous and thinking things of me, but I was not like that.

The day that Juan Pablo left, Graciela was conflicted over her feelings for him. "He had such a desire to go to the jungle, to uproot and take me with him, so I had pain. At times, I cried too. Juan Pablo was always encouraging and cheered me up." In addition to not understanding her own feelings toward Juan Pablo, Graciela also believed Juan Pablo rejected her for being apparently barren. "I did not have children. For three years, [while on the run] we did not have children. Therefore, when Juan Pablo went to the jungle, we did not have anything in Andahuaylas. We did not have a field, nothing." Graciela assumed that Juan Pablo left out of jealousy and because she had not become pregnant. Without land or children, there was nothing to tie him down.

Alex's Educational Challenges in the City

While Graciela was unable to attend school in Andahuaylas, as she needed to work to support her family, after several years in the city her younger male siblings eventually began to take classes. Her brother Alex described how challenging it was to earn an education, given his advanced age in comparison with his peers and their unstable living situation:

> Because of the political violence, I did not study until I was about ten or eleven years old, because up to this point, I was living in the mountains in the war. After then, when the military captured us and brought us to Andahuaylas here, I [eventually] studied. I entered the first grade, and I was the oldest and I was big starting first grade, but I was in different schools in different institutions, not just one in one place. Why? Because for a while we would live there, for example, in Kichkapata. At times, we would go to Talavera, and then leave there because we did not have a stable living situation because we did not have our own house. We just lived in a rented house, and at times the landlord kicked us out, and when they kicked us out, we had to go to a different place. I tried to study in different places and could not just end first grade and then start second grade. I studied in Andahuaylas, another time in Salinas, other in Talavera.

As Alex shifted around to different schools, he became the target of bullying.

> When I was twelve years old and entered first grade, there were children who were six years old, five years old in first grade and seven years old. I was the only person that was so big at twelve years old and I was bullied, I was discriminated. "You are old, huge. You are *burro* [dimwit, blockhead, stupid]. Why did you not study? For sure you do not know anything, that is why you are so big in first grade," they would say. They discriminated against me horribly, my classmates. They hit me hard and beat me up, everything. They would beat me up and say that I was a terrorist. They continued to do this to those who came from our land, various people, they beat up badly. There is a memory I have. One time three people, three

brothers, I was walking in the street and they came at me and hit me hard. I fell and was almost dead. They repeatedly hit me all over my face and hit everywhere. I did not understand why they hit me so hard. I escaped from various [boys].

Peers also discriminated against Alex for speaking Quechua. "We only spoke Quechua, like our mother. When we arrived at the age of seven, eight, and nine years old, we did not know how to read or write Quechua. So, at twelve years old I was put into first grade. Little by little, I learned, but it was not easy. Almost I did not understand. For this until now, it is hard because I do not speak correct Spanish." Alex explained that most of the people from the campo spoke Quechua, but those who had migrated to Andahuaylas were spread out in different schools. "Yes, the people from the campo spoke Quechua, but here in the city, the majority spoke Spanish, and I spoke Quechua in the school, and also there was a lot of bullying for this. If you did not know how to speak Spanish, [they would call us] 'mote, mote, mote.'" *Mote* is the name of a fat kernel of boiled maize that people commonly eat in rural highland households. By calling Alex "mote," the students were insulting him for being from the campo.

This hurt a lot, very strong. They would discriminate when you would say a word. They would make fun and repeat this word and it made me feel really bad. . . . They would fight us, our classmates. They would hit us hard because we were not from here. "Go to your land!" They would discriminate against us badly when we could not talk well.

From working in the fields, Alex's parents knew a man who needed help in the city of Lima, and so they sent Alex there to continue his studies.

We were working in the fields, and so we were known. To my mom and my dad, they said, "Señora, your son can support us in Lima. I will send him to Lima and there he can get an education. He can get everything," they were saying, but it was a lie. When I arrived, there was no education. When I went to do the things of work, he began to hit me. . . . In Lima, I studied first and second grade and third grade and fourth, fifth, and sixth

I finished in Lima. The man took me to finish my studies, but not just to study; he exploited me. I had to work hard day and night. I had to mop the floors. I had to clean bathrooms, many things I had to do, but he also did not pay me.

In addition to exploitation, Alex experienced even worse discrimination at school in Lima than he did in Andahuaylas. "In Lima, it was worse because I was a little older, so I was fourteen years old there. I was an adolescent, and they would treat me ugly when at times in Lima I studied with students from Lima itself or residents that all agreed to discriminate against those who do not speak Spanish well. Ugly."

Alex ended up escaping from the house where he was living and survived on the streets.

When I escaped the place that was hitting me where I was working, I fled to the street. In the street, I was selling to the cars. I was selling candies, buying and selling sweets to survive. . . . In the street, in the parks I was sleeping because I had no choice, and the work was not easy because I was a minor. At times people thought I was a thief; they accused me.

Alex was living in the streets for what he thought was about three weeks. Soon Alex met an individual who requested his labor. "When I was walking in the streets, I knew a man and he asked me to work for him. He would give me food and a roof if I worked to study. I accepted and I was helping him and studying. I finished fifth and sixth grade." Alex explained his work in the house. "In the house to make all the things of the house, cleaning the house, mopping the floors, cleaning the bathroom or helping with cooking, cleaning, everything." Again, the man did not pay Alex for the work but rather compensated him with "a roof and a plate of food."

After finishing sixth grade, Alex was unable to continue his studies. "I finished my fifth and sixth grade, but I could not continue there because the man had his family there and needed to invest more in education, because in Lima the schools are more expensive. I was a child, and I did not have capital or money to support myself to continue studying." With few options, Alex attempted to join the military, yet continued to face further discrimination.

When I was fifteen or seventeen years old, I presented to military service. I presented to the Marine Corps in Callao, in Lima. I wanted to be a military person to serve my country, but they discriminated against me badly because I could not speak correct Spanish. Therefore, for this I left the institution of the marine infantry.

Without financial support and with limited options in Lima, Alex returned to Andahuaylas.

My mom said I could stay and work in the fields. So I returned, but I returned from Lima completely sick. I think I was sick from the work, but I do not know. I continued in hunger. For ten years, I was sick. I do not know what the sickness was. A lot of blood came from my mouth. It started when I was about eight or nine years old, but I was [eventually] treated and I cured only with time. Thanks to God now, I am okay.

Alex visited various doctors while sick. "I went but they never found what sickness I had. They could never touch it. None of the doctors knew. They could not find it." Once back in Andahuaylas, Alex was unable to continue his studies due to their family's ongoing instability. "Only I worked and did not study, and so there were not motives to continue onto secondary school. My parents did not have money to have stabilization. We did not have our own home, so we were living house to house." With few other options, Alex returned to work in others' fields to help support his family.

Graciela's (Limited) Work Opportunities

With Juan Pablo gone and Graciela's brothers helping other people harvest potatoes, Graciela needed to find work.

All my siblings had to work to eat. This is all we had, so my mother and my father told me, "Daughter, you go and work." They said, "We all need to work to eat." So there above, they found me work with a man who had a shoe shop and many gardens. I did not know how to speak Spanish, so I went above to work in his house.

The man with the shop and Graciela's father agreed that she would help care for his extensive patio gardens.

There were four girls. There was one woman who was of an older age; she was about forty years old. So, three young, minor girls were there. They were working for him, employees. I asked, "What are these girls doing? There is hardly anything to do." So, one night he said, "Here is your room. Here is where you will sleep," the man said to me. "The girls have their room, so this is your room," he told me. The following day he said the other girls were bathing so I needed to bathe, so I went to take a bath. So, I went to the bathroom and the man yelled at me, "Come, daughter, from your room," he said. Therefore, I obeyed and went to the señor. "Sit," he said. He had a bed and he had chairs, so I went to sit in the chairs. So, he said, "Come here!" He said to sit here on the bed. "Come and talk with me," he said, so I went to sit. He grabbed me. The señor grabbed me. He said, "I want to be with you." At this moment it was humid, and my clothes [outer layers such as pollera, sweater, and llikilli, as opposed to underskirt and blouse, which Graciela was wearing] were hanging [on a hook], so the señor wanted to abuse me. I was scared. He made me uncomfortable. "No, señor, I have to go!" I said. All my clothes were together, and I ran to where my mom was. . . . When I was putting my clothes together by the door, I lost one of my skirts. It was lost. So the señor told me, "Do not go, girl. Do not go. You are not like the other girls. Other girls when we talk, they trust me and stay," he told me. "I will pay you well. Do not go." I left. At this moment, I put all my clothes that were hanging in the bag. The fear! The fear to face my mother! Therefore, I did not tell my mother anything, that he wanted to abuse me. I did not tell her anything. So, she said to me, "Oh, daughter, we have nothing. What are we going to do to eat? When you work, you can have money to buy your clothes. You can have money." This is what she told me, my mother. She was crying. "We are not in our pueblo. Here we have to work," my mother told me. I also was crying. I came with pain, but my mother did not know why I left.

Graciela believed her mother had no idea what had happened with the señor but did not want to divulge the truth.

[She knew] nothing. I did not tell her anything. "Maybe you need to get accustomed to it," she told me. I can get accustomed, but I did not want to be abused by the señor. I did not want it. . . . He was fifty years old or more. He was old. When I arrived at the house, my mom cried. "Oh, daughter, how are we going to make it here? We are not in our pueblo. We do not have money, nothing. We need to buy things. You have to become accustomed, you have to work," she told me. I can work with a shovel and pick. For me it is not difficult to work. Only that in this case he took advantage of my body. He wanted to take advantage. He wanted to abuse me. This I did not like. When we were talking, I was AFRAID, Nicole!

Graciela refused to go back and reclaim her skirt (pollera) and knew she would need to find alternative employment.

I left [the skirt] behind and was so scared. . . . Other girls are loose and leave their bodies. These words [the man said] until now are recorded in my head to say to my daughters when they work, I tell them. At this time, I was only seventeen years old! I was afraid to tell my mother. Crying, crying, so I did not tell my mother anything, only my conscience knew. So, I cried too when she was crying. What can I say? I was crying, "Mother, do not cry, do not cry." "Another person will need you to work," she said. I did not want to work for this man, so I said I would work for someone else. So below, there was a known person who worked there in Chapi.[2]

Graciela's following place of employment did not prove to be much better than the first.

Continued Exploitation

As mentioned in chapter 4, Graciela's maternal grandfather was a hacendado. A woman within the hacienda family lived in Andahuaylas. This woman knew Graciela's mother and offered Graciela work washing clothes. This woman of the house, or dueña, gave Graciela continuous mounds of clothes to wash by hand in cold water, which Graciela said contributed to her developing bronchial pneumonia and coughing up blood.

Yes, I had bronchial pneumonia. It grabbed me, the bronchial pneumonia. Therefore, [at first] I was fine there, I was fine, right, but hunger grabbed me. I had a little water in the morning. I had a piece of bread and a little cup of water is all. At noon, they also just gave me this [water and a piece of bread]. However, I was also cooking lunch, rich food I was making, but they did not serve me. In the kitchen, all of them ate in the dining room with all the family. They did not give me the leftovers. They gave me nothing. Therefore, I suffered a lot.

Graciela felt she was not able to protest her mistreatment. "However, I was afraid because they had money and I did not at this time. I did not know about human rights. Now I know, but people with money can defend their rights more than the poor can."

The dueña also had a small store window from which Graciela sold cakes and sandwiches.

The police would come, old people, many came, sometimes with their wives. How they looked at me [knowing I was] lacking and sad looking. I did not know the people, but they would buy food and offer it to me. "Here, eat it," they would say. Therefore, this señora, the boss, saw this. "No, you all eat, she is eating," she would say. At times when they did not finish the meat, pork sandwiches, also in their plates they would leave a little food, as you see in a restaurant. Therefore, when I had hunger my patrona, the dueña of the house, my boss, she would put it all in a pail. This clean garbage. I was so hungry, so at times I would take out things. There was meat and fresh vegetables, so I would take them out to eat. However, the woman would sell good food and did not offer me anything. I liked everything, but she would not offer me any of the good food. The dueña's daughter was there who was studying. At times, I would be crying, and this girl was studying in Chispa. She was studying to be a teacher and she said to me in Quechua, "Gracielita, I am studying to be a teacher. Do not cry. *Hijita*, do not cry. My mom is a *renegóna* [grouchy, cantankerous person]." She was good, this daughter. She was trying to lift me up, this girl, at times when I was crying. However, her mom did nothing when I was spitting up blood. She did nothing. She had no compassion for my pain. I had much pain in my chest. Therefore, the daughter who was studying said, "You are sick. You are washing too many clothes and it is cold. I will go buy you some pills," she told me. However, nothing made me better. After a month, she [the dueña] took me to my mom and said I was not accustomed to this work. I was sick. "Your daughter is spitting up blood," she said to my mama. My mom saw that I was sick and asked, "How could you bring her like this?" "Yes, she is sick from washing my clothes for my work." The dueña did not say anything else. Therefore, my mom brought me a juice of ground garlic with onion and honey to drink. With only this, my mom cured me.

The dueña told Graciela that she could continue working for her when she fully recuperated. Graciela wanted to buy a watch, so the dueña told her that when she completed one full month of work, she would earn enough money to buy a watch. However, once Graciela's health returned, the dueña said that Graciela was to go work for her son in Lima. "'So, bring your daughter to me,' the señora said to my mom. 'I will send her to where my son lives in Lima. He only has one daughter. It is not like here where there are skirts to wash. It will be nice for her to go to Lima,' she told me." The señora lectured Graciela about the importance of learning Spanish to work in Lima. She also told Graciela not to bring her polleras (skirts) to Lima, otherwise people would call her names in the city. "It was Saturday, and I was talking with my mom about having to go Sunday at six in the morning with a plane. The señora was going to send me. The son would be waiting for me in the airport in Lima. He had a daughter who was three years old." With little choice in the matter, at seventeen years old Graciela prepared to move to an unknown city of over five million people to work for an unfamiliar son of an unkind woman.[3]

Juan Pablo's Return

The day before the dueña was going to send Graciela to Lima, Graciela walked to the market to buy pork to prepare sandwiches for the dueña's son and his daughter. Juan Pablo's brother-in-law from his late ex-wife worked in this market and Graciela greeted him upon her arrival:

"Good morning tío [uncle]," I said at seven in the morning. "What are you doing?" he asked me. "I am buying pork," I said. "Oh yes, and where are you working?" the señor asked me. Other days I had seen this man, but he had never asked me questions. "So where are you working? What are you doing?" he said to me. "I am buying pork to cook," I said in Quechua. I did not know how to speak or understand Spanish, nothing. He was also speaking Quechua. "Oh yes, Juan Pablo is here. He has returned," he told me. I said, "You are a liar." "No, it is true," he said. "Yes, he went to your mom's house, Juan Pablo, at three in the morning. He then returned to Talavera at four in the morning," he said. "So, what did Juan Pablo say?" I asked. "He wants to get back together with you to return together," he said.

Graciela was in disbelief. "What is this? I did not believe anything. I did not think he would return. He was very jealous and angry when he left. When I was crying, and he left. No way would he return." Then Graciela began to laugh, saying, "But then again, I could see him doing so. Unusual, right?" However, ultimately not believing what this man had said, Graciela returned to the dueña's house to prepare for her trip to Lima.

Graciela's mother and her brother Alex came to the dueña's house to say goodbye. When hugging, Alex quietly reiterated to Graciela what the man in the market had said: that Juan Pablo had arrived the night before in search of her. Graciela could scarcely believe what he had said. Graciela explained what she later learned had occurred the night before:

> Juan Pablo arrived at three in the morning. I could not believe it! He arrived to my mom asking at three in the morning, "Where is Graciela?" There was a big door where you would enter my mom's house. In there he knocked on the door, it was a big door. "Who would arrive at night with a lantern?" my mom said. It was Juan Pablo. "What do you want?" my mom said. "Graciela. Where is she?" he said. "Why do you want my daughter? My daughter is not here. She is far away in Lima." She was lying.

Alex ended up inviting Juan Pablo inside the house to spend the night. "So, when he could not enter [the house], my little brother Alex invited him inside. I could not believe it. [Alex] was a little, skinny boy." Graciela's mother was not pleased and instructed Graciela's siblings not to tell Juan Pablo anything about Graciela, but Alex did not obey. "'Where is my wife Graciela?' Juan Pablo asked Alex in hushed whispers. 'Below she is working, *papay*,' he said to Juan Pablo." At four in the morning, Juan Pablo left the house to go to his brother-in-law's home in Talavera. It was mere hours later that the brother-in-law then relayed the message to Graciela in the market that Juan Pablo indeed had returned for her.

Here was Graciela in the dueña's house about to travel to Lima the following day to work for an unknown man and his daughter, but Juan Pablo had returned for her. Graciela's mother was saying, "'He is older, he is a widower. He will leave you when you have children. Tomorrow much later, you must leave. You must study.'" Graciela had mixed feelings. "Therefore, I was going to go to Lima on Sunday. This afternoon he arrived. He arrived at my house. He was crying and crying, they said."

Graciela told the dueña that she was just going to go home with her brother for a short time. She returned to her mother's house and found Juan Pablo there waiting. "There we conversed. There Juan Pablo was saying, 'I will not hit you. You will not suffer. I will treat you well. Go with me to the jungle,' he was saying." When he had left two months prior for Chanchamayo, Graciela did not think he would return.

> "So now I go, and you will never see me again," he told me. He said he would go to the jungle. When he went in the car, I was crying. How I did not have a baby also. I thought maybe because of this also he left me. . . . I did not think he would return. I did not think he would come back for me, but he told me with passion, "Because I thought you did not love me, I left." I cried. . . . So, I said, "Why did you leave me? What were you thinking?" Juan Pablo said, "What were you thinking of me? For sure you did not want me." "I do not know what I was thinking. I cannot explain myself," I told him. However, I had pain. Juan Pablo did not want me to go [to Lima] for this woman. He wanted me to stay.

Graciela asked Juan Pablo what they would do for work, and he replied, "'In the jungle, they plant coffee. We can go and work as contractors. Let's go.'" However, Graciela did not want to leave her family. "I did not want to go. I had pain to leave my mother. I said, 'I do not want to go to the jungle. We will suffer there. My mother and father said you should go alone.' My mom said for me not to go. I also did not have a DNI [an identification card needed to pass through police patrols on their way to the jungle]."[4]

Graciela's mother and father did not want Graciela to live with Juan Pablo, believing that he would mistreat Graciela, and preferred that she go to the city of Lima to attend school. Yet when faced with moving to the bustling city of Lima to work for an unfamiliar person or traveling to the jungle alongside her jealous and older, yet devoted, partner, Juan Pablo, Graciela decided on the latter, and her parents eventually relented.

> I went to the jungle with Juan Pablo, and in the end my parents were saying, "Whatever will happen, we are the authorities of our lives, and we give authority to Juan Pablo. She is a minor. Take care of her. Do not let her suffer. Do not hit her." My mother and my father said this to Juan Pablo. He said, "I will not let her suffer. I will not mistreat her." He did not hit me. We were peaceful. For this, we went to the jungle.

The following day, Graciela's mother walked to the dueña's house and explained that Graciela would not be traveling to Lima to work for her son. As expected, the dueña of the house was angry with Graciela for leaving. "'But how? My son is waiting in the airport. The liar!' she said with loathing." In fact, Graciela stated, "Until now I think she is angry."[5]

———

Upon reuniting with her family and surviving a challenging adjustment to life in the city and various exploitative work situations in Andahuaylas, Graciela ultimately reconciled with a man she previously loathed, Juan Pablo. While Graciela's siblings faced challenging adjustments supporting their family while striving to acquire an education, contending with acute discrimination, instability, and poverty, Graciela also strived to find her way. Facing a fork in the road of whether to travel alone to Lima or to take a risk and rejoin Juan Pablo to work in the tropical lowlands, Graciela veered toward Juan Pablo. It was 1990 and Graciela was only seventeen years old when she left her family and headed to the Amazon rainforest with a widower sixteen years her senior. "When I was seventeen, I went to the jungle with Juan Pablo. My mom did not want me to go to the jungle with Juan Pablo. They said I would suffer, and Juan Pablo would abandon me because I am a minor. However, he did not abandon me."

Chapter 6

Dislocated Motherhood in the Tropical Lowlands

Adjusting to the Lowlands

When Graciela and Juan Pablo initially arrived in the Amazon, Graciela was pleasantly surprised with life in the lowlands. According to Graciela, the Amazon was a place of plenty on various levels.

> At first, we lived deep in the jungle. In the jungle, you can grow ullucu [Andean root vegetable], tomatoes, camote [sweet potato], all. There is fruit, avocado, sugarcane, *uncucha* [Andean root vegetable]; all is there, even bananas.[1] It is beautiful. Juan Pablo worked and the two of us lived there. We did not have kids. We lived there almost two years.

Numerous people traveled to the Amazon from around the country for employment, and Graciela found the work not overly demanding and the inhabitants friendly and open. Graciela spoke fondly of the older workers who looked out for her in the fields: "Older women were there, and they cared for me a lot. They would say to work, they gave us food." Graciela and Juan Pablo worked for others cultivating coffee and could cut some trees from the surrounding forest to grow crops of their own. "More than anything, we cultivated pure coffee from the jungle. All coffee in all directions that you could see."

Graciela said the most challenging aspects of living in the jungle were the animals of the rainforest and adapting to the language.

> I was afraid of snakes in the forests. At times, there were snakes in the fields. There were also worms called *caspydo* [scorpions]. This would bite you with its tail. With its tail it would be inside [the coffee leaves] and if you touch

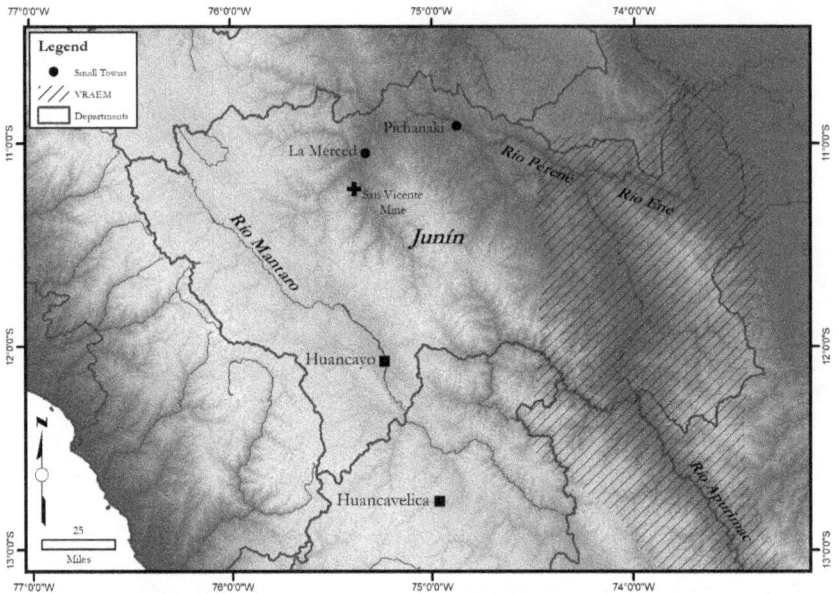

Figure 13. Map of the Department of Junín showing principal locations discussed in the text. Map created by Lucas C. Kellett.

it, it will bite you. . . . There are black, red, and green ones that grow where you produce coffee in the leaves. Therefore, in the leaves there would be its hairs. When you do not see it, when you grab the coffee and you touch it, it itches badly. It hurts really badly.

Even though mestizos in the highlands spoke Spanish, many also spoke Quechua, and nearly everyone from rural highland communities spoke Quechua as their first language. Conversely, in the jungle, Spanish was the dominant language spoken.

More than anything, the language was the most difficult. Working in the fields planting, this for me was very easy. More for me the difficulty was Spanish because I did not know it . . . Yes, I did not know Spanish—I knew nothing. I cried. All the people from old people to babies spoke only Spanish talking to me, but I could not understand. It was difficult for me, like a bucket of water spilling equally [the Spanish washed over her like water and she felt drowned by her inability to comprehend the language].

Eventually Graciela began to pick up the language. "People told me to ask God. Told me that I will learn. For this, I had faith in God, and I learned Spanish. In my dreams when I was sleeping, I spoke Spanish correctly."

Motherhood

Although Graciela believed she was perhaps barren because she experienced so many years of not becoming pregnant while on the run, once settled in the Amazon her status shifted. "I could not eat all of the food when I went to the jungle. All of the food gave me *asco*." A direct translation of *asco* in English is "disgust." However, people often use the word to describe the tendency for pregnant women to have an aversion to certain foods or smells.

> The señora of the patrón asked why I was not eating—was it dirty? The wife of the patrón said I had parasites. She did not know that I was pregnant. She said I had asco from the parasites. . . . She said to drink these herbs to get out the parasites. Therefore, she had me get the herbs, boil them, and drink them in a glass to get rid of the parasites. Juan Pablo also said to drink it. He also did not know I was pregnant. The patrona did not know I was pregnant. She thought I had parasites and that I was anemic, and for this, I could not eat, but it was not parasites, it was Sumac Killa!

Graciela began to laugh explaining how her first child named Sumac Killa was mistaken for a parasite! Soon the patrona realized Graciela was not sick with parasites but rather she must be pregnant.

> Therefore, [the patrona] told Juan Pablo I was [actually] pregnant, and it is better not to drink this herb because it could abort the baby. It is better not to drink it. I did not drink it. I did not think I was pregnant. I did not know I was pregnant. When will my period come [I asked], but it was not coming and I was growing.

When Graciela became pregnant, harvesting coffee proved more challenging. "For me it was a little difficult to harvest coffee, to put it in a basket. You would collect it like this [Graciela imitated carrying a basket on the side of her hip] and I was pregnant with Sumac Killa. Therefore, this part hurt a little as it was pressing the basket filled with coffee. It bothered me a bit."

Graciela gave birth to her first child, Sumac Killa, at home with Juan Pablo and a traditional midwife.

> Before in the campo there were not hospitals like here [in Andahuaylas]. There were *sanitarios* [health clinics] that would send you to the hospital, but I did not go to the sanitarios. I was just in the chacra and in the house where I gave birth. A *partero* [midwife] attended me too and the baby. Therefore, [before the birth] Juan Pablo asked this midwife, "Is she going to give birth well or is she going to suffer?" Therefore, the señor looked at the coca leaves and said, "She will give birth in three days." So, with a rope they moved my stomach around. They moved it around, but I could not give birth. They moved it around and I could not give birth for three days. I did not have any strength either. So, he put his knee in here [Graciela pointed to the middle of her lower back]. Her head was stuck so he [the midwife] was taking his knee and putting it in my waist and still I could not give birth. It was as if my daughter was fainting. Her head was stuck.

In the Andes, a common practice of midwives is to manipulate the position of the fetus manually before birth by placing mantas or ropes around the back of a woman and vigorously shaking her back and forth.[2]

The midwife had been working with Graciela for three days and she still could not give birth.

> This midwife was pushing with his knee in here on the waist and this midwife was saying, "If she does not give birth, I do not know what to do." Juan Pablo was saying, "If you are attending her well, why isn't she giving birth now? Do we need to take her to the hospital? She is sick and it has been three days!" He was discontent discussing it. He talked with the midwife who attended me who was a little old. It was a man. He was discussing this in the corner. . . . When I could not give birth to my daughter, he

went outside and looked at his coca. "How beautiful, *atakaw*," [he said] in Quechua, which means how beautiful. The midwife was saying "atakawi" in Quechua. . . . He left and returned inside. I was awake all night and so he was sitting there tired, this midwife. "Atakawi!" He said this waking up. Therefore, he looked at his coca and said, "Wata rosas."

Technically, *wata* in Quechua means "year" and *atakaw* translates as "What a fear!" while *ataw* means "fortune or luck." However, according to Graciela, the midwife was expressing the premonition that Graciela would give birth to a daughter as beautiful as roses. The midwife described what the coca leaves were telling him:

It will be a girl. All will go well, and she will be beautiful like a rose. . . . Yes, he knew this from his coca, from his dreams, I do not know. . . . I was in such screaming pain, and I was not able to give birth. Therefore, he kept putting his knee in my back. He said, "Wata rosas, your beautiful daughter." She was beautiful when she was born. What pain when I could not give birth, but when he put his knee in my waist, I gave birth to my Sumac Killa. . . . Beautiful was my baby girl, my Sumac Killa. I bought her clothes before she was born. I loved the clothes that I bought before she was born so much.

After three days of hard labor, Graciela finally gave birth to her first child, Sumac Killa, and life overall seemed relatively problem free.

For Graciela, their initial time in the jungle was peaceful. There were only about seventy people living in the area, there was little corruption, they had a school, and Graciela found her employer to be a generous and kind woman.

When my Sumac Killa was very young, when she was a baby, the señora took good care of me. I would be carrying the baby and she would tell me to go get the milk when I was carrying the baby. . . . She did not have a daughter, she had little kids, but they were boys, so for sure she wanted to adopt this girl. She only had boys, older ones. "I want to carry your baby," she would say. Her cow gave milk so she would say to me, "You go take the milk and I'll carry your baby *ñañay*," she would say to my Sumac Killa carrying her.

Ñañay is a term of affection that the señora used frequently with Graciela's family and that Graciela recounted fondly. "She would tell me to go get the milk from the cow to help my baby grow. Therefore, she gave me lots of milk from her cow. So then, I would take the milk and make cheese. This is what I wanted." Graciela had warm memories of living with the señora.

> They had a big house and they dried coffee—they had coffee dryers. All they had. They grew a ton of coffee. We loved them a lot. . . . They were good people. For my Sumac Killa, they bought her clothes. "*Ñañay*," they would often say. They loved us. I would be fine helping them with anything, for the señora. When she asked me to wash the clothes, I helped. I loved her for this. . . . When she was traveling to the city, she would come down and say, "You can take care of my animals." She did not have mistrust in me. Nothing. "You go take care of our rooster; you go take out milk from the cow," she would tell me. I would stay with her child when she went to work. I made her breakfast, her lunch, and her dinner. They worked with Juan Pablo too.

Graciela remembered this señora with tenderness because she was kind and trusted Graciela, and she also helped Graciela and Juan Pablo escape when they were once again faced with violence.[3]

Strengthened Resistance against Sendero Luminoso and Increased Violence

In 1991, the death toll reached at least twenty-two thousand and Sendero was dominating political influence in about 40 percent of Peru (Strong 1992, 222). However, during this period, communities began to become more organized in their fight against Sendero by fortifying or creating even more rondas campesinas (Starn 1994, 17). In 1991 and 1992, President Alberto Fujimori issued Legislative Decrees 740 and 741, which "recognized the counterinsurgency militias as part of the state's official counterinsurgency campaign" and "extended to *ronderos* the legal right to bear arms," handing out 15,179 Winchesters, Mossbergs, and MGP-43s (La Serna 2012, 199–200). Armed with these weapons, "*ronderos* were empowered to escalate violence against their own neighbors" (200).

Lima became further embroiled in violence throughout the early 1990s. In

1991, the Grupo Colina, a death squad made up of Peruvian armed forces that operated out of the Servicio de Inteligencia Nacional del Perú (SIN, National Intelligence Service) and Servicio de Inteligencia del Ejército (SIE, Army Intelligence Service), killed fifteen and wounded four individuals mistaken for members of Sendero in the Lima neighborhood of Barrios Altos (Burt 2006). According to Burt, under "Fujimori's chief advisor, Vladimiro Montesinos, the SIN became the regime's political police and the Colina Group its instrument to intimidate and silence regime critics through often macabre spectacles of violence" (47).[4] In 1992, an explosion, known as the Tarata bombing, left over forty dead (see Pike 1992; Thoma 2006). Two days later, the SIE and the Dirección Nacional Contra el Terrorismo (DINCOTE, Counter Terrorist Directorate—a branch of the National Police of Peru charged with antiterrorist law enforcement) abducted nine students and one professor from the Universidad Nacional de Educación Enrique Guzmán y Valle, otherwise known as La Cantuta (see Burt 2006; Jara 2017).[5]

Not long after the invasion at La Cantuta, major headlines reported the capture of the leader of Sendero, Abimael Guzmán, within the neighborhood of Surquillo in Lima on September 12, 1992 (Starn 1994, 17). He and eight other Sendero leaders were apprehended, including a key organizer, Laura Zambrano, as well as Guzmán's female partner, Elena Iparraguirre.[6] While Fujimori's administration was celebrated for capturing Abimael Guzmán, a group of Peruvian military officers exposed the brutality of the SIN and DINCOTE in April of 1993 by anonymously releasing a document that claimed members of Grupo Colina, under orders by Vladimiro Montesinos, murdered and then buried the victims from La Cantuta.[7]

Unfortunately, despite the capture of Abimael Guzmán, violence continued to escalate in isolated areas, particularly in the Amazon region of the Department of Junín. On August 19, 1993, in Santa Rosa de Shiriari (Department of Junín), fifty-two Asháninkas and *colonos* (homesteaders, tenant farmers, or colonists, non-Native people who work the land) were killed. Extreme conflict and violence occurred in the towns of Chanchamayo, Oxapampa, Satipo, and Gran Pajonal, where Native Amazonian groups—including the Asháninka, Yanesha, Machiguenga, Nomatsiguenga, and Yine, as well as colonos—resided, not far from where Graciela was living at the time. Graciela found herself once again immersed in an epicenter of conflict and violence.

Violence Returns

Sumac Killa was only about two months old when Graciela and Juan Pablo's period of stability was disrupted. Graciela explained how at first, the Indigenous populations in the area were targeted: "*Ch'unchus, nativos.* People of the selva [rainforest]. These they killed. The *provinchos* killed the Natives." In Quechua, the word *ch'unchu* means "forest dwellers" and refers to the Asháninka tribe of lowland South America, yet people also use the term in a derogatory fashion to reference "savage man" or "uncivilized," and it is therefore largely rejected by Asháninka individuals. Graciela explained how the violence began:

> When Sumac Killa was just two months old this happened. The pain in my head returned with the violence in the jungle. The provincial people killed the Natives. They thought that they were terrorists. We were afraid. They said we were Túpac Amaristas [MRTA]. This is a *partido* [political party]. First came the Túpac Amaristas.

At this point in the conversation, Juan Pablo interjected and said, "No, it was Senderistas that came and killed the Natives. In the jungle, also they killed. Therefore, they also escaped. They were against the Natives. The Natives killed the Senderistas and the Senderistas killed the Natives." Juan Pablo further explained that the people of the province would kill any Native Amazonians without proper documentation. Túpac Amaristas, Senderistas, and government forces targeted Indigenous peoples. "They [government] tried to pacify the Natives, and then when Senderistas came, they came looking for the Natives and killed them." The Túpac Amaristas had established a rural *foco* (guerrilla vanguard) in the Department of San Martín back in 1987 and made headlines by establishing a broad network of student and peasant support and attacking town after town (La Serna 2019, 346). According to Juan Pablo, it was not only Indigenous inhabitants who were pursued but also local nuns. "There were nuns. They lived there. They had a pueblo also with a guinea pig farm and a coffee deposit. Therefore, they came, burned, and killed all the nuns. Other people also came and killed them."

Graciela described how shortly after the nuns were attacked, the peace and stability Graciela and Juan Pablo so deeply cherished was abruptly altered:

We were sleeping one night in the house where we slept. We slept on the second floor. We were workers, so we slept on the second floor. The terrorists arrived at our house to kill us. Juan Pablo reported that the señor of the house was sleeping in the direction of the window and said that the Senderistas were coming. . . . "There are two Senderistas coming," he said.

They were yelling the name "Amillino," and a huge number of Senderistas were heading toward their house. Graciela explained: "They began yelling and we were listening. 'Amigo! Amigo!' they said. Their [señor's] son was named Aigue, Amigino." Graciela was not aware what connection, if any, the señor of the house and his family had with the Senderistas.

They were speaking very fiercely! I think that the señora had talked with them before, but we did not know anything. Our sentiment was just to work. Each afternoon we left to look after the cow. What they had done, we did not know. We just looked after the cow. I cooked in the house for their older children who worked in the fields. If they had talked [with Senderistas], we did not know. [Trapped on the second floor of the house] I was crying that we needed to escape to the mountains. Juan Pablo said, "Shut up, shut up, or they are going to grab us!" My heart was paralyzed with fear. The baby was sleeping, my Sumac Killa. How are we going to escape? I was afraid. . . . We stayed, and we were just listening to their voices. I wanted to escape when we were sleeping on the second floor, but Juan Pablo said, "If we do, they will kill us," and my Sumac Killa was sleeping. I had to keep her quiet, but I wanted to get up to escape. We could not do anything, but my heart was filled with fear.

Fortunately, no one attacked Graciela and her family that evening.

Graciela explained how nervous the señor was the following day: "He was so preoccupied chewing his coca, drinking his trago, crying. Nothing to eat. They took all the food that we had grown. We could not eat. He said they had to leave. Juan Pablo agreed that it would be better to not stay and go to the city of La Merced." The wife was also distraught. "She was saying that they were for sure going to kill her and was crying. The señor was also crying with fear and said, 'We need to go too or for sure they will kill us. Go with us to Merced.'" La Merced is a city much larger than Andahuaylas. The family had another house in Chanchamayo, outside of the city of La Merced, where they planted coffee. The family was saying they had to flee and asked if Graciela and Juan Pablo wished to go with them. Later that afternoon, one of the señor's older sons arrived from Lima. "He was studying engineering and he was about thirty years old. He was young and came from very far away." The family was urging the son to leave, to return to Lima, as they feared the Senderistas would kill him. "They said he needed to leave and to not delay even an hour. Our patrón was saying to his son, 'You have to leave and return [to Lima] or the Senderos will kill you!'" The son left, only to return later that night with a vehicle to help them all escape.

> In the night, they came with their truck. Their son came with his car and with his wife. Therefore, when we were sleeping, they called, "Compañero!" When I heard this word, I got very, very scared. They said, "Light it up with a lantern!" so we were on the second floor sleeping, so inside there was a garage. In there was their car. "Now we must go below," they were saying. They were conversing freely. They told Juan Pablo, "We need to go." "Yes, ma'am," we said. "Go below to get in the car to go" [they said]. We were watching them. We saw their lights coming from their trucks. From the second floor, we jumped. From the second floor to the patio, we jumped. From very high up we jumped. "If we stay, we die," they said. Therefore, in this we went for three hours beginning when we heard bullets. They said that in their house they killed many people.

Having no other viable option, Graciela and Juan Pablo fled in the middle of the night to the city of La Merced with the señor. "So, we went to Merced, but I knew nothing of La Merced, but we were in the city in the day. With the señor, we went to La Merced." Once in La Merced, the family quickly abandoned Graciela and Juan Pablo and they became greatly disoriented.

> When we went to La Merced from the field, we were abandoned. The owner of the car and the señora also left. Therefore, we were in the city of La Merced. We said, "Where are we going to live? What are we going to do?" We did not know where we would stay. . . . There were people, but in the city, all runs purely with money. It is not like in the campo. It is not like in the field.

Juan Pablo described their predicament: "We just walked and walked and had no support. The first time in our pueblo, we had cows and calabaza, but with nothing, we escaped. Then we found a place where we had some new things to live. Then we had to leave that all behind. So much suffering." Graciela described the added challenge of escaping with a baby:

I had my baby, and we were hungry, and I was lactating so, "We have to eat in a restaurant," my husband told me. Therefore, when we went to the restaurant to eat, the owner of the restaurant asked me, "Where are you from?" "I am from Andahuaylas," I said. "What things are you doing?" the señora asked me. "We are not doing anything, señora. We are just looking for work," I said. "We are not terrorists or anything," we advised the señora that had the restaurant. "We are looking for work. We came from Andahuaylas," we were saying. "Help me," she said. "But I have my baby," I said. She said, "I see, but help me." Therefore, I helped in the restaurant for us to eat and Juan Pablo helped in the fields.

Juan Pablo and Graciela could not foresee the long-term viability of staying in the city, and Juan Pablo had a sister who lived outside of the town of Pichanaki, so they considered searching for her.

So, in La Merced we did not have money, only enough to eat and the food that the woman in the restaurant gave us. "So, let us go to my sister's," my husband said. "Now we do not have money and you are not being paid well. It is better we go to where my sister lives in Pichanaki" [Juan Pablo said]. "But where do we go? We do not know where their house is," I was saying. "For sure we will find it," he said.

Juan Pablo asked the owner of the restaurant how to find Autiki (a small community just outside of the city of Pichanaki), explaining that his sister lived there and they wished to find her. "The señora said Autiki was below and directed us to where it was. So, the following day we went, and we met my sister-in-law."

Moving On

Graciela and Juan Pablo were only in La Merced for about one week before taking a car to Pichanaki in search of Juan Pablo's sister, Felipa. Felipa had also previously fled Oronccoy and lost her husband during the violence. She had resettled in Autiki with another man and worked planting coffee. Graciela and Juan Pablo soon found Felipa, and they met a woman who let all of them work in her fields. In recounting her good fortune in finding work once again, Graciela stated, "Always there are good people, right?" Graciela helped in the woman's home and Juan Pablo planted coffee alongside Felipa and her partner. Soon Graciela and Juan Pablo built a small house of their own out of the wampee tree. Unfortunately, once again, the peace was not long lasting.[8]

It all began one morning when Juan Pablo traveled to a nearby community to buy coffee plants.

> When we were sleeping, still he would be up at 5:00 a.m. and I would stay sleeping. I would wake up slowly to make breakfast and Juan Pablo would say, "Stay sleeping, wake up slowly to make the breakfast. I will return. I will bring plants. I will buy them," he would say. However, he did not return, my Juan Pablo. I was afraid and I was crying when he did not return. On the other side of this neighbor, there was a river and when there was rain, it would grow a lot.

Grabbing a tall stick that rose well above my head, Graciela demonstrated how high the water would rise.

> All the way to the top of this stick it would get, this river. Therefore, I was thinking maybe he fell into the river and maybe the river took him. Until 10:00 a.m., he did not return. I made breakfast, but he had not returned. So, I was crying. "Now, where is he?" I was saying to my sister-in-law, "He went down to the river and why hasn't he returned?" I was crying. I was alone with my baby in my field, in my house. Therefore, I was looking, and he still had not come.

Graciela's brother-in-law eventually returned to the house. "He said, 'Imata wachkanki mamai.' They say in Quechua, 'What are you doing, mama?' 'I am sad Juan Pablo has not come,' I said." Graciela's brother-in-law assured her that he had just seen Juan Pablo.

"He is below in the school. There are tons of Senderos, and they have captured many people. All of the community is in the school" [the brother-in-law said]. He came to advise me of this, my brother-in-law. He said, "A man grabbed him. Juan Pablo is also in there." "I thought he had gone to the river," I was saying. How I was worried. "No, mama, he is below. Below there are many Senderos who have captured people" [he said]. "The Senderos rounded them up, Juan Pablo too," he told me. Therefore, I had such fear when my brother-in-law told me this. "For sure they will kill him," I said to my brother-in-law. "No, they will not kill him," [my brother-in-law said]. "What can we do? What is this person that grabbed Juan Pablo doing?" I asked.

Later that day, Juan Pablo returned to the house and told Graciela what had happened. That morning when Juan Pablo and Graciela's brother-in-law had gone to the community of Anampiari to buy coffee plants, Senderistas intercepted them.

Therefore, [Juan Pablo] stopped in this corner and there was a Senderista. He was looking and wondering, who is this person. It was a surprise. So, the Senderista was yelling, "Come! Come! Come!" What can I do [Juan Pablo was thinking]? Is this a thief? "Come, do not escape," [the Senderista] was saying. So, with fear [Juan Pablo] got closer. "Enter! Enter below. They are having a reunion, enter," [the Senderista] said.

Having no choice, Juan Pablo followed the man's instructions and went to the reunion in the school. "There was a school in this community and in there were men, women, young people, children. All the women were inside the classroom. In here, they were having a reunion in the school. So, all of the community was there in a reunion."

The Senderistas told everyone gathered that Chati was hiding in the jail. Chati was the nickname for a man who oversaw constructing a road that would facilitate the transportation of coffee to urban markets. Senderistas had come to stop the road construction and, as a warning to others, toward the end of the reunion they took Chati out of jail, chastised him, and then publicly executed him. "They killed him because he was working for the state. . . . 'You are a dog of the state!' they were saying.[9] They said this when they ended the reunion and took [Chati] out of the jail and killed him. They were in the school from 5:00 a.m. to 12:00 p.m." Following this event, the people in the region, especially those who had been working on road construction, felt they needed to flee. "Therefore, the people who were working on the road said that they should escape. The community was preoccupied. They thought they would be killed. We cannot advance this road, we must keep it as it is, but we cannot stay here. We cannot continue to work. So, for this reason we also were afraid and felt we had to go."

The entire community began to organize a plan of how to respond to the recent threats.

> Therefore, when they killed this person, [community leaders] said to the others that we would need to escape to the caves. "We will have to leave this pueblo, desert this" [they said]. I was thinking, to where will we disappear? "For sure in this community we will be killed by the military. We will be killed by Senderos. We will be killed by both. What can we do?" they were saying.

Graciela lamented having to uproot and flee once again. "We had our clothes, and we also had our little animals, our guinea pigs, our hens. We had it all that we had to leave. Again!" Graciela also lamented the loss of her friend, Susana, who left the following evening. "We would bring lunch to our husbands together, the two of us. We treated each other like sisters." Susana and Graciela had planned to flee together if the violence returned, and Graciela felt abandoned by her friend. "She was my friend and I missed her. The following day she was not there. Her house was silent, and I cried. I was so used to her so when she left, I was so sad."

(Re)Resettlement

Graciela and Juan Pablo remained in the community for a few days following the execution of Chati, then once again they escaped.

> We were there three days. There was a big truck like to haul wood trunks.

In this, we put all our clothes, all Sumac Killa's clothes, and we left with Juan Pablo and with my brother-in-law. We left many of our hens and we brought some in a *costal* [bag]. We also brought the largest guinea pigs to sell in Pichanaki.

Graciela laughed describing trying to stuff as many hens and guinea pigs as possible in their bags, as they did not want to leave any behind. Juan Pablo also explained how they had to abandon everything they had fought so hard to obtain:

When this violence started, we left our fields. We abandoned everything. We had to carry our baby. We tried to carry our baby and plants, platanos. We had a hole where we had planted things, so we tried to carry those plants with us. We had to make so many sacrifices for fear that we would die. We had to abandon everything. We had to throw it all out.

Graciela further clarified the relative plenty they had to leave behind: "We had a lot of chickens. We had new fields filled with maize, *ayucu*, platano, and yucca. We had everything to live well and peacefully. We had hens, guinea pigs. All the chickens we abandoned. Also, we had to leave everything in the community—our house, everything." Juan Pablo added, "Fortunately no one from the Senderistas met us. If they had found us escaping in a truck, they would have killed us. . . . If we stayed for sure they would have killed us, the Senderos." With the clothes on their backs and a few small animals and plants to sell, Graciela and Juan Pablo once again left all they had created behind and headed toward a jungle mining town in search of work.

Past La Merced and San Ramon lies San Vicente, a zinc-lead mine in the Department of Junín. "Yes, close to the mine there is a town called Bella Vista. In this town live the miners only. Further above there is a town Antaloma." Following traditional Andean settlement patterns, the miners and their families lived in the town of Bella Vista. Antaloma represented the rural fields lying above the town where the executives and managers of the mine and other large landowners had estates and campesinos lived and worked the land. When Graciela and the others first arrived, a man offered them work hauling wood, and after completing this task, they walked along the road, where they met another man who offered them a more long-standing work opportunity.

Therefore, on the road, we met a man and he asked us where we were going. We told him how there was still a little violence in this place, and we were afraid to be walking. Juan Pablo talked with this man. In Bella Vista, all the miners lived with their wives and with their children. When we arrived, this man asked if we were looking for work and we said, "Yes," so he said, "You can live in my field. I have my own fields with fruit with platanos to eat—it is all there. If you work in my fields, I will pay you." Therefore, we worked. I had only one child, but my sister-in-law had three children, so he said that Juan Pablo, Sumac Killa, and I could stay in the house and the others had to go stay in the field. He gave us rice, sugar, and noodles. He had a cow also with a calf so my sister-in-law could get milk. Therefore, we lived for a while in this field.

Graciela, Juan Pablo, and Sumac Killa stayed in the miner's house with him and his family while Felipa, her partner, and their three children stayed in another house in the fields. During the day, Juan Pablo and Felipa's partner worked in the fields and Felipa managed the cattle while Graciela "stayed in the house to cook and to wash the clothes of the señora and her children. She was good. . . . They paid us because we did not have money."

Marriage and More Children

Graciela and Juan Pablo continued to work in the fields above the mining town and eventually built a small house of their own. Life was relatively stable for quite some time. Graciela and Juan Pablo decided to wed officially when Sumac Killa was nearly three years old. "There with my husband, Juan Pablo, we made a house in Bella Vista. Here is where we got married. . . . So, we had our wedding there." Graciela and Juan Pablo traveled to the *consejo civil* (local commission) to be married.

We did not go to the church. How do you say, municipality? We went to the civil and the municipality. We were young and we did not know anything. My sister-in-law, according to her religion and her father, said that we should marry as God has asked. . . . My sister-in-law said, "Juan Pablo is your husband, so you have to get married, otherwise it is not valid," she said. "You have to have a wedding, a marriage." I did not know anything, and so she looked for my godmother.

The only people present at the wedding ceremony beyond Graciela and Juan Pablo were Felipa and her family, as well as Graciela and Juan Pablo's godparents for the wedding. Graciela did not know her godmother before the wedding: "I did not know where she lived, where her house was, nothing. Only my sister-in-law knew her. A surprise. My sister-in-law knew her, but she was very pretty."

For the wedding celebration, Felipa prepared pachamanka with guinea pig and soda. Graciela explained that while in the city guests give wedding presents, "in the campo, people will typically gift a cow, sheep, or pigs" and the parents and godparents give the couple advice. "They give advice about what you should do. The godparents give advice. Maybe when you are like this you will live well [they say]. Always they *llamar atención*." To *llamar atención* in this context means to give advice to someone about appropriate conduct, a common term used throughout Peru referencing the value of providing advice or enacting justice. The godparents serve almost as a second set of parents for the couple. "The godmother and godfather have to have responsibility like you are their child." After officially marrying one another, Graciela and Juan Pablo soon welcomed another child into their lives.

Considering the complications Graciela had with Sumac Killa's birth, Juan Pablo was extremely nervous about the second pregnancy. "Always my stomach hurts a little bit before I give birth, so Juan Pablo was preoccupied like with Sumac Killa that maybe I would not be able to give birth." Given Juan Pablo's worries, he consulted with a Native healer.

> Ch'unchu, like Natives, they were telling Juan Pablo [about] the fruit of my stomach when I was with Augosto [name of Graciela's second child] before I gave birth. . . . Two months before [I gave birth], Natives came, and we asked them if I was going to give birth well or not. . . . [Juan Pablo asked] "How is my wife going to give birth? She is a little sick. Maybe she will die, I do not know. She suffered a lot with my daughter, giving birth. Maybe we need to go to the hospital," [Juan Pablo] was saying. When I was only seven months along, this elder Native arrived and said, "Give me your pulse." [While holding Graciela's vein and analyzing her pulse], this elder said,

"You will give birth alone. You will not suffer. You will give birth quickly," she said. She also claimed, "It is a boy. You will give birth well."

Nevertheless, Juan Pablo was skeptical. "Juan Pablo told me, 'She was a liar. With Sumac Killa you suffered, we should go to the hospital. I will take you to the hospital.'"

Graciela did not end up going to the hospital and began to giggle describing how Juan Pablo took such good care of her throughout her entire pregnancy:

> He took care of me like a cow giving birth. . . . He took care of me, but this one day he did not care for me, he met his friend in the field. "How can we plant the *rocoto* [spicy red pepper, *Capsicum pubescens*] without falling the flower?" [Juan Pablo asked]. When the flower of the rocoto falls, it does not produce. Therefore, he was talking with his friend about this.

Juan Pablo and his friend had to fumigate the rocotos to make sure they flowered correctly, and "so he was delayed that day until 5:00 p.m. or 4:00 p.m. in the afternoon when I was home alone."

Graciela continued to describe how upon being left home alone, she went into labor. "In three pains, no more, I had him. I had three strong pains that grabbed me, but there was no one to yell to. Therefore, I fell to the ground in the kitchen on my knees, and I was grabbing at the door, and I gave birth on the floor. There was no one there to help me, to grab me or the baby, no one." Having just given birth completely unassisted, blood covered the dirt floor of their home. "Yes, a lot of blood on the floor. I could not grab anything; my baby was crying. Thankfully, in a half hour Juan Pablo arrived. When he saw me at the door, he came running. He was yelling when he saw me. He hugged me later and my baby Augosto." Graciela explained that at this point the labor was not entirely over:

> The placenta was hanging. . . . Still, it was trapped hanging. The cord from the baby was hanging. It had not passed. Just the baby was on the floor. The placenta was still inside me . . . [Juan Pablo] grabbed me and he sat me on the bed. He attended to me and at this point, the placenta came out. . . . After he grabbed me, he called a person. Elia [a midwife] came and cut [the umbilical cord] when my placenta came out.

Laughing, Graciela continued to reflect on the entire situation: "How could I give birth alone? With Juan Pablo in the field! I was thinking [the Native healer] was a liar, but in the end when I was having my pain, I thought it is the truth that this woman told me!" Just as the Native healer had predicted, Graciela gave birth to a boy quickly and alone.

Upon describing this most unique birth story, Graciela continued to discuss her second child, Augosto's, unusually good health. "Until now he is never sick. When he was a kid about five years old until seven or eight years old, he was a fat baby, round face and everything, but now he is a little skinny and tall, a little tall. His siblings call him *tallarin* [noodle], they say spaghetti." Graciela credited eating many carrots and drinking fresh cow's milk while pregnant for Augosto's good health. "When I was pregnant with him, I ate a lot of carrots. I made carrot juice. I cared for the cows and Juan Pablo worked in the fields. I cared for the cow of the dueña, so in the morning I would drink the boiled milk of the cow for breakfast. For this, my son came out fat."

Graciela soon gave birth to another child, her daughter Eufemilia, while living in Antaloma, without incident. "With Eufemilia, I was peaceful. The neighbor, my husband attended me well and she was born. There were no difficulties." I asked if there was a midwife present. "No, there was no midwife. Only my neighbors were near me. There was not a doctor, no one." Although Eufemilia's birth was problem free, about three days after giving birth Graciela became ill. Juan Pablo was working with cauliflower in the fields and wanted to sell it in the market before it spoiled, and Graciela was intent on washing her clothes after the birth. "My clothes were all dirty, so I was washing my clothes, but I had an infection and great pain in my head. My neighbor said to rest, but I did not obey." Graciela's neighbor found her too sick to work and brought her to the hospital where the doctors discovered she had an extremely high fever. "They said I had *sobre parto*—an infection." Juan Pablo returned from the market and met Graciela at the hospital where they gave her an injection, which helped restore her health.

By this point, Graciela and Juan Pablo had lived in the same place for quite some time and had three children and some sense of stability.

We lived peacefully and there was not much violence. There we worked and planted coffee, platano, and cauliflower . . . Big ones we grew, huge, a lot.

This cauliflower was the size of hearts and so we would grow this to sell. We would grow it in the field to sell it in the market. . . . Here we planted coffee and it was beautiful flowers, big ones to little ones. Therefore, the platano was beautiful when it would give fruit. We were working with others too, in my godmother's field.

Although life had stabilized, Graciela deeply missed her family.

I had pain. I had no contact with my mom, with my dad. "How are they? Is my family still alive or are they dead?" I would say, crying in the jungle for my family. I wanted to return, but from Antaloma, from the jungle, I could not return. We were good there. Then there was talk of them killing police officers, that the terrorists had killed the police. People were talking.

Once again, upon acquiring a sense of plenty, violence disrupted the peace for Graciela and her now growing family.

The area in which Graciela and Juan Pablo were living had a police control center, and Graciela explained her first interaction with violence entering the area:

Here we lived and there was a control where you would enter the mine. The police control. It was like a *comisaria* [police station]. When we were a little distant, I heard the bullets. . . . They said that the police were killed in Antaloma in the mine, San Vincente. We did not see it, but people were talking about it. My neighbors were saying, "The terrorists have come! They killed the police!" This is what people were saying, and my body was shaking.

Graciela explained that a group of Senderistas arrived, passed through the control station, and killed two police officers. The entire event yet again fostered fear and uncertainty. "I was afraid. We thought they would kill us too. If they killed the police, why wouldn't they kill us, we thought."

Graciela and Juan Pablo described the confusion with so many groups active in this area at the time. Graciela stated, "It was terrorists. It was Senderos. Later it was Túpac Amaristas. Then it was military." According to Juan Pablo, "the political movement of Túpac Amaristas organized like Senderos and there was also a ronda campesina in this pueblo. The campesino people had arms." Juan Pablo continued to describe how, during this time, many communities in the region had rondas campesinas, which he credited for the eventual pacification. "In different communities in all of Peru, this is how they pacified them. Militaries killed the people. Police also killed the people. In contrast, [rondas campesinas] did not just kill, they looked for the enemy. This is the pacification." Juan Pablo explained that during the night the Senderistas passed the police control, "This group of ronda campesinos lost," as they were unable to prevent the entry of Senderistas and the subsequent killing of two police officers. This event ultimately caused Graciela and her family to flee, yet again, but this time back to the highlands.

———

While living in the tropical lowlands, Graciela learned Spanish, found kind employers, officially wed, and became a mother of three children: Sumac Killa, Augosto, and Eufemilia. Graciela and Juan Pablo's initial experience of tranquility in the jungle was continually disrupted with the presence of Sendero and then other groups fighting for control and sovereignty, including MRTA, the military, and rondas campesinas. Graciela and Juan Pablo were able to continually rebuild their lives as they cared and provided for their three children. Yet, with further threat of violence, Graciela and Juan Pablo, alongside their growing family, once again were forced to abandon what little they had (re)(re)created. This time they left the jungle behind to retreat to the highland city of Andahuaylas. Although unaware of it at the time they left the jungle, their time in Andahuaylas would be short lived.

Chapter 7
An Altered Homecoming

The Revolution's Demise

By 1993, nearly all villages across hundreds of miles of rugged terrain between Andahuaylas and Junín had a ronda steering committee (Starn 1995b, 553). Thousands of peasants took turns patrolling their villages, towns, and checkpoints along the potholed highways. To curb the continued violence, in early 1993 the government of Peru instituted a Repentance Law that lasted until November of 1994. This law enabled Sendero Luminoso cadres and sympathizers to turn themselves in, along with their weapons or information, in exchange for "support, retraining and progressive reintegration into society" (Palmer 2007, 208). Because of the law, more than five thousand individuals, primarily low-level supporters and sympathizers, came forward, resulting in further intelligence.[1] The organizational structure of Sendero subsequently weakened and the movement, along with associated violence, began to diffuse.

Following the capture of Abimael Guzmán, the government sought to enact justice on a larger scale; however, on June 16, 1995, the government of Peru declared an amnesty law, Ley de Amnistía (No. 26479), that absolved military, police, and connected civilians from grave violations of human rights abuses.[2] An "interpretive" law (No. 26492) that obliged judiciary to apply this amnesty (Coordinadora Nacional de Derechos Humanos 1995) followed the amnesty law. In effect, the passing of these two laws cleared of accountability the arms of the state who the Comisión de la Verdad y Reconciliación later deemed to be responsible for nearly half of all deaths during the war.

Although the leader of the MRTA, Víctor Polay Campos, was captured in 1992, the group was not entirely disbanded and it made headlines in 1996 by invading the home of the Japanese Ambassador of Peru.[3] Alberto Fujimori gained international attention for the capture of MRTA militants in the Japanese Embassy hostage crisis; however, in 1999, there was a public manifestation against Fujimori, and in 2000 he sought refuge in Japan. He attempted to resign from the presidency via a fax from Japan, which the Congress of the Republic rejected in favor of impeachment. The amnesty law (Ley de Amnestía) created under the presidency of Alberto Fujimori was repealed in 2000, and on March 21, 2001, Attorney General Nelly Calderón filed charges against Fujimori for "coauthoring" the La Cantuta and the Barrios Altos massacres. He was also charged for working in concert with SIN supremo Vladimiro Montesinos in exercising control of Grupo Colina as part of counterinsurgency policy that grossly violated human rights (see Human Rights Watch 2001; Krauss 2001). Amid major political upheaval in Peru, Graciela once again returned to the highlands, this time during a period of established peace.

(Re)Adjusting to the Highlands

When Graciela left the Amazon with Juan Pablo and their three children, she was about twenty-two years old and the year was 1995. Upon returning to Andahuaylas, Graciela sought help from a woman who had a house in the neighborhood of Kichkapata on the edge of the city, the same woman who had helped Graciela's parents when they first came to Andahuaylas following their capture.

> We lived in Kichkapata. In there, the woman knew us. When I was young, they knew me, so she had confidence in me. Therefore, I said, "I have re-turned, and let me stay here, please." She knew me so she asked, "Where have you been all this time?" I told her I had been in the jungle. . . . We returned with three children. They said that we could stay there. They had a room they gave us. There we lived. She is like family.

Similar to Graciela's parents and siblings years before, Graciela and her family helped care for this woman's fields and animals in exchange for a place (one room for a family of five) to live.

In contrast to Graciela's difficult adjustment learning Spanish in the

Figure 14. A photo of the city of Andahuaylas taken from Graciela's home
in the neighborhood of Pochocota. Photo by Nicole C. Kellett.

Amazon, Graciela's children, having been born in predominantly Spanish-
speaking lowlands, had a challenging time understanding Quechua once they
returned to the highlands. Sumac Killa was about five or six years old when they
returned to Andahuaylas. "And my Sumac Killa was studying below in a girl's
school. It was very painful to become accustomed because she did not know
how to speak Quechua. She spoke pure Spanish. So, when my mom would say,
'Llanta apamuy' ["bring me firewood" in Quechua] she did not understand."
Sumac Killa could understand limited Quechua, but the younger Augosto and
Eufemilia could not communicate at all.

> Sumac Killa understood, but Eufemilia and Augosto would cry. They
> would say daily, "Let's go to our house in the jungle. When are we going?"
> they would say crying. They were not accustomed. It was very difficult.
> They would say, "What things are they saying?" when people would speak

in Quechua. When the women would speak in Quechua they would ask, "What is she saying to me?"

Most of their peers also spoke Quechua. "For them it was very difficult when they wanted to play with other kids, and they spoke Spanish and others spoke Quechua and did not understand." I asked if Graciela spoke Quechua with the children when they lived in the jungle, and she said:

> I spoke, but they did not answer me. For example, I say, "Trae apamuychic llaquta" [Bring me water] in Quechua and they would say, "Agua, mommy" [Water, mommy] and bring it to me, but they did not want and could not speak [Quechua]. They understood but did not talk. Eufemilia, Sumac Killa, and Augosto now know Quechua.

It is notable that Graciela's children struggled in Andahuaylas for not knowing Quechua, surrounded by Quechua-speaking peers, likely due to the influx of agriculturalists seeking refuge in the city of Andahuaylas throughout the 1980s. Conversely, less than a decade earlier, Graciela's brother Alex was bullied for speaking Quechua among Spanish-speaking students, underscoring a dearth of Quechua spoken in the schools at that earlier time. Given the difficult adjustment to the city of Andahuaylas, Juan Pablo and the children initially wanted to return to the jungle. Longing to leave the city, they ended up living in Andahuaylas for only about six months. However, instead of returning to the Amazon, the family was able to return to Oronccoy: a community Graciela's children had not yet known.

A Return to Oronccoy

Following Abimael Guzmán's capture, the government of Peru encouraged individuals to return to their home communities. Graciela explained the situation, "The government declared a return of the people who were victims from the pueblos." When the government first called people back to their home villages, Graciela's mother and father returned to work the land. Graciela's brother Edolo, however, stayed in Andahuaylas with Graciela's sister Mia so she could continue her studies. At the age of fourteen, Edolo took charge of supporting his twelve-year-old sister.

My other brother Edolo, he at times worked in the fields to maintain, to support, my sister. He helped at times. He had his tips, and, at times, he washed cars. He was also young, fourteen years old. Therefore, my brother Edolo helped my sister Mia. My mom said, "I have to return, but you stay and study," she told my sister.

Graciela explained that Mia was so young when they first left Oronccoy, only three years old, so she was not accustomed to life in the campo.

In discussing campesinos' return to rural communities, Graciela recalled the work of a particular individual, Marcos Williams, who was from Belgium and worked for a nongovernmental organization in Andahuaylas, ProAnde.[4]

They [Marcos Williams and others with ProAnde] worked to *capacitarnos* [trains us]. So, they went to Huancavelica, they came to Oronccoy. We went to Huancavelica together, united. Not in jealousy, nothing. To train us. Marcos Williams was the boss. They said to build houses, to rest, and not to worry.

People in the area referred to Marcos Williams as "Papa Williams," and he worked with other individuals from various countries to help survivors return to their rural communities, often hosting large forums in the cities. "Other people came from Bolivia, Colombia, and Brazil. 'You need to care for your water, environment, and be united' [they said]. This happened in a stadium with people from all different places. I could not read or write, but with my ears I listened." When people returned to their communities, they did not even have a seed to plant, but Marcos Williams gave them a pot filled with kitchen supplies, which soon people called a *gringoolla*.

My mom still has it. All families have them. He gave them out in the stadium. Tons were given out. If he returned to Oronccoy, all would mound up flowers to throw at him. Much respect and honor for him.[5] When I was in the jungle, a woman had a gringoolla. I asked where it was from. She said Marcos Williams, and she was from San Francisco, in the jungle!

According to Graciela, Marcos Williams helped the displaced, living not as a distant outsider but rather equally with campesinos, illustrated by the sharing

Figure 15. The Kutinachaka Bridge was formerly known as Puente Pampas.
It, along with many other bridges, was destroyed during the violence. Years later,
the bridge was rebuilt and renamed Kutinachaka, which means "bridge of return."
Photo by Max Altamirano Molero.

of food. "He lived here about seven years. He lived equally with people. He did not eat alone; he ate with us."

For Graciela and her family to return to Oronccoy, it was necessary to fix a bridge that the violence destroyed. Before the war, a footbridge crossed the Pampas River, a wide, deep, roaring river at the bottom of an intensely steep mountain gorge. Pointing to a map, Graciela described how to reach Oronccoy from Andahuaylas you take a vehicle for about three to four hours to the bottom of the gorge, cross the river, and then ascend ninety-seven curves on a narrow dirt trail to the community of Oronccoy, a roughly eight-hour journey by foot.

This trail to the community of Oronccoy is a zigzag, zigzag in here, more zigzag. This is a big river. This is Pampas and this is a big river deeper than all, right? Therefore, at the river from here to pass there is a bridge that you pass with a horse. Here there is a big bridge. So what is this bridge called?

Graciela explained that before the violence, the bridge had no name and they called the river Pampas Grande; however, when the community rebuilt the sixty-five-foot bridge, it acquired an official and quite symbolic name: Kutinachaka, or "bridge of return."

> When you pass it like this [demonstrated walking across a narrow foot-bridge], it moves. . . . There were not people practically [living in the region], but when Marcos Williams supported us, they returned. Before this bridge was not there. It burned, but all built it with cables. It is big to pass. It is not a small bridge. There was no one living in La Oreja. My paisanos who once lived there. No one was there. The area that ProAnde worked was completely depopulated. The Oreja zone was completely de . . .

At this point, Graciela grew silent, and I interjected, questioning if she meant "*destruido*" (destroyed). She replied, "Yes." The somber mood quickly shifted, however, with Graciela reanimated through her memories of Marcos Williams.

> With this [bridge], we returned to my pueblo. They wanted the people from my community, of this entire zone [to return]. So, [Marcos Williams] said to return to Oronccoy, the people to Yerbabuena, to Mollebamba, to Huallhua, to all right. . . . Therefore, Marcos Williams said we needed a bridge for all the people to return to their places. Therefore, when we returned, there were not seeds, nothing. These dates Fujimori was president, so Señor Marcos Williams made this bridge. He protected us a lot. He said to carry all the seeds from here to plant. So, Marcos Williams helped us a lot with maize, potato seed, haba [flat bean], of all with beans too. Little by little, the people brought them. They produced them. He also gave cows and animals.

Graciela relayed with enthusiasm the details of the return bridge and the various pueblos' dedication to its maintenance. "With cables and boards [it is made], but when the horse crosses it, always the wood wears out. So just this we must replace. We come together in a faena [to replace it]. Juan Pablo last year also went to renovate it. Always the community goes to renovate it." Various communities come together to repair the bridge when needed. "Yes, they come

Figure 16. A panoramic view of the ninety-seven curves that lead from the Kutinachaka Bridge toward the community or Oronccoy. Photo by Max Altamirano Molero.

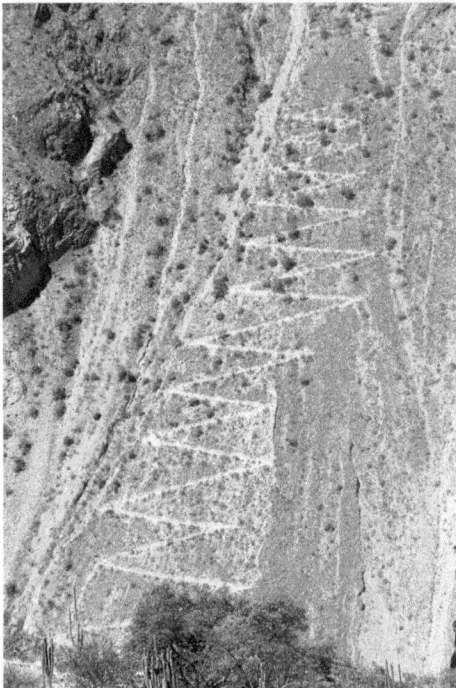

Figure 17. Closer view of the steep terrain and switchbacks leading toward Oronccoy from the Kutinachaka Bridge. Photo by Max Altamirano Molero.

down for a faena. This road has over ninety curves!" At this point, Graciela's eyes glossed over, and a small smile crossed her face as she began to sing a song in Quechua about the bridge. "We would sing this from the river going up and while constructing the bridge."

Orphaned Community

In discussing her return to Oronccoy, Graciela asked about my perceptions of home when I am away. "You miss your country [when in Peru], right?" I responded that yes, at times I do miss my own country. "When you are here you miss it. Since you were little, you had your friends who you would play with in high school, in kindergarten. Nice, right? However, my friends died, two neighbors, two uncles. It is sad, Nicole. So, it is like an orphan, our community now." Graciela continued to describe how her community had changed:

> Everything has fallen down. There are only a few houses, and they do not have roofs. Everything is depopulated. Arriving here there is a quantity of houses—houses that do not have roofs. There are corrals without animals.

Figure 18. Looking out from the community of Yerbabuena; a sacred cross and the peaks of Azulcocha and Panta. Photo by Max Altamirano Molero.

Seeing this makes me cry, Nicole. I believe it, but if I did not know it, maybe I would not believe it.

After a long pause, Graciela continued, "But, Nicole, very sad. You can cry when you arrive to this community. From this community you pass Liampata, in there it is equal. There are not houses, only there are corrals. In the patios, there are plants, trees. There are corrals for animals, but there does not exist an owner. All is destroyed." Graciela continued to describe the challenge of returning to a largely deserted place:

> In all these communities now, there are hardly any people. . . . Us that lived in these parts walking, pasturing animals. We always knew who lived in this community. When I was little, I knew my neighbors, but these neighbors are no more. Their houses have now fallen down, their plants, their door has fallen down.

Graciela claimed that some had resettled in other parts of Peru, however, "others are no longer."

> They are not here. They are no longer. There are not people to return. Only a few returned who are living. For example, in [a community near Oronccoy] there live like only five people, but before there were two hundred or three hundred people. It is painful that there are only three or five people. There are more animals [than people]. They are augmenting buying cows, pigs, sheep, but there are not people. . . . We are in different parts, but more than anything more are dead.

When Graciela was explaining the destruction of the homes in her community, she shuffled through a pile of pictures and pulled out a photo of Oronccoy, apparently taken from a high vantage point, likely a nearby mountain. She enthusiastically pointed out about twenty different houses, naming the residents and, in most cases, their relation to her.

> In this corner, there is a plaza, right? This last house is mine. Below here is the house of my grandmother. This is the house of Angelica. Angelica continues to live there. She returned, but four years before this photo was

taken, everything was destroyed. So, they are now rebuilding to make new for Angelica. Here is my uncle in this house. This is another uncle of mine. In this part there are four houses following. Here below the church that continues in the corner is the house of my mom's sister, Paulina. Yes, my aunt Paulina, her house is here, and if you continue, there is a little house of my mom's, another house here, another house here. Then continuing is the house of my grandmother who died now. This biggest house is the house of my grandmother. This is my house.

Graciela then solemnly pointed out what seemed to be countless rectangular shapes throughout the photograph, explaining that they were the remnants of abandoned houses that were home to the hundreds of additional families who once called Oronccoy home. Graciela explained how all the homes were mud brick construction with thatch roofs, similar to what you see today throughout the Andes. During the time of violence, the thatch roofs were burned, and the rains quickly deteriorated the mud brick foundations, leaving merely countless bases of a once thriving community dotting the rich landscape. According to Graciela, another community, called Esta Calloq, was also burned to the ground. "So, in there were people waiting in their houses when the military arrived. Therefore, they closed the doors and burned the houses. All of them were killed, turned into carbon and ashes. Many of these things happened. The telling does not end."

After much discussion, Juan Pablo, Graciela, her brother Alex, and father all agreed that in the Oreja de Perro region before the war there were about five thousand people and that only about a quarter of them survived the violence. While many were displaced, most were unable to return as they had died during the violence. Juan Pablo described the tragic demographic shift because of the violence: "Twenty-five percent or less survived. For example, in my pueblo there are few people, like twenty families, no more. But before there were almost three hundred families."[6] Peruvian anthropologist Luis believed that this region was by far the most fragmented, claiming, "They lost their origin" (Luis, pers. comm., August 10, 2018). Moreover, the CVR declares that "as with the Asháninka case, countless communities and peasant families in the *Oreja de Perro* ended up living in a state of slavery and precariousness after the withdrawal of *Sendero Luminoso* for many years" (CVR 2003, 5:13).

Those who currently reside in Oronccoy continue to hold the land for survivors who live elsewhere in case they can return, yet few people have resettled in Oronccoy, and the entire demographics of the Oreja de Perro region of Peru has shifted as young people are the ones who are slowly repopulating the area.

> In Oronccoy, there are no elders. There are a few from before like Juan Pablo, my aunt, my father, other people like five only are there. The young people that are there are now populating it. . . . However, there are not people from before. Only the future is populating.

Juan Pablo also described how a community near Oronccoy consisted of only five families and the overall demographic shift in the region.

> All of this zone. It is all young people because the old people were killed. There are just two old women, one who is eighty years old or so. . . . Before, when we lived in our pueblo in the 1980s, we had cattle and fields to live. We had a quantity of people. These people are no more. Now live the children that suffered in this violence who had escaped, who had hidden from the military. Some children have come, only these have returned. Only these are now the population.

Graciela discussed how traumatic memories and ongoing fear initially made it difficult to adjust back to life in a largely abandoned Oronccoy:

> It appeared different when I returned. It was very difficult. When the dogs barked in the night, I was afraid that maybe they had returned. I was very, very scared. . . . I always was afraid sometimes when the dog would bark, a little time of violence I would remember, and maybe these people would return. It made me very afraid. . . . When I would see, for example, on a hill, a car that has lights, right? When we would see on the road light, we would think maybe it was these people [military or Senderistas], but liars, our imagination.

According to Graciela, although some people wanted to return to Oronccoy, it was difficult to do so because of persistent memories and fear. Graciela described a neighbor in Andahuaylas who was afraid to return to Oronccoy:

There is a young woman below from the community of Oronccoy also. When I was in the violence, she was [about ten years old]. We were children still. She had pretty blond hair like yours, so her nickname was Sarita [*sara* signifies "maize" in Quechua] out of affection. Now she is a señora and has two sons. "We can return to Oronccoy," I say to her. "Oy auntie, I do not want to go. I am afraid to return" [she says].

I asked if Sarita had ever returned to Oronccoy since the violence ended. "No, she hasn't wanted to and is afraid to return, as she thinks the violence will recommence." For some, fear was so great, death was preferable to reliving the violence. Graciela described the sentiments of another neighbor in Andahuaylas, who had fled to the city during the war:

> From the community below there is a señora. At times, she remembers this violence, so we talk. We say that hopefully this will not happen again. At times, she says if this violence returned, she would prepare a poison to drink and to give to all of her children. She says this to me. For all that had happened during the violence, she says. Therefore, we talk. "Do not talk like this," I say to her. "If you drank the poison and gave it to your children, you could not be presented to God. God would not recognize you. No God would permit" [I say]. "However, I would die," she says. "Do not think of giving all of your children poison," I say.

The abandonment and traumatic memories contained in Oronccoy made it challenging to readjust to life in Graciela's natal community. Yet Graciela also recognized how fortunate she was to be able to return, unlike others who died or whom the war permanently displaced.

Orphaned Survivors

Returning to La Oreja was particularly challenging for those who were taken during the war. Graciela claimed that during La Violencia nursing children were typically killed and other children were often captured by the military and brought to cities far from La Oreja, which often resulted in cut ties with the region.

There are some in Lima, in the jungle; they want to return from the jungle to Oronccoy, who left when they were young from the military. They are now big, right? Like those who the military took [when young children], they want to return to their pueblo. They ask, "How is our pueblo, paisanos?" "It is good," I say. "You can return," I say. The young people who ask me, they are young and have families, but during this violence their moms, dads were killed, so the young people continue working as *empleados* [servant/maid], they want to return.

Many who were taken have not been able to reconnect with biological family. Fortunately, Graciela's aunt was able to locate her son who the military captured during the war. "For example, my cousin was taken by the military to the Ciudad Blanca, Arequipa, they say.[7] He was brought there young." Graciela described how the military captured him when he was about six years old: "So, one woman was carrying my cousin, so the military, an official said, 'Give me the boy to raise,' and brought him to Arequipa." Once peace was established, Graciela's aunt from Oronccoy searched for her son, not knowing if he was alive or dead. "My aunt was saying, 'Where did the military kill him? Where did they discard him that we will find him?'" Graciela's aunt eventually found him alive. He had been adopted and given a different last name but still remembered his parent's names. "He knows the names of his mom and dad, but he is now adopted. A señor raised him and my cousin has his last name." He had been working in Arequipa, but he returned to meet his biological family. "So, my cousin has a profession, electrician, works with cables. Yes, he had come, and we met him, so he returned." Graciela reminisced about her cousin as a young child and their eventual reunion. "He was with my aunt for six years or maybe four or five years. He was little and fat. We were so happy when he arrived. We did not know whom. 'You are Julia's son?' we said."

As previously mentioned, Juan Pablo's youngest son, Lazaro, was stolen during the war. Juan Pablo claimed the people who took his son were from Pallqas, not from Mollebamba. "They took him to Ayacucho, but these people were from Pallqas, not from Mollebamba, Pallqas. These are good people. They are not bad like those from Mollebamba. [People from] Mollebamba grab people and kill them. They [from Pallqas] were peaceful, people with conscience." Many years following the capture of Abimael Guzmán, when peace had been established for some time, Juan Pablo began to search for his son. He asked various people about his son's whereabouts. Graciela described how "a person told Juan Pablo that he was in Ayacucho." An authority figure from Yerbabuena accompanied Juan Pablo to Ayacucho to search for his son and they found him in the community of Matara in the town of Sachabamba. When Juan Pablo eventually located his son, he found that Lazaro had the same first name but had changed his last name and denied that Juan Pablo was his father.[8] Graciela explained the situation: "[Juan Pablo] cried a lot looking for him, but he no longer had his father's last name. . . . They said he was adopted, so they gave him their last name when he was a child." Graciela continued to describe their initial encounter: "When they found Lazaro, Juan Pablo said, 'This is my son.' She [adoptive mother] said, 'This is your son? Yes, he looks exactly like you, my son,' she was saying. . . . The adoptive parents said to Juan Pablo, 'He looks just like you!'" I asked if the adoptive parents were angry, and Graciela claimed that they were not. "Yes, they were conversing with him. Therefore, the señora that adopted him, they are conscientious. They have a conscience. 'It is your son. We adopted you,' they said." Although the adoptive parents were accepting of Juan Pablo, Lazaro initially reacted negatively to his biological father.

"What will you do, my father?" he said when he was crying tears. "You are my son," [Juan Pablo] said. Juan Pablo knew and was crying. What pain, no? "What do you do, my papa? You are not my papa!" [Lazaro said]. "I am your father," Juan Pablo said and [Lazaro] said, "What are you going to do?" to Juan Pablo. "You want to know me?"

Even though the son had denied his biological father, Juan Pablo knew Lazaro was his son, as Graciela explained:

[Juan Pablo] knew in his mind that this is my son, but he had a different last name. Juan Pablo was crying and returned to Oronccoy alone. People asked, "Where is your son?" "He didn't want to come," he said. He did not want to come when he was eighteen years old still, he did not want to come. He was seventeen or eighteen, I believe. So, [Juan Pablo] returned alone because [Lazaro] did not want to come.

Juan Pablo had been listening to Graciela describe their initial encounter. When there was a pause in conversation, Juan Pablo shifted his position in the creaky wooden chair and kept his focus on the bag of coca leaves, avoiding eye contact, then stated, "He did not believe that he was my son. He thought, 'Is this my father? I think no.'"

In 2018, Graciela showed me a photo of Juan Pablo's son, Lazaro, taken alongside two of her children. Even though Lazaro denied that Juan Pablo was his father when he was an adolescent, Lazaro began to search for and eventually reunited with Juan Pablo as a young adult and periodically visited his biological family. When I asked Graciela if Lazaro maintained a relationship with his adoptive parents, she replied, "Who knows. Maybe."

Although one of Graciela's cousins and Juan Pablo's son were able to reunite with their biological families and return to their natal communities, many individuals who were stolen during the violence have not. "Yes, and now they are twenty-five years old, thirty years old, like my age too. My cousins are in Maldonado and in Cuzco. They are like lost people in different places. In Lima, in Chanchamayo, other places." The long-term separation of children from their birth families served to sever ties and trust. For instance, Graciela had not seen her brother Alipeo, who the military took during her family's capture, for many years. Although Alipeo was able to reunite with his biological family as an adolescent, he was later taken to Argentina to work for a mestizo family. Given their limited physical proximity over the course of their lifetimes, Graciela questioned their relationship.

> For example, who knows my brother in Argentina, we do not know. He could be him or he could be another, right? We have not seen him with our own eyes. We cannot hug him. We cannot caress him. We do not know. Maybe he is another person, right? Is he my brother or is he dead, or maybe it is the truth that my brother is in Argentina? I do not know, but if he arrived, I would see.[9]

Jessaca Leinaweaver cites Fermín Rivera, a Peruvian anthropologist, who stated that due to extended family networks in the rural Andes, even if parents perish, no one is ever orphaned. However, during the war, tens of thousands of children lost their mothers and fathers, never obtained godparents, and, in some cases, their communities were completely wiped out through migration and massacre, leaving no one to care for children, thereby crystallizing the concept of *wakcha* (orphan) (Leinaweaver 2008, 78–79). According to Graciela, hundreds of thousands of survivors have lost ties to their extended family networks and entire regions have been largely abandoned, causing individuals as well as communities to become *wakchakuna* (orphans).

Regaining a Livelihood

When Graciela, Juan Pablo, and their three children initially returned to Oronccoy, they had little to support themselves.

> When we returned to Oronccoy, we did not have one animal. To feed my children, there was nothing. We did not even have a hen—nothing when we returned to Oronccoy. We also did not have a house either. . . . My mom had her little house. My siblings also had houses, but very little ones. For this, my mother also returned without anything.

Having worked for others throughout the violence and disruption, survivors returned to their rural pueblos with nothing to restart their lives.

> We worked for other people, merely just to eat. We only lived in other people's houses. My mother also. We just worked to feed our children, but children were working for shoe stores and other places. . . . Therefore, everyone from Pampachiri, from Pomococha, all from Lakai, from all these parts, returned to their pueblos but did not have animals, cows, horses, and sheep.

For individuals to be able to return to their rural communities and once again raise animals and crops, people began by renting others' animals.

> Returning to Oronccoy, to Chapi, to Yerbabuena. Each community, when everyone returned to these communities to augment our animals, they gave to the people ten sheep, fifteen cows for them to care for. Giving them just to care for them. Like a caretaker, they were. . . . For example, I have nothing, so this person says, "Take care of my cow in your community to augment it." After one year, maybe they will pay one hundred soles

[US$30.00], at times only fifty soles [US$15.00] for the people. Therefore, we did not have them, but my mom had them. My mom rented fifteen cows from a far place near Pampachiri, Pomacocha. From Pomacocha is where the owner of the cow was from. They came with a car and my mom cared for that cow happily. At times when you are taking care of a cow, you can take out milk and cheese to eat that you do not have to give the owner. Only they want the animal, and the calves were also rented.

Given limited options, various individuals returning to La Oreja cared for others' animals, and after about a year, the animal's owner would pay the individual for this care, with the amount ranging drastically.[10]

Graciela's mom rented a cow, using the milk to make cheese as needed, and Graciela and Juan Pablo began to question if they could also rent a cow. "So, with Juan Pablo we discussed that there is nothing, nothing for our kids to grow. How are we going to maintain them? Maybe we could rent a cow too, we said. Therefore, there was a *quermis*. Do you know quermis, Nicole?" Graciela continued to explain quermis, which is a soccer competition wherein players from various communities come to compete. "Once a year in Yerbabuena, Oronccoy, Tastabamba, they always come and earn the first prize, a bull or cow, for second prize a sheep or pig, the winners get a prize." Graciela explained that the community selects a godparent to support the game. "You have a godparent for the ball, to baptize the ball." The godparent is expected to buy the ball and bless it before the game by pouring beer over it and saying a prayer. They also provide beer or chicha for the players and spectators to drink and prepare potatoes and sometimes mazamorra to eat.[11]

> Therefore, there was quermis in my community of Oronccoy. In this community of Tastabamba, my father's cousin arrived. We were playing with this ball and this man, when we were playing with the ball, he kicked the ball and broke [his foot] completely. Therefore, we were in our house, in my father's house. He was badly hurt; he could not walk, nothing, he was just in the bed. A man and his wife also arrived and said, "How is this man? We need to take him to the hospital."

The family of the man who broke his foot while playing soccer was worried about who would care for their animals while seeking medical care. "So, my mom said to this señora, 'It is okay, you can leave them with my daughter. My daughter also has her children and does not have anything. You can leave them with her. So yes, leave this mountain of animals.' The owner's cows, they were good cows."

The family did not own the cows outright, rather they were caretaking or renting them, so Graciela called and asked permission from the animals' actual owner in Ocobamba to transfer their care to Graciela. The owner of the cows agreed that Graciela could care for the animals and said that they would bring whatever she wanted from Ocobamba when they were next in Oronccoy. "They said, 'I will bring you whatever you want from Ocobamba. You are from the chacra. Please take care of my cow.' I was very thankful to this señor. 'The cows give milk,' he said, 'that you can give to your kids.'" So Juan Pablo met the caretaker halfway between Oronccoy and Tastabamba to hand over fifteen cows. Graciela was thrilled to have so many animals to care for and help support her family. "Fifteen cows! Yes. So, we were happy!"

Although Graciela was relieved to have work to do and a means to support her family, she was preoccupied with her children's lack of educational opportunities in Oronccoy. "So, I had another worry of where my daughter is going to study. Now there is no high school. There is only primary, but when you finish primary there is no secondary." When Graciela and her family returned to Oronccoy, Sumac Killa had finished primary school, which in Peru ends after fifth grade. Augosto and Eufemilia, however, had not yet completed the fifth grade, and postwar there was no secondary school in Oronccoy for the children to continue their education.

Unexpected Education

Approximately one month after the animal transfer, the owner of the cows met Juan Pablo halfway to ask about his animals. "After a month, the owner of the cow arrived. The señor gifted Juan Pablo his watch. Yes, this owner of the cow met Juan Pablo in the middle of the road and gave him his watch!" Another month later, the owner traveled all the way to Oronccoy to check on his animals. Upon arriving in Oronccoy, "the cow owner saw how well his animals had been cared for and asked, 'How much is it worth that you are taking care of my cows?

How much?' he said to us." Throughout this negotiation, Graciela and Juan Pablo mentioned that they might return to Andahuaylas for their children to attend school.

> About the cows, we were conversing and conversing. In this we said, "Here there is no secondary school. Maybe we [the children] will study in the high school in Andahuaylas. I will stay here and care for the animals," Juan Pablo said to the owner of the cows. So there the señor said, "Don't worry. I will take them with me like a family, like a brother. I will take your children. They will study." We said, "I will take care of your animals as if I was you." Therefore, in this he took my children.

The señor insisted that he take Graciela's children back to Ocobamba to attend school. "'You are like family. Let us take your children to study in Ocobamba. Leave my animals here. Your children are suffering, and they should not suffer at all. They are children and they should study. Care for my animals' he said." In payment for taking care of the animals and to ensure that Graciela and Juan Pablo did not abandon his cows, the cow owner took Graciela's three children— Eufemilia, Sumac Killa, and Augosto—to Ocobamba to attend school.

The transfer of Graciela's children to the cow owner's family reflects a common practice of "child circulation" in the Andes (Fonseca 1986, 15). Jessaca Leinaweaver (2008) looks closely at the practice of circulating children in the Andes, underscoring how the physical movement of children to different homes entails material, moral, and relational responsibilities. As young people *acompañar* (accompany) older individuals, they are often expected to share daily household tasks in exchange for access to education, shelter, instruction, or affection. Through the process of cohabitation, household members actively formulate and transform relatedness and sociality. As evidenced throughout Graciela's and her family members' various residences while living on the run, as well as upon returning to Andahuaylas and then to Oronccoy, in some cases the relationship mirrors close kin relations often predicated on compadrazgo (godparent) relations of reciprocity (still power laden), and in other cases it can be more transactional, hierarchical, and even exploitative. In this case, Graciela's children were exchanging the opportunity to attend school with Graciela and Juan Pablo's continued care of the man's animals. Undoubtedly, Graciela's children were expected to also contribute to household tasks in exchange for *propinas* (tips) that helped pay for school fees.[12]

When Graciela's children left to attend school and reside in another home, she missed their companionship gravely. "But always I have pain for my children. I was crying for my children. Where are my children? Looking for them in the fields, looking for their clothes drying, crying! Since they were born, I have had pain for my children." Because Graciela was so worried about her children, Juan Pablo went to Ocobamba a week later to check on them. When he arrived, he said to the cows' owner, "How are they? I am looking to see how my children are doing." When Juan Pablo returned, he told Graciela, "I saw they are doing well, so do not worry." While Graciela was relieved, she still suffered from the absence of her children.

> Nevertheless, always I was missing them so much. . . . So much, I complained about missing my children. Looking at their clothes. There was no one to talk to. I missed them so much at times, I cried hard. Just from this, I think made me sick, my sickness. When it was almost half a year, I was sick. At times when Juan Pablo would come, and I was crying. "Do not cry, our kids are fine," he would say when he returned to Oronccoy, but I did not believe him. Maybe he . . .

At this point, Graciela's voice trailed off and she looked down at her hands lying in her lap.

At another point, Graciela told me how she becomes worried about her children when she is not with them, imagining what horrible things could be happening to them due to her own traumatic experiences with sexual assault and exploitation. Due to her ongoing concerns, Graciela needed to check personally on her children. "I wanted to see with my own eyes. I wanted to see my children. When I was crying, so much Juan Pablo said to me, 'Let's go so you can see them then. Let's go. They are fine.'" Graciela and Juan Pablo went to Ocobamba to check on the children.

> I went one time to see my kids in Ocobamba. My Eufemilia was very little at the time and I missed her so much. I arrived at the house of this señor. There were my children. I cried. "Don't cry, mommy. We are just fine. Let's walk,"

they said. So, we walked to the señor's fields and there we took garlic and there were many nisperos [small, native Andean citrus fruit, *Mespilus germanica*], so we took much of this and ate this while we walked. "Let's walk, mom. Do not cry," they said. "We are okay. He gives us tips too that we use to pay for the school. This señor is good and the señora also. Do not cry. We are not suffering," my daughter said. The three. We slept three nights with my kids in Ocobamba. Arriving and seeing my children, I cried. The woman saw my tears and said, "Do not cry, señora. Your kids are not lacking anything," she told me. However, I missed them a lot. After three days, I returned, leaving my children, but always I had this pain in my heart and I missed them.

Graciela continued to long for her children, but more children soon accompanied her as she and Juan Pablo expanded their family.

Birth of Rous, Hermenegildo, and Nayely

While living in Oronccoy, Graciela gave birth to three other children: Rous, Hermenegildo, and Nayely, all at home. "Before, only in our houses we gave birth. All my children I birthed just in the house. Never did I go to the hospital." Rous's birth went rather smoothly, *tranquilo* (peaceful), according to Graciela. Graciela's mother encouraged her to seek help from her aunt, the woman who had raised Graciela's mother as a young girl, as she was a partera (traditional midwife) and could read coca leaves.

> Paulina was her name that cared for my mom. She is a little midwife. She looks at coca also. Yes, Paulina is her name. Therefore, my mom said, "Maybe you cannot give birth. It is better to call your aunt, and she could come to the house to attend you. Maybe you will not be able to give birth," my mom said. "I will call my sister. She could return to help you give birth."

Fortunately, Graciela's fourth labor and delivery went smoothly, and she gave birth to a healthy baby girl, Rous. "I also gave birth very quickly with Rous. Paulina was there. Paulina, my mom, my aunts, Juan Pablo were there to help. She is like a midwife, Paulina. She is old now."

About two years later, Graciela gave birth to another child, her son

Hermenegildo. Graciela described Hermenegildo's birth as a rather quick process as well, which happened at home assisted once again by her aunt, the midwife Paulina. "With Hermenegildo, I also gave birth very quickly." A lightness immediately came over Graciela as she described Hermenegildo and Rous as young children. Hermenegildo "was very funny when he was learning to walk. He had these little shoes, and he was dancing when he walked. Very funny." Graciela began to giggle as she described Rous. "Rous was very fat. It was hard for her to learn to walk because she was so fat! Hermenegildo was skinny and learned to walk fast. In one year, he was off and walking. . . . He was walking and dancing when he was little. And Rous was so fat it was difficult for her to walk, so she would just sit happily."

In discussing Hermenegildo's and Rous's births, I asked Graciela how they cut the umbilical cord, and she said that she realizes most people cut it with scissors, but in her pueblo, they cut it with carrizo. In describing carrizo Graciela said, "You know this? You bring it for the roofs of the house. It cuts like a knife, so with this you cut. For this, they say your clothes do not wear out quickly. Understand?" I was completely confused and responded that I had no idea what she was talking about, so Graciela explained further:

> You do not wear out your clothes quickly when you cut the cord with this [carrizo], the person [whose cord was cut]. It is a custom of the pueblo. I will cut this umbilical cord and when I cut it with scissors, they say the person will quickly wear out their clothes. This child when they play, they will destroy their clothes when they [cut the umbilical cord with] whatever. On the other hand, if I cut with carrizo, they say the child will not wear out their clothes.

Graciela then said that although the midwife cut Hermenegildo's umbilical cord with carrizo, he quickly wears out his shoes. "My Hermenegildo, he wears out his shoes very quickly. I buy them and he breaks them. He breaks them because when I was pregnant with him, we brought little calves." In seeing my confused expression once again, Graciela explained that when she was pregnant with Hermenegildo, her father brought her little baby sheep. Because Graciela was caring for the baby sheep that walked around her while pregnant, Hermenegildo would also trot around like baby sheep, wearing out his shoes.

"Also, the sheep walked very quickly and so does Hermenegildo. The sheep walked very strongly. For this reason, Hermenegildo is like this. He also walks fast." Graciela claimed that Hermenegildo acquired the characteristics of baby sheep given their proximity to him while he was in the womb. Graciela discussed how Hermenegildo was also more mobile in utero and is unique in other ways. "Yes, more intelligent, my Hermenegildo. He is more thoughtful, more conscious, and he is more caring. At times he will say, 'Do not worry, mama. Do not suffer. I will work. I will study.' At times I cry, and he says, 'Do not cry. I will work. I am big,' he says."

After giving birth to Hermenegildo, Graciela and Juan Pablo experienced strain in their relationship. As previously described, Graciela and Juan Pablo's relationship did not begin on equal footing; however, once they began their life together in the tropical lowlands their situation improved for many years, yet they later experienced periods of turmoil. Graciela described how in the beginning of their relationship, while in the Amazon, "It was happy. We were happy, but it changed [for the worse] for about four years. When I had my baby Rous, [along] with Hermenegildo, in these times a little had changed. . . . [Now] he says, 'I am sorry, forgive me,' he asks me." Rolling her eyes, Graciela said, "Men always ask for forgiveness." From living in the rural highland community of Sacclaya, I found when a couple was having marital problems, they first consulted the godparents from their wedding. If the situation did not improve, they then talked with their parents. As a last resort, the community became involved in the marital dispute. For issues of domestic violence or infidelity, it was common for the community to enact justice via a public lashing or permanent expulsion from the community.

Graciela and I had previously discussed how Oronccoy handled marital disputes, which was like the process followed in Sacclaya; however, community leaders charged offenders a fine in Oronccoy that they then channeled into community projects or to support a community member in need. I asked how those in Oronccoy responded to their tense relationship and Graciela stated, "A little bad." She then clarified that the community did not respond, because the treatment never warranted community engagement. "He did not mistreat me. He just bothered me, scolded me, but I did not tell anyone, only in my heart . . . The things that had not happened well with Juan Pablo, I did not tell anyone. I guarded it in my heart." I asked if there was any abuse and Graciela responded, "Yes, with words. With fists, no, but with words. My stomach was also uncomfortable. I also felt bad in my stomach when I was pregnant, so it made it worse when he *renegarme* [deny, renounce, gripe about, or detest me]." According to Graciela, this tense period eventually passed, and Juan Pablo has become more peaceful in his older age.

Illness Strikes

Life shifted for Graciela's family following the birth of Graciela's sixth child, Nayely. Nayely's birth was much more challenging than that of Rous and Hermenegildo.

> With Nayely, it went a little bad. With Augosto, Rous, and Hermenegildo, when I gave birth I was not on the floor or on the bed, no. I was squatting, but with Nayely I had no strength. My whole body was shaking. I was nervous. For this, I had great fear. It was very different with Nayely to give birth.

Graciela's experience with Nayely also differed from her previous births in that a traveling nurse had seen Graciela prior to labor, as opposed to the midwife, Paulina.

> The practicing nurses come. They do not use meds either. Only when you are going to give birth, they tell you about birth control. "In Mollebamba there is a pharmacy where you can buy birth control," they told me. They said to get it a month after you give birth. . . . The doctors that attend in the hospital, they live in Mollebamba, so they come every month to the pregnant women. With Nayely, they came to check on me. They said to come in a month to give birth to Nayely. The following day, I gave birth. I did not complete a month.

I asked if Nayely was small, given that she may have been born a month earlier than the doctors expected, but Graciela said she was born a normal size, same as her other children, and that the doctors and nurses do not know anything: "The coca leaves know more."

Graciela's description of the nurses' focus on birth control is reminiscent of forced sterilization of hundreds of Indigenous women under Alberto Fujimori's so-called family planning program.[13] The Peruvian State targeted Indigenous and peasant women because they were understood as seeds of insurrectionary groups and poverty that must be eradicated (Koc-Menard 2015). As part of its policy for demographic control, Fujimori's family planning program gave service providers goals and quotas in terms of the number of sterilizations to carry out. Medical practitioners frequently gave biased information to women and their families and threatened some women with imprisonment, fines, or the withdrawal of state food aid if they did not agree to undergo the sterilization procedure. Moreover, many women did not receive adequate postoperation care and consequently suffered health problems, some even dying (Amnesty International 2004). Between 1996 and 2000, an estimated 294,032 people were forcibly sterilized, including 22,004 men, yet such gross violations were not mentioned in the CVR report and continue to be ignored (Kovarik 2018; see also Leinaweaver 2005).

After each birth, Graciela registered her children at a nearby *posta* (health center), so they could receive their DNI (national identification card). When Graciela gave birth to all of her children, there was not a posta in Oronccoy. Currently there is a posta in Oronccoy, but there is not a regular attendant, and few give birth in the posta because it is too far away from their homes. According to Graciela, "They do not oversee many births. After a month, there is an attendant. It is not established." Paulina, the one surviving midwife in Oronccoy, is becoming quite elderly, and Graciela is concerned that she is not passing her knowledge on to others.

Although Nayely was born healthy, soon after delivery, Graciela became ill, and so the older children that had been living in Ocobamba returned to Oronccoy.

I was sick still, and they came from Ocobamba carrying their backpacks full of nisperos and little potatoes. These things they were carrying for me. When I gave birth to Nayely, I was sick. I was sick in the bed in Oronc-coy. ProAnde arrived, an association. The señora visited me. "How are you?" they asked. I said, "I am sick." Juan Pablo asked what they could do. They said if I did not go [to a hospital], I would die. Therefore, Juan Pablo brought me carrying Nayely. My head hurt so much! We arrived to the Cortina aside the river and there was a car from ProAnde, so they brought me to Andahuaylas in a car. They brought me quickly to the emergency room. There were many bumps in the car. It was worse. I could not talk. I could not walk. I could not take steps like this. [Graciela stood up and demonstrated barely shuffling forward.] I could not move anything. My head hurt so badly. I could not do anything. I walked so slowly. They carried me below to a private doctor at the emergency.

Upon examination, it was determined that Graciela had a urinary tract infection and chronic gastritis. The doctors gave her a series of shots and pills and she recovered relatively quickly.

Juan Pablo, Hermenegildo, Rous, Nayely, and Augosto came to Andahuaylas when Graciela went to the hospital. Once Graciela left the hospital, she stayed with her brother Alex and his wife but felt uncomfortable since she was unable to work and earn her keep.

When we came, below by the hospital lived my brother Alex. He had a room he rented. His señora [wife] had another room, but I was not healthy to work, and I felt uncomfortable with this. When I got out of the hospital, there in a room I lived with my brother Alex. There I stayed and Juan Pablo stayed too. "Your sister is not well. Until she recuperates, can she stay here?" [Juan Pablo] said [to Alex]. "Yes," my brother said, but his wife was uncomfortable and wanted me to return. She was bothered and I was uncomfortable too. I said, "Perhaps it is better I live somewhere else." However, just my brother said, "But you are sick, mama. You are not well."

Juan Pablo needed to return to Oronccoy to tend the animals and fields and brought Hermenegildo and Rous back with him. Graciela stayed in Alex's room with Nayely and Augosto. Graciela had brought what little money they had to "buy noodles and whatever thing. I bought [other] things too, but my brother's wife was angry with me." In the end, both Alex and Juan Pablo realized that perhaps it was best if Graciela and the children found another place to live. Luckily, Alex knew a woman who was looking for people to help care for her house.

Alex and Graciela's other brothers had worked for a woman by the name of Sara for many years. "Sara knew my brother. He had been working for her since he was [about ten years old]. Other brothers of mine had worked on her house since they were little. . . . So she knew us." Sara wanted someone to care for her plants and dogs that lived at her house on a hill overlooking the city of Andahuaylas. "At that point, I did not have a dog. I had nothing. Therefore, señora Sara said, 'Please return to my house. My plants are drying and need to be watered. All of my dogs have been forgotten too,' she said. So I said, 'Yes another day we can talk,' I told her." After talking it over with Alex, Graciela decided to help Sara and live in her house to care for her plants and dogs.

> So at seven in the night, she arrived. My brother said her husband was below with the car. Therefore, he said, "Let's go. They are going to take us." However, I did not even have a blanket, nothing in the house, so my brother lent me two blankets to sleep. Therefore, with these two blankets, my manta, and my *lliqta*, we slept on the wooden planks. We did not have anything. My daughter, Augosto, and I arrived in the night. . . . I felt bad for the señora because I did not have money, nothing. I told this all to Sara. "I do not have anything to buy anything. I do not have a pot to cook in," I said. Therefore, that night she brought an olla [pot] and spoons and she left me a kilo of noodles. "This you can cook," she told me. I said, "I do not have money to buy me anything." Sara also left me ten soles (US$3.00). "With this you go and buy things," she told me. . . . The money she gifted me, ten soles, and later the kilo of noodles she gifted, but she lent me the pot, spoons, and bowls. Therefore, I could cook with this, but I could not do anything. I could not even walk.

It was at this point I met Graciela. "We were there a short time before you arrived, Nicole. When we were living in Sara's house, we were there just a week before you arrived."

Graciela was eventually able to recuperate her health and managed to care for the plants and dogs, as well as work in the fields adjacent to Sara's house. Graciela was in the house with Augosto and Nayely for about one month before Juan Pablo returned with all the other children, except Eufemilia, who returned to Ocobamba to attend school. For the following year, Juan Pablo spent most of his time in Oronccoy tending their fields and animals, while Graciela and the children remained in Andahuaylas selling what little produce they could grow in the local market, washing clothes for money, and attending school.

> Selling our arroba of carrots and *habitas* we would earn sometimes twenty, thirty, fifty cents is all we would earn to survive.[14] At times, I would bring the kids, and at times, I would leave them at home to wash clothes. More than anything, they would wash clothes.

I spent the following year conducting research in the community of Sacclaya and living alongside Graciela and her family in Andahuaylas. Although Graciela and I came from extremely divergent backgrounds, I like to believe that our friendship brought us both a strange sense of familiarity and comfort, if only for a relatively brief period.

———

Once peace was established in Peru, Graciela continued to seek stability as she returned to Andahuaylas, then Oronccoy, and once again to Andahuaylas in a continual quest to educate her children. Returning to Oronccoy was challenging, as she and her family adapted to a changed physical and social landscape. While resettling into life in Oronccoy, her family grew through the birth of three more children. She struggled to support her family and contended with heartache from periodic absences of her children yet maintained happy memories of their earliest years. It was at a particularly challenging point in postwar life while contending with physical illness that I had the rare opportunity to meet Graciela. Graciela and I were able to share stories on the patio of our home and at our kitchen tables, during which we developed a rare and beautiful friendship for which I am forever grateful. Upon leaving Peru a year later, the one person I feared losing touch with the most was Graciela, which is what happened. Fortunately, I was eventually able to reconnect with Graciela to learn about how she continued to navigate life as a survivor of political violence in postwar Peru.

Chapter 8

Postwar Survival on the Margins

Seeking Stability

Graciela remained in the house we shared on the side of the hill in Andahuaylas for less than a year after I left Peru in 2006. According to Graciela, the proprietor was not pleased with her care of the gardens. Graciela admitted it was challenging to care for the property and sell produce in the market while caring for her young children. Having no other viable option for work and housing, Graciela and her family returned to Oronccoy. They worked in the fields and raised animals with the perpetual goal of purchasing land and building a house in Andahuaylas, thereby providing the security necessary for their children to continue their education.

After several years raising livestock, Graciela and Juan Pablo sold their animals, effectively liquidating all their assets, and bought a small plot of land on the steep hillside overlooking the city of Andahuaylas in the neighborhood of Pochocota for 2,000 soles (about US$606.00). They constructed a home by hand with mud bricks and a corrugated tin roof amid a sea of other makeshift homes gripping the steep hillside. Because they had no surrounding land to raise crops, to support themselves they rented a tricycle cart to sell raw sugarcane juice on the side of the road.

Three years after building their home, the municipality of Andahuaylas notified the residents in Pochocota that they deemed the region a dangerous zone, as the land was unstable and at risk of major landslides during a heavy rainfall, and ordered all residents to leave. Graciela described their predicament:

> Now the municipality is saying that we must leave the land. However, this is my worry because we sold our animals to buy this land. For this, my mom said that if you want to sell this land, you could get some animals

back to augment in the campo. Nevertheless, no one will want to buy this when this land is a dangerous zone.

The person who sold Graciela and Juan Pablo the land claimed they could not return the money, and the municipality was not offering any form of compensation.[1]

> The owner that we paid the money does not want to return the money. He has already spent it. This is our land, but the municipality says it is their land. However, the owner says it is our land. So, all of the people here are saying to give back their money. He says he already spent the money. We say, "Where did you spend it?"

Even though residents of Pochocota paid fees to live on the land, the municipality refused to invest in the neighborhood, so there were no running water, electricity, or sewage services. "Many people are working to bring water and drainpipes. Many work, but until now we still do not have light. But we pay punctually to the municipality, but they do not want to bring electricity." Graciela, along with many other families in Pochocota, did not trust the municipality, believing that the government wanted the land to mine gravel for roads and the construction of a new hospital, and refused to leave.

> Other neighbors of mine say that they are not going anywhere, that they are going to die here. . . . They do not want to move. We are many in this part. Here we live and we bought this land with our money. They said, "We will leave as dead people," this my neighbors say. . . . For this, we are constructing with materials.

While most tightly packed homes in Pochocota were constructed with mud brick and had corrugated tin roofs, a few houses were being built with more enduring materials, such as brick and metal rebar framing, signaling a sense of permanence.

Depeasantized Workers

Many of the people who had resettled in Pochocota were originally from the

Oreja de Perro region, and about thirty to forty families formed the Asociación de Desplazamiento por la Violencia Residentes en Andahuaylas (ADEVRA) to fight for their rights with the municipality, but they lack government support.

> We have an association that right now I attend with my paisanos. We are from La Oreja. For example, there are people from Tastabamba, Chillihua, Totora, Oronccoy, there are various pueblos. We come together in the association from Putucunay, from Occoro, from Huallhua from Chapi, Yerbabuena—the people that survived, that still live from the violence, we come and reunite. We are an association. . . . Because we all know each other from there. We suffered. For this, we come together to help with whatever big thing we need. We meet about every two weeks to help us between us when we need help. For example, when I fell from the car, they supported me with noodles, with whatever thing, a kilo of sugar.

Graciela was in a car accident in 2018. She was traveling to the Kutinachaka Bridge in a large potato truck that overturned on the side of the highway. Various passengers were injured, and Graciela was brought to the emergency room in Andahuaylas. Fortunately, she did not break any bones or sustain major injuries, although she was unable to work for some time. Individuals from the association pulled together resources to assure Graciela and her family had food to eat. Graciela argued that the government did not support the association and that any attention given to the association was merely for political reasons.

> With their mouth only they support us. For example, they said they would give us proper roofs. For example, close to the campaign for mayor, they come with their promises and they bring us chocolate, but they do not complete it. . . . We are bringing our votes, we are bringing our DNIs [identification cards], but they do not help us with anything.

The hundreds of thousands of individuals directly displaced from the violence, such as many of those living in Pochocota, represent what has been referred to as the "new urban class of depeasantized workers, merchants and entrepreneurs" working whatever jobs available and barely scraping by (Mitchell 1994, 6).[2] Hernando de Soto (1989) heralds support of the informal sector in

Peru to fight against terrorism and poverty, which has since proven ineffective. Overall, in Peru the availability of formal jobs that offer benefits, stability, and pensions has declined. In the 1980s, Peru's informal sector was 48 percent, which expanded to 58 percent in 1990 and then to more than 74 percent of economically active adults in 2012 (Instituto Nacional de Estadistica e Informatica 2014, 113). Younger adults are facing fewer opportunities to secure formal employment, yet children increasingly need to work to support their families economically (Campoamor 2016; Vincent 2016). Graciela described how most people who live in Pochocota work in the informal sector, illustrating their depeasantized situation:

> For example, other paisanos, my neighbors, my compañeros, are selling in carts. Some are selling soup, and some are selling guinea pigs. This is how we survive. For example, my sugarcane I am selling. For example, some of my compañeros are working as carpenters. Others when they come here clean rivers because we do not have other work. We are not supported with other options.

By 2018, the municipality relented their fight for the land and began to invest in Pochocota by providing materials with residents providing the labor. "For half it is from us. For half we give our money and our labor. There are two posts for electric lines. These they put in. But the rest is our own work." In addition to bringing electricity to the neighborhood, the steep dirt road I had previously walked up to the foot of Pochocota had been paved, and the government constructed a cement staircase from the main road at the bottom of the neighborhood to where the housing construction ceased at the crest of the mountain. The municipality also built a water system, allowing most homes to have one basic water pump. Like throughout Andahuaylas, it was necessary to boil water before consumption, and there was no access to water during the middle of the day. There was no sewage infrastructure in Pochocota, and most homes had merely a hole in the ground serving as a toilet.

With the advent of electricity by 2018, Graciela enjoyed listening to the radio and they had purchased a television. From working at an appliance store, Graciela's eldest daughter, Sumac Killa, won, through the ever-popular raffles in Peru, a gas stove for their kitchen, which drastically reduced cooking time as compared to using firewood.³ I also noticed an addition of two wooden dressers. Graciela credited these investments to the limited profits they were making with the sugarcane cart and the older children being able to earn money as well.

> Now I think there is almost no suffering for my children. To buy their clothes, I have my work. I feel peaceful to work to pay their school fees and to pay for their uniforms. So, I feel a little happy. However, before I did not have work. At times, there was no money to buy clothes either. I had to try to round up just fifty cents. At times, I could not buy anything. It was a total failure. So Eufemilia, when she was in high school, at times she could not eat lunch when she was a girl. All of this was such a shame. However, I would want her to go so she could drink water. With this [sugarcane cart], I can now buy bread, rice, and sugar for my children. You know, Nicole, because you met us when we had nothing. Yes, much suffering.

Someone from the family worked the cart every single day of the week, typically Graciela, Sumac Killa, and Nayely when Juan Pablo was in Oronccoy. Accounting for costs, the family earned approximately 41.5 to 111.50 soles a week (US$12.50 to $33.78) from the sugarcane cart and constantly sought additional means to earn money.⁴

Discrimination of Depeasantized Workers

Graciela described how she continued to face discrimination for being from Ayacucho, which exacerbated her already acute marginalization: "At times, the people of the pueblo are treated as terrorists. Always the people treat us in this manner. We are always *humilde* [poor]."⁵ Juan Pablo believed that people continued to discriminate against campesinos and those who the war displaced because they were unaware of what they had suffered. "People who did not suffer in this time in this stage do not know. They know generally, but they do not know critically at all. Maybe they do not know what happened in our pueblo. . . . People from the city do not know these problems. They do not know why we are suffering." Graciela described poor treatment from the municipality when she began selling juice in Andahuaylas and authorities demanded payment for working with her tricycle cart:

I did not have [money], for that reason I was selling. I am not a thief. At one point, the boss of this municipality came, and he hated me. Bad words. My Augosto was there. [Augosto said] "'*Upa*' you say to my mom, 'upa'! You fucking upa who sells sugarcane juice!' This municipality was discussing with me badly. Augosto began to argue with the man. Therefore, for this Augosto was saying, "'You are calling my mom 'upa'!' and he grabbed a stick of sugarcane and acted as if he was going to hit the police.

The Quechua word *upa* translates into Spanish as "bobo" (idiotic, simple, innocent, clown) as well as "sordo" (deaf, dumb, insensible, and uncompliant). In this region of Peru, it is used in a derogatory fashion combining fool and ignorant, particularly referencing someone who became involved with Sendero due to a lack of knowledge (Koc-Menard 2015, 216). Graciela said that fortunately relations with the municipality had gradually improved over the years. She claimed they did not want her to sell in that particular spot, "But yeah, now no." Laughing, Graciela said, "Now they are my friends. Yeah, they come and drink sugarcane juice. They buy sugarcane from me. More peaceful." Graciela did not know why it changed and said, "Maybe a favor from God?"

Graciela's brother Alex described how "people from the campo" are immediately identified, and discriminated against, for their use of Quechua, accent, or lack of fluency in Spanish:

It is very bad. It is too much, this psychological damage. There are people who are nervous. There are people who do not want to talk. At times until now, I go to an institution; I go to an office where there are engineers or lawyers, people that are superior to me. I think that I am speaking badly or talking very badly. Psychologically this hits me. It is very bad, the bullying and the discrimination of the language, or that you speak Quechua, because in reality until now a little has changed, because some people understand here in Peru there are various languages, and they must accept this, and what you speak is a vocation and you should not discriminate. It is something normal because all have the same rights to live the customs that we have, to speak and to express ourselves. More than anything, it is Quechua, our languages, which must not disappear. It must be cultivated because it is a culture.

As indicated by Alex's experience with discrimination, in Peru race is malleable and performed with dress, education, and language being key indicators of whether a person is considered an "Indian" or "mestizo" and where people thereby stand in the social hierarchy. Quechua is tied to "primitiveness, backwardness, and ignorance" and how one speaks Spanish is linked to determination of individuals as ignorant or *motosos* (Huayhua 2014, 2,401). In fact, throughout the war, language followed an itinerary like that of lost lives. "'Shining Path' became 'terrorist,' which later became synonymous with 'Ayacuchano,' which in turn meant anything that was Indian or mestizo, dressed poorly, and spoke deficient Spanish. To say you were 'Ayacuchano' was to admit breaking antiterrorist law" (Flores Galindo 2010, 241).

Alex believed that Quechua speakers had more pride in their culture than they did in the past and that the situation was improving with the younger generations, yet discrimination continued.

> At times, there are people who treat each other well, but then there are others who treat [one another] badly. They are professionals, but they do not have ethics. They do not have an agreeing behavior toward others. This is very bad because there are poor, there are sick people, there are women with skirts of the campo, that come, and the treatment should be equal, because all humans are equal.

When I asked Graciela her opinion on how discrimination may be changing, if at all, she responded, "It is improving a little." I then asked why she thought it was improving.

> Why is it improving? I do not know how to explain it. Maybe some have compassion for poor people, the rich people that have money. I cannot explain it. Yes, but we are thankful that people with money are starting to change a little, that want to be good. Those with money that believe, a few understand.

Graciela believed that perhaps now people are starting to understand what had happened in the 1980s and therefore have greater compassion for the victims of the violence, whereas before people were acutely discriminatory of all campesinos. Nevertheless, Graciela continued to face discrimination at public institutions, namely due to her illiteracy.

> More than anything, when I take my kids to the school or to the hospital, they ask me, "When did you give birth to your baby?" I do not know. "How do you not know, woman?" they say to me. Therefore, I cannot. I do not know. I cannot respond. I do not know. "How do you not know?" they say, and I feel bad. I cannot respond.

Graciela explained that there were no calendars in Oronccoy or in the various places she lived in the jungle when she gave birth to her children. "I cannot. I cannot read and I cannot record it in my mind."[6]

There is not merely individual discrimination but also institutional discrimination in Peru, according to Alex.

> The government or Congress make a mountain of laws, but there are laws that are practically only for the rich, for those who have money, not for the poor. Yes, there are the same things that continue, the same *atropellas* [knock down, run over, abuse], and the same form of slavery of the children. How many children live in the streets cleaning shoes, shining, selling? However, who protects? Of whom are they? There are authorities. In Peru, there is money, but it is only for the rich. The poor continue to be poor. Like I told you, there are laws, but the laws are no value for the poor, only for the rich. There is a mountain of children, more than anything in the capital of Lima. There are children that sleep in the streets, that take drugs, live their destiny sleeping below the bridges, sleeping in old cars. They do not have roofs and they do not have anything to eat. There are children that suffer from being drugged. Many things. There is a law that says there is a lawyer for the children, but for the people nothing changes with all of this suffering for the children or for the human rights that they say they make laws. There are laws, but they serve no one.

In line with Graciela and Alex, according to Rubio-Marín, Bailey, and Guillerot (2011), due to the conservative oligarchy that dominates the Peruvian military, press, and business sectors, "Peruvian society still expresses little empathy for victims of the conflict—who are Quechua-speaking or speakers of other native languages, illiterate, rural, too often still portrayed as 'terrorists'" (34). As Graciela continued to seek stability and faced discrimination as a depeasantized survivor of the war, she (along with countless others) also struggled to access due reparations.

Truth, Reconciliation, and Reparations

Even though 75 percent of those who testified at public hearings were Quechua-speaking victims, the CVR argued that the civil war did not qualify as an ethnic conflict because the parties involved (insurgents and the state) did not identify themselves ethnically but rather politically (Lambright 2015, 9).[7] An exception to the CVR's claim that the civil war was not an ethnic conflict was its acknowledgment that Sendero included the physical and cultural disappearance of part of Amazonian peoples, "pointing to the possibility that *Sendero Luminoso* was responsible for a crime of genocide against the Asháninka people" (Rubio-Marín, Bailey, and Guillerot 2011, 25). About ten thousand of the fifty-five thousand Asháninkas were forcibly displaced, six thousand died, and about five thousand were held captive by Sendero Luminoso. Additionally, thirty to forty Asháninka communities disappeared (CVR 2003, 5:241). Even though the commissioners did not define the overall war as an ethnic conflict, they did address the profile of the vast majority of the victims, stating, "It is not surprising that this Peruvian rural, Andean, jungle-dwelling, Quechua and Asháninka, peasant, poor and uneducated was left to bleed for years without the rest of the country feeling or assuming as its own the true extent of the tragedy being endured by that 'alien people within Peru'" (CVR 2003, 1:163). In effect, the war unveiled deep-seated racism and scornful attitudes that persist in Peruvian society. As the CVR concluded, "two decades of destruction and death would not have been possible without a deep disdain that both members of PCP-Shining Path and agents of the state displayed towards the most dispossessed population of the country, that disdain that is interwoven in every moment of the daily life of Peruvians" (CVR 2003, preface, 12–13).[8]

Given that most victims were poor peasants, the report called for reparations and encouraged a national reconciliation and acknowledgment of Peru's multiethnic and multilingual population.[9] In 2004, the government formed a high-level commission to follow up on the CVR's recommendations for peace, reparations, and national reconciliation, and in July of 2005, Congress passed reparations legislation (United States Institute of Peace 2001). The Plan Integral de Reparaciones (Comprehensive Plan for Reparations) was designed to help victims of the conflict regain their personal dignity, tranquility, and security, as well as their self-respect and physical and mental well-being, with a focus on symbolic, health, education, citizenship, and financial reparations. The plan also outlined institutional reforms regarding state presence, security forces, administration of justice, and the education system (Amnesty International 2004). While clearly articulated, the ability of the Peruvian state to enact the reparations and reforms has been limited.

Remote Reparations

The CVR addressed not only the violence during the war but also the historic marginalization of peasant and Indigenous communities who were most affected by the conflict and continued to suffer its consequences (Correa 2013). The CVR recommended reparations to bring reconciliation to the country and address deep-seated inequality in Peru, thereby providing redress for crimes suffered individually, as well as equalizing disparities regarding economic, cultural, and social rights and citizenship to historically marginalized populations. In a commitment to establish human rights as a core principle guiding state activity, the government also approved a National Human Rights Plan. Nevertheless, ironically, yet not surprisingly, due to their marginalization, peasant and Indigenous communities face the greatest challenges in accessing reparations designed to equalize their long-standing exclusion.

In early 2004, the Toledo administration partially implemented the Plan Integral de Reparaciones (PIR, Comprehensive Reparations Plan) that the CVR had recommended. To implement such visions, the Toledo administration established a Comisión Multisectorial de Alto Nivel (CMAN, High-Level Multisector Commission) to follow up on state action and policies for peace, collective reparations, and national reconciliation (Correa 2013). Within the first few years, the ability of CMAN to effectively design, coordinate, and supervise implementation of reparations policy was limited due to inadequate funding and no clear long-term funding strategy. The government approved a more complete version of the PIR in 2005 and detailed an executive decree that the government implemented in 2006. The plan identified various programs, including restitution of civil rights, education, health care, collective reparations, symbolic reparations, promotion, and access to housing, and economic reparations of compensation.[10]

During this time, the government enacted a registry program for displaced persons and the disappeared.[11] The plan defined *beneficiaries* to include "victims of displacement, arbitrary imprisonment, torture, rape, and kidnapping, as well as members of the military, the police, and self-defense committees injured as a result of the conflict" (Correa 2013, 6).[12] Certain relatives of the killed and disappeared were also eligible as indirect victims (e.g., children born of rape, children conscripted by self-defense committees, those unjustly indicted under terrorism charges, and those who became undocumented because of the conflict). The state's definition of *victim* specifically excluded subversives, thereby contradicting the United Nation's definition of *victim* (Guillerot 2008, 12, 26) and challenging the assumption of human rights as inalienable (Correa 2013). The negative public view of anyone associated with the Sendero Luminoso or the MRTA reinforced political pressure to not "register terrorists," and the government passed a law in 2013 expanding the definition of *victim* to exclude "those charged with having committed crimes of terrorism or terrorism apology" (7).

The government created the National Council for Reparations to build a unified registry of all categories divided into individual and collective beneficiaries (e.g., peasant and Indigenous communities, organized groups of displaced people). To register individual victims, the Reparations Council reviewed and validated previous registries and conducted fieldwork to access not yet registered victims.[13] The Reparations Council provided opportunities for community leaders or witnesses to give public testimony, and individuals could also travel to one of the main CMAN offices to give their personal testimony. Prior to a finalization of the victims' registry, the government assessed collective reparations based on the Peace Censuses (preliminary registries of affected communities collected by MIMDES). Collective reparations acknowledged how the unrest compromised or broke communal ties by sowing distrust within and between communities, as well as with the state. The collective reparations program focused primarily on small infrastructural projects with investments of up to 100,000 soles (approximately US$37,000) per community.[14]

Giving Testimony

Graciela described the process of giving one's testimony to be a registered victim of the war. "[People come] from each pueblo. Like I am going to give my manifestation, right? To say who were killed by militaries, people, for example, from Mollebamba, [to say] there were people that raped me, they continue to live. So, with these words they are trying to reconcile what happened." Graciela said years ago people from other countries came to Peru to take people's manifestations. "Yes, before gringos came below at the Kutinachaka [Bridge]. We were giving our declarations like testifying our manifestation, as I am giving this. It was equal and they were crying." Graciela described how emotional the foreigners became listening to individuals' testimonies. "They were crying. So many tears were falling off their elbows. Like four had come." Graciela demonstrated tears streaming down their faces, along their arms, falling off their elbows. Graciela's daughter Sumac Killa chimed in, "I think it was an international organization. They were supporting the reparations. I believe it was an NGO or something. They had come to give their support." Sumac Killa said that most individuals from Oronccoy had given their manifestation, yet Graciela had not. "The great majority have done it. My mom is the only one that has not, I think." Graciela explained that she had not yet given her manifestation because when people came to take them, she was afraid. "But in these dates, I had shame to tell, fear. For this I did not tell . . . I was very weak, I think."[15]

Outside of fear or shame, a lack of trust, suspicion, and opposition to giving one's testimony also prevailed in war-torn regions. According to Caroline Yezer (2008), rural villages in Ayacucho hardest hit by the violence were used to being *engañados* (tricked and betrayed) by the state and rebels, making them suspicious of members of the truth and reconciliation commission (275). The close-ended neutral survey questions used by the commission investigators did not allow villagers to relay their full side of the story and further raised suspicions. Moreover, villagers often did not see the point of laboring through the painful memory work of a past they already knew for the benefit of *ciudadrunakuna* (city folk) and national healing, which they understood as another example of extracting rural labor for the benefit of others (Yezer 2008, 280). In addition, due to the lack of clear division between perpetrator and victim with continually shifting alliances within and between communities, along with the explicit exclusion of any member of subversive organizations in the victim registry, people were relegated to adopt the role of passive and innocent victim during the war, distancing themselves from any sympathy with Sendero or political engagement of the past (Theidon 2010). Given that the government had not yet registered Graciela, there are likely countless other unaccounted-for victims throughout Peru.

Registered victims are eligible for economic reparations or compensation; however, defining the amounts and modalities for payment is difficult due to various notions of restoration and reparation and then implementing them on such a massive scale, resulting in serious gaps in payment.[16] Graciela's brother Alex claimed although he was a registered victim, he had not received reparations.

> Yes, I went to the human rights office, how do you say, to give my manifesta-
> tion, my declaration, but they have not given me any reparation from the
> state, but other people received their reparation. A small incentive like one
> thousand soles, two thousand soles I believe, but in my case no, only a certifi-
> cate that this happened, the violence, nothing more. However, other people
> of my time who are orphans who lived during this violence have received it.

Alex believed that the inequality in receiving reparations was due to changing political whims. "More than anything, nothing happens, because this happened in the time of the government of Alan García, but nothing happens for reparation for the rest, but the rest simply receive nothing. But others get nothing, not even ten cents." Various scholars I met in Ayacucho similarly discussed how dedication to the reparations has waned with subsequent administrations following that of Alberto Fujimori and Alan García. In fact, the Humala administration made explicit efforts to decrease financial commitment to reparations.[17] According to Gisela Ortiz, head of a group of family members of victims of the 1992 La Cantuta massacre, "There isn't any real political will to tackle this problem that should have been resolved years ago" (Chanduví Jaña 2015, 3).

A lack of government priority is evident in continued limited resources allocated toward reparations. The five regional reparations offices in Peru have limited staff and service incredibly expansive geographic regions. For example, according to Peruvian American political scientist Adriana, in 2018 there were a total of thirty-eight workers nationwide in CMAN charged with implementing reparations for tens of thousands of victims (Adriana, pers. comm., August 12, 2018). Adriana asserted that there were committed individuals working in reparations, however, given the limited offices and personnel, victims faced immense challenges in accessing them. For instance, by the end of 2013, 1,946 communities were projected to benefit (Correo 2013), while 5,609 of an estimated 9,000 communities had been registered in the Unified Registry of Victims (Rubio-Marín, Bailey, and Guillerot 2011, 33). Moreover, within its thirteen years of existence CMAN has changed its state apparatus and location four times, and the resulting institutional weaknesses have hampered the execution of many of its decisions (Guillerot 2019). A Peruvian anthropologist, Fidel, claimed that even with such gross gaps in community reparations, even more requests for individual reparations go unaddressed. As a registered victim of the violence, Fidel stated, "the state has made a promise to families from the work of the Truth Commission, this is a promise, but this is not assumed by the state. They do not want, they do not value." He said that people have waited years to receive financial and other reparations and have since died.[18] According to Cristián Correa (2013), although the PIR passed in 2005, changes in policy and competing narratives have caused delays of over twenty years, underscoring the government's low priority of Indigenous peoples.

In addition to a lack of commitment on the part of the Peruvian state, Alex and Graciela expressed frustration that reparations were not equally distributed due to the country's entrenched power dynamics. Alex claimed that with the Repentance Law, "leaders of terrorism, they could present themselves to bases or commissions to surrender and have less fault—be forgiven—less at fault." Once absolved of guilt, those political leaders who initially fostered violence received reparations, while campesinos continued to receive nothing.

> They came from [afar] to organize the left, the terrorism. They can receive reparations even until now, but us the people, the innocent people that are illiterate, until now we are not receiving reparations. It was worse for us. We were tortured, and with all forces, we were taken. Our land was exploited, totally until now from the year 1980, what happened until the year 1990, when the government of Fujimori made this law of repentance, until then there is reparation, but in our cases, there is nothing. I think there is money, but they do not want to give anything. They took information, they took statements, but until now, there are no reparations from the Peruvian

state, as I told you. The people for human rights came saying there was reconciliation and wrote this in actas [record-keeping books]. They all took our statements, but until now there is no support for the same place, for the same site, that we are very far, we are forgotten. Nothing to make of our reparations. Nothing, no form of reparation normally or personally.

The Repentance Law (Ley de Arrepentimiento) that Alex mentioned did in fact help detain and imprison people who had been unjustly accused of being a part of armed opposition groups. Under the Repentance Law, members of armed opposition groups who provided information leading to the capture of other members were granted benefits such as reduced sentences. This led to people making false allegations against others, and even though the 1993 Repentance Law Regulations (Reglamento de la Ley de Arrepentimiento) required police to verify the applicants' information, they rarely did, which led to further unsubstantiated arrests (Amnesty International 2004). Graciela contributed the unequal distribution or lack of reparations to overall corruption.

There is support, but the authorities are thieves, grabbing and not sharing. More than anything, the authorities fill their pockets with the money. They do not give it. They rob so much money. . . . More than anything [it is] people from Ayacucho. The workers that are paid forty soles, thirty soles are conforming [following the rules], but the others put the money in their pockets. Much corruption!

In fact, the implementation of the individual economic reparations program has been severely criticized. Only direct victims receive 100 percent of allocated funds, which was set at 10,000 soles (about $3,300 USD). For other cases (death or disappearance of the victim) the amount is divided among the entire family, which results in negligible amounts. This is particularly problematic considering members of self-defense committees have received 39,000 soles (about $9,685 USD), and some officials and public servants have obtained up to $30,000 USD (Guillerot 2019, 35). Adding to, or perhaps because of, ensconced unequal power dynamics, Graciela expressed her belief that she and other campesinos lacked the capacity to fight for their rights to receive reparations. "For the authorities when we are from far, we do not have a lot of vocabulary, the government rejects us. There is no one that can speak well that can demand from the government also." Graciela continued to describe feelings of incapability when journalists came to Oronccoy from the city of Ayacucho and asked her and others to speak on the radio about their experiences during the war. "In Oronccoy, when I still lived in Oronccoy, a team came from Ayacucho. They wanted to communicate with Ayacucho. . . . I could not do it." Graciela said no one would talk with the journalists, and when I asked if they did not want to, she replied, "It is not that we did not want to. There is not much capacity for this. For this no one did it."[19] Graciela's fear of giving her personal manifestation and perceived inability to speak to outsiders about the war underscore power engendered in language practices. As Ashley Greenwood states, the scarcity of highly developed literacy, language fluency, and translatability of language ideologies limits the ability of marginalized individuals and groups to access reconciliation, compensation, and inclusion, as well as to justify their own authenticity (Greenwood 2019, 751).

In addition to feeling incapable due to limited communication skills, Alex believed they were at a disadvantage in advocating for themselves given their geographic isolation. He described how people from pueblos closer to the cities had received reparations. "More than anything, for the same communication, for the same day, because they are close to the road. They can travel quickly to Lima to communicate, but in contrast, we must walk on foot two days. There is no way to communicate, there is no road." Graciela agreed with Alex: "They do not complete these promises. For example, there is a government organization that is supposed to help us victims of the violence, us poor, to help us construct our house, but there is nothing. In other [less isolated] places they are making [houses], but for us there is nothing." Moreover, each reparation entailed stipulations that impeded their delivery. For example, Peruvian anthropologist Fidel claimed that he was denied help with housing:

It does not happen. It is a fraud. I went to get help, for example, with housing for a free roof that the state said I could have as a victim, so I went, and they said I had to have my own land to build a house. I had to have public register of the land [akin to a deed], and many people do not have this. They do not have their own land that is registered, so then what can they do? (Fidel, pers. comm., August 11, 2018)

As evidenced with Fidel, it can be challenging for someone with a university education living in an urban area to secure reparations, yet alone someone living in an isolated community with few resources. In fact, the PIR did not define a housing policy for victims and "little has been done to compensate victims beyond the benefits provided to families of police and armed forces personnel killed during the conflict" (Correa 2013, 25; see also Zapata and Scott-Insúa 2019). As Alex said, "Only in our case there is not reparation, only there are promises, promises. For many it is just your name but no reparations. At times you need a lawyer, but you need money to secure [one]." Further reinforcing Alex's claims, Cristián Correa (2013) argues that securing civil rights and documentation, which assists individuals whose registries were destroyed, "is not sufficiently accessible to victims, especially those living in rural areas" and "obtaining a judicial declaration can be a complex process requiring a lawyer" (21). Not having personal registry or civil documentation is a critical matter for communities affected by the war, as Sendero Luminoso destroyed and burned civil registries in its battle against the state. Peruvian anthropologist Raul also described a lack of follow through with the reparations, particularly regarding those from the campo:

> So, there are recommendations of the truth commission to make changes, but this is on paper. I do not know how they are realizing these concretely. For example, rural education, education for peace, educational rights of city people, gender equality, they do not take seriously. It is on paper, but there are no concrete changes, so the inequality continues. There are some programs in the city, but they do not think of the campo. The campo is excluded. (Raul, pers. comm., August 10, 2018)

With a lack of long-standing dedication on the part of the government, limited allocated resources, and continued physical, economic, social, and political marginalization of rural communities, promised reparations to close gaps in inequality remained largely out of reach for the most marginalized and negatively affected by the war.

Search for Human Remains and Memory

An objective of the symbolic reparations program entailed "restoration of the social bond broken by the process of violence, between the State and the people and between the people themselves" (Guillerot 2019, 41), which has largely taken the form of memorial spaces and museums. More recently, an important component of the symbolic reparations policy has included the search for and identification of victims of enforced disappearances, as well as the facilitation of coffins, funeral rites, plaques, and public recognition (Guillerot 2019).[20] Graciela described how the government sought to exhume, identify, and reconnect human remains with surviving family members: "They are looking for the cadavers. To know how many families were lost, all of this . . . They carried those [human remains] from Oronccoy to Ayacucho. For sure, the government is giving money to take out DNA [to say] for sure this is your family or no, to know. Others know their family from Ayacucho from their cadavers. From this they are taking out DNA." According to Graciela and her son Hermenegildo, once the government retrieved the remains, they brought them to Ayacucho for DNA analysis and then sought to reunite them with living family members. While the government supported identification of loved ones through DNA analysis, a nongovernmental organization (the International Commission of the Red Cross) assisted individuals in claiming and reburying the remains of their loved ones. Yet according to Graciela's son Hermenegildo, the nongovernmental organization claimed they did not have financial resources to support this process.

> It is possible that the government gave the money to the NGO to return the cadavers free to Oronccoy, but the NGO says that they do not have funds for this; each family has to return their family's cadavers with their own money. Therefore, if there are people without their own money, they cannot return them.

Graciela and her family members argued that even with the collaboration of various government and nongovernment agencies, a gap existed in covering all costs associated with the return of human remains, making it unattainable for many to reclaim and rebury their loved ones. Moreover, Graciela believed much more work needed to be done to recover those lost during the war. When I mentioned that the CVR claimed roughly seventy thousand people died in the violence, Graciela shook her head side to side and responded, "Many, many more."

Undoubtedly, there is still much to uncover regarding human remains and lives lost during the war. For example, since 2002, out of 3,202 recovered bodies, 1,833 have been identified and 1,704 have been returned to their families, out of more than a presumed 16,000 buried in more than 4,500 common graves (Chanduví Jaña 2015). In Oronccoy alone, forensic scientists found five common graves with sixty people believed to have been killed in 1985 by Los Sinchis. A Peruvian anthropologist, Luis, served as a coordinator for the Comisión de la Verdad y Reconciliación for this region. He discussed the population loss in Chungui, claiming at least two thousand household heads died during the violence, probably more. As part of their investigation, they exhumed three hundred mass graves, many of which they had not yet excavated. In 2013, the biggest exhumation to date was taking place in Chungui. As described by Rodrigo Abd (2013), at least 1,384 out of a total population of 6,000 were killed in Chungui, and this is where "the worst of its carnage occurred in these hills between the Andes ridge and Amazon jungle." A fifty-two-year-old survivor, Teresa Vilchez, told reporters that rebels killed her husband and raped her mother and cut off her breasts and that she herself still suffers occasional vaginal bleeding from a gang rape by soldiers in 1984 at the Mollebamba barracks. Thirty years later, the government has not arrested or prosecuted one individual for crimes committed in Chungui (Abd 2013). Another factor complicating the assessment of lives lost during the war is the fact that so many of the Peruvians who were killed during the war were not "integrated" into the nation without birth certificates or identity cards. Journalist Mirko Lauer notes that with the discovery of tens of thousands of victims, "these Peruvians did not exist for the nation long before they ceased to exist in reality" (cited in Milton 2018, 8). Ironically, they only became citizens of Peru upon recognition of their death.

For Graciela and her family, identification of human remains was particularly important for the younger generations to recognize and remember the atrocities of the past to prevent their repetition in the future. Alex described how younger generations do not have similar memories yet must understand the past to avoid repetition of its dark history:

> Some are surviving, and this is the new generation. Now the kids do not know this violence, they have not seen it. In my case it is I, my sister, almost all of us saw this, but my children or those other kids do not know. They have not seen this. . . . It is important that they know what happened in Peru, the external war that was done for what. It is important that they know these problems, this violence, to not repeat it because they are our future. . . . At times, most of the young people in Peru do not know a lot

because they did not suffer as we suffered. They do not value what happened to us.

Graciela described a level of detachment among the younger generation. "Yes, at times they believe us when we cry and they tell us not to cry, but they do not feel anything, nothing." Graciela's memories of the war shaped how she experienced violence in the media as opposed to the younger generations: "Much, much happened. For this, I do not like to watch the movies. I do not like when they fight with guns, this I do not like. It is very bad. However, for those who did not experience the violence, they are normal in watching it. When there is blood from fighting too in the movies, I am afraid." Graciela discussed the importance of seeing in believing among the detached youth and credited Sumac Killa's belief in Graciela's stories to seeing exhumed human remains. In a community near Oronccoy, "There they killed people and they have found their remains." At this point Alex added, "Their craniums." Graciela continued, "In complete. They have found people. For [seeing] all this, Sumac Killa believes me. Her father tells her what happened to her uncles, and she believes a little." In 2019, more physical proof of the loss of life was brought to Oronccoy with the return of sixty-four individuals who had disappeared from Oronccoy in 1985. Of the sixty-four people who had disappeared, twenty were identified by family members, and the remaining forty-four unidentified bodies were given codes to continue identification work. The International Committee of the Red Cross supported the construction of eighty niches for proper burial, and the community performed a ritual wake to honor the return of their loved ones.[21]

For Graciela, the identification of human remains was important for people from other countries to understand what had happened in Peru and to prevent similar events from unfolding across the globe. In fact, Graciela felt a particular sense of kinship with those experiencing violence in other parts of the world that she heard about through the radio.

When I hear the news [stories], how the people are suffering in these zones, and people are crying from hunger, and children are crying with hunger, I feel this pain. Very sad. . . . For this, I think between brothers, why do they kill us? Why? I ask. Why does this happen in other countries too? If you believe in the word of God, at times I think, why did they kill us? Between us, between brothers, for what I say. It is difficult to comprehend. Until now, it continues from the jungle in other places and other countries also. . . . For them we say, "We want peace, and we are shedding tears for you."

Graciela's brother Alex recognized shared experiences with others throughout the world as well. "The people [in Peru] lived how other people in other countries are living now. We say like in Iraq there is total violence in Iraq and the children will grow up with a psychological trauma and physical pain." Graciela and Alex felt compassion for others at war and believed exhumations were a necessary warning of what to avoid to future generations in Peru and abroad.

While Graciela and Alex argued for the value of locating human remains in shaping memory as well as the future, Juan Pablo described the complexities of memory. Juan Pablo argued that some people suffer because they cannot forget lost loved ones and others agonize over their inability to remember cherished individuals who perished during the war. "For this dirty politics, they lost their mothers, their fathers, their brothers, their houses. At times, they suffer. They cannot forget how their pueblo was before. Like me, I am thinking, maybe it is better to forget I say. *Así pues.*" It is difficult to translate the simple term *así pues* with which Juan Pablo ended many of his explanations. Literally, it means "therefore, hence, or thereupon," but in practice, it is often spoken as an expression of defeat as well as passive agreement. In English, perhaps a more suitable equivalent would be "therefore, that is just how it is" or "it is what it is." In Juan Pablo ending many of his statements with "así pues," he conveyed a sort of relinquishing of his past, which perhaps also demonstrated a struggle with how to engage with his own memories as he recognized the dangers of forgetting yet found little utility or solace in remembering.

Juan Pablo's internal conflict reflects a dichotomy between reconciliation efforts focused on remembering and justice versus the Andean cosmovision of to forgive is to forget (Alayza and Crisóstomo 2007). In Andean cultural representations, reconciliation refers to forgiveness or *pampachanakuy*, which refers to burying something in the Pampas, evoking the concept of letting the past go. This concept of forgiveness and reconciliation can work to ensure coexistence (Jara, Tejada, and Tovar 2007), particularly in regions in which opposing sides were not clearly delineated and were constantly shifting.[22] In a similar vein, José Carlos Agüero (2021) argues, "Ultimately the use and abuse of memory is something that has no clear limits but rather, perhaps, only moments and needs" (37). As illustrated through Graciela and her family members' reflections, she and other survivors struggle daily with what to remember and what to bury in order to continue forward.

Lost Opportunities and Future Generations

In addition to reconciling the past, the state also created reparations to provide future opportunities for war survivors, which proved challenging with entrenched systematic inequality. With the displacement of hundreds of thousands of Peruvians, an entire generation lost the opportunity to obtain an education. According to Juan Pablo, "Without this violence maybe Graciela would have studied. In our pueblo, there was a secondary school; however, it was all destroyed. So many young people could not go to school and now have sacrificed their future." Juan Pablo described others displaced to Andahuaylas whose futures were sabotaged by the violence: "My neighbors now below are also from the pueblo. They do not have education, nothing. Younger people do not have education and suffer. They do daily work for a tiny sum. We cannot benefit from a profession. With how many sacrifices do we make to eat? We have forgotten how to study."

When discussing the future, Graciela repeatedly focused on the importance of their children acquiring an education. "I want that they study. I only think about this. I do not want them to be like me. I do not know how to read. I do not want this for my children. I want them to learn how to read so they can be professionals." Juan Pablo supported Graciela's sentiment of wanting a different life for their children than what he had led. "Therefore, they do not suffer like us. Yes, for this, we think and is our worry. That they study to make a tomorrow like other people so they can have the path that they want." Graciela then continued: "This is what I tell my children, that they can become a professional. 'When I am old and I am walking with my cane, who will give me ten cents? Who will take care of me when I am old?' I say." As Carlos Iván Degregori (1991) argues, Peruvians have understood education as vital to social, political, and economic advancement and modernization since the middle of the twentieth century. Peru did not provide state-funded schools in the Andes until nearly a century and a half after independence from Spain. Calls for education by rural highlanders have been linked to demands for land and citizenship, yet there has been a historic reluctance to franchise Indigenous peoples through education, beyond becoming barely literate agricultural workers and soldiers (Oliart 2019). Consequently, low quality of education and limited accessibility, as well as mestizo models of knowledge that reinforce hegemonic values, along with entrenched structural hierarchies, offer little opportunity for poor people to experience social mobility (see García 2005; Oliart 2003 and 2010; Van Vleet 2019; Yon 2014). Such barriers to social mobilization are particularly acute for war survivors from Ayacucho.

For Graciela and Juan Pablo, a university education would guarantee that their children would become "professionals." When pressed about what a professional represents, Graciela and Juan Pablo stated it is someone who does not suffer like them working the land and "does not work just to eat." I had heard others refer to a professional as someone who earns a salary, not working in the informal sector. With professionalism as their goal, Graciela expressed some sorrow that none of her children had yet entered the university or obtained a steady position.

> Always in my heart, there is a little pain. Until now, none of my children are professionals. None of them. For this, I feel sad. . . . I miss. I have this missing in my heart. So much suffering has passed from all the violence. All the terror that has passed, but even with all of these problems, I have my children. However, still none of them are professionals. For this, I am a little sad, but someday they will continue. Only one, to be a professional. This would make me happy. This would make me happier from now.

As of 2018, all but Graciela's youngest child, Nayely, and her older son, Augosto, had graduated from secondary school, yet none of her children had entered the university. Public universities are essentially free in Peru. The challenge for students is to pass the exam to enter university and to cover living expenses in costly cities.

Educational Reparations

The Reparations Plan included an education program designed specifically to redress the interruption of educational opportunities for war victims and their children.[23] The program included adult education and literacy programs; access to primary education and vocational training; waivers for tuition, certificate, and exam fees; student meal and housing stipends; and a full scholarship program covering tuition, transportation, food, and books for technical and university studies (with regional quotas for students from affected areas) (Correa 2013, 7). The eligibility of beneficiaries had shifted with various administrations, with the García administration excluding children of all categories of victims except for victims of killings, enforced disappearance, forced recruitment, or rape, which was later overturned.[24] As part of the reconciliation process, registered victims of the war, or one of their children, could access a scholarship to help cover costs to attend university, which was limited to a number of beneficiaries per province and to programs at public institutions.

When we were discussing the victim registry, Graciela climbed the ladder to her second floor and returned with a piece of paper in a plastic cover that represented Juan Pablo's official victim status. Sumac Killa explained that Juan Pablo received a scholarship as a victim of the violence:

Therefore, they also gave my dad a scholarship when he got his reparations. They gave him the scholarship, and if you do not want to study, you can give the scholarship to one of your children, only one. Just one you can give this scholarship. Give to me, or Hermenegildo, or Nayely. One of them, whichever. But just one. This is for him, but if he does not want to study, it will be given to Nayely or me, whoever wants to study.

According to Sumac Killa, regardless of the scholarship, students from the campo do not have the training or attention necessary to succeed at the university: "Sometimes some do not have the attention in the campo that you need to study in the city. . . . They take one course and leave. They do not finish the course." In other cases, students dropped out for personal reasons, which happened to Graciela's neighbor in Pochocota.

She entered with a scholarship in Lima. She studied there for three months with the scholarship, then she returned for a lover, and so they do not have trust. What anger! She is now with baby, so her mother is crying. Without studying, she returned from Lima. Her mother said, "This is free. You need to study. The government is paying for this. What are you doing, my daughter?" She returned for this young boy and now she has this baby also, and this young man is behaving badly. For this, her mother said, "For this you returned! You should have studied!" Yelling, her mother says this. At times, she cries.

Graciela and Sumac Killa said that once a student drops out of college, their family loses the opportunity to use the scholarship.

Graciela explained that professionals often visit rural communities promoting the scholarship, but they fail to realize the challenges that campesinos face in even entering the university.

> But, Nicole, they come from Lima, the engineers, the doctors, giving this paper that they are explaining, that there is an ease for our children to enter with this scholarship, to study, but most of us from the Oreja . . . only how many, three people, are studying with this scholarship. Why, Nicole? For us, almost us, how do I tell you . . . For us, it is not easy. Because? Because more than anything they are entering with this scholarship people, important people that have money, their children are studying in the best universities, but for us we cannot get in, because we cannot pay.

In discussing students not being able to pay, Graciela was referencing not only the costs associated with attending university but also the preparation and investment necessary to pass the entrance exam.

It is common for middle- and upper-class urban families to pay for tutors or special courses in preparation for the university entrance exam. Friends of mine in Andahuaylas, for example, paid approximately one hundred soles a month for a nine-month course merely to help their son pass the entrance exam. That sort of investment is out of reach for Graciela's family due to the cost of the course and lost wages in the informal sector when in class. "Our kids are not entering the university. How are we to enter when we are selling things on the street? When we are working to survive, when we do not have money?"

According to Peruvian anthropologist Raul, barriers to college entry also exist due to a lack of dedication on the part of universities to support this scholarship. He claimed that out of approximately six thousand students entering La Universidad Nacional de San Cristóbal de Huamanga, only about three to five students enter on the reparations scholarship. "There is a scholarship in name, but in reality, it is nothing. Few each admission. Sometimes there are two, but two is nothing. Not many enter because the administration does not help. It depends on if the university administration helps, but it appears there is no interest by the authorities to prioritize this" (Raul, pers. comm., August 10, 2018). Reinforcing perceptions that there is limited dedication to education reparations, the Peruvian State has provided minimal guidelines to enact educational benefits for registered victims. While the education reparations program was created in 2005, CMAN did not approve guidelines on educational reparations measures until 2012, which eventually led the Ministry of Education to draft the 2016–2020 Multiannual Plan for Reparations in Education. As of 2018 only 12,082 people had been registered in the Special Registry of Beneficiaries of Reparations in Education, yet universities and institutions continue to operate within their own criteria and autonomy regarding admissions (Guillerot 2019, 39).

Graciela's son Hermenegildo could not pass the university entrance exam, so he chose to study in a local institute. "Hermenegildo took the exam but missed the points. He said, 'What can I do? I do not want to waste time. Now I am studying in an institute.' For this, he works on Saturdays and Sundays for twenty soles [US$3.00]. His professor pays him twenty soles when he helps in the hotel." Hermenegildo cleaned a hotel that his previous teacher owned and another individual's house on the weekends, changing sheets, mopping the floors, cleaning the rooms, and performing other duties as needed to help pay for his school fees at an institute in Andahuaylas, El Instituto de Educación Superior Tecnológico Privado La Pontificia (the Private Technical Institute of Higher Education–Pontificia). Because Pontificia is a private institute, it costs money. "It is not free. We pay every month. For this tomorrow, I must go to sell my sugarcane to pay. Each month we pay 150 or 180 soles [US$45.00 to $54.00]. First, we paid 150 soles and now it is 180 soles. . . . Each person."[25]

Sumac Killa was also attending Pontificia, as she was unable to pass the entrance exam to study at a university. When not in class, she helped her mother with the sugarcane cart or cared for her son, Kennedy.[26] Rous also took the exam to go to university but could not pass it. "When she could not do it here, she was crying, 'How could I not do it?' she was saying. My Rous was crying. So, my sister lent me money, so for this we went to Abancay to take the exam for the university." Graciela took Rous to the city of Abancay to retake the test, but she failed to pass it once again. Graciela did not understand why her children could not pass the exam.

At times, our children do not learn a lot. I do not know how to say. Lack of money, lack of nutrition, and it is far to study in the university in Lima, Cusco. . . . [Rous] did not have the grades [scores needed to pass the exam], so she was here and saying, "What can I do? I studied for this. I studied for ten years primary and secondary school and I have not learned. What can I do?" I was praying for her and she was crying.

From her research in rural Cajamarca, Tara Patricia Cookson describes the persistent staff shortages, poor quality of instruction and inadequate infrastructure common in rural schools in Peru. Due to teacher shortages, students spent up to three hours of the five-hour school day without classes (Cookson 2016, 1,194). Without resources for an initial investment to enter university, and likely poor preparation to effectively pass the entrance exam due to neglected rural schools, impoverished rural families faced further financial strain to acquire an inferior education that would ultimately yield a lower-paying job, thereby perpetuating the economic divide.

Rous ended up moving to the lowland city of Kimbiri to help her sister Eufemilia sell plantain chips and study civil engineering at a private institute. While visiting Graciela in 2014, I learned that her daughter Eufemilia had given birth to a son and had temporarily stopped her studies, which concerned Graciela greatly. In 2018, Eufemilia had returned to school and her partner was helping her manage her extended obligations. Graciela's son Augosto was also living in the same jungle city as Eufemilia and Rous. He was not married, had one three-year-old son, and continued to work construction jobs.

Graciela expressed how she maintained hope that her youngest child, Nayely, still in secondary school, would be her one child to attend university. "I tell my children that one of them, Nayely for sure; she will be able to enter." During our discussion, Nayely walked into the room and Graciela continued to describe how she was their last hope. "I hope that she does not fail me." Nayely had a solemn expression on her face, as if she was feeling the weight of her family's expectations. She just nodded shyly and walked up the ladder to the second floor of the house. Graciela then stressed, "It is not for me, it is for them. So many sacrifices they have made to study. It is for them; it is not for their mom." While Graciela longed for a brighter future for her children, she also worried about potential developments in her beloved Oronccoy.

An Unknown Future of the Forgotten "Red" Zone

Although Peru experienced immense economic growth after the war, large swaths of the population have not experienced financial improvements. Between

2002 and 2013, Peru had one of the fastest growing gross domestic products in Latin America at 6.1 percent growth rate, yet the Amazonian regions and rural highland communities such as Oronccoy continued to struggle with poverty.[27] For instance, as of 2017, in the Peruvian highlands 66.7 percent of the population lived in extreme poverty, as compared to 12.2 percent that lived on the coast. Those who spoke an Indigenous language (Quechua, Aymara, or Amazonian languages) had double the poverty rate as those who spoke Spanish as their first language: 33 percent versus 18.6 percent (Instituto Nacional de Estadistica e Informatica 2018).

Following the war, the Oreja de Perro continues to represent the most impoverished region in one of the most economically depressed departments in Peru, making it particularly susceptible to neglect and exploitation. Much of its neglect is due to its geographic isolation. It is easier to travel to Andahuaylas from Oronccoy, which still takes multiple days, than to the capital of its own department, the city of Ayacucho. Yet Andahuaylas does not have jurisdiction over the Oreja de Perro region, so it does not offer support or resources. Graciela argued that they are also continually associated with terrorism:

> Until now, they say in my pueblo, a red zone, an emergency zone, they say of us, but we are not like that. . . . They thought we are [terrorists]. However, we are peaceful, we do not think of that. Still, they do not understand. In their imagination, we are terrorists, but we are not terrorists. Liars. It was complicated. . . . Where did the terrorists go?

A "red zone" (*zona roja*) is an area deemed to be dangerous due to kidnappings, theft, the growing drug trade, and other crimes. The expansion of the cocaine drug complex in Peru, including agriculture (coca growing), manufacture (cocaine production), trading (narco trafficking), and banking (money laundering) began in the 1960s, grew in the 1980s, and has continued to expand as the success of Plan Colombia, a US military initiative to tackle Colombia's drug cartels, effectively pushed cocaine from Colombia into Peru and Bolivia (Crabtree and Durand 2017). Approximately 70 percent of Peru's cocaine is produced in the region called VRAEM, the Valle de los Ríos Apurímac, Ene, y Mantaro. The Oreja de Perro region lies in the drug corridor between VRAEM and the Department of Apurímac, and the city where three of Graciela's children live, Kimbiri, is in VRAEM. As of 2014, the VRAEM was the most important coca-producing (*cocalero*) area and had the highest production of cocaine paste in the world (Beriain 2014). This is also the area housing a holdout of the last Senderistas, and reported uprisings of Senderistas continued to haunt those from the region.[28]

> However, in the news, what is continuing to happen in the jungle that they say are Senderistas. So, we hear this on the radio and are afraid. . . . Or they are narcotraffickers? This happened about four months ago. The radio news said that in the jungle they grabbed some Senderistas and that it is continuing to be dangerous, and for this, I am afraid. . . . Until now, I feel bad, physical and mental worries. Always I have thoughts I am afraid of these problems. I think maybe at any moment they will return. I am afraid. At times when they make fireworks here, I am afraid. It scares both Juan Pablo and me. Much worry of the violence that causes pain in my stomach.

The development of youth gang activity and continual formation of rebel groups that have occurred in other Latin American countries, such as post–civil war Guatemala and El Salvador, have largely not occurred in highland Peru.[29] Nevertheless, the media continues to cite local uprisings of rebel groups with supposed links to Sendero, and violence associated with a growing drug trade in Peru has reportedly been on the rise.[30] Francisco Ferreira argues that even though this area has been notorious for drug trafficking and for housing the last remnants of Sendero, it has been unjustly demonized in the national imaginary, which serves to justify inefficient and harmful state policies while ignoring the complex reality of peoples' lives (Ferreira 2016), thereby deterring outside support from government or nongovernmental organizations.

In 2016, the Peruvian government declared Oronccoy a district seat, which should entail greater government support. Alex described the myriad unmet needs of the new district of Oronccoy, including investment in infrastructure, education, and health care. Teachers travel to Oronccoy from urban areas and Alex questioned their dedication to instructing children in Oronccoy, as well as the overall quality of education:

> The kids also study what they can with the teachers who are contracted. At

times some years, they teach three or four months and then leave. Sometimes they teach fifteen days, after twenty days, they have a rest and there is no control of anything because it is not a place that is accessible for the teachers to agree to teach there. The education is very low. It is not like in the city.

Overall, educational conditions have remained poor in Peru, with the average salary of teachers being the second lowest in all of Latin America. The situation is particularly acute in rural areas, where three-quarters of all schools lack running water, proper sewage system, or electricity and where 92 percent have no access to the internet (Crabtree and Durand 2017).

Peru has experienced some headway in expanding health-care services. The Toledo administration created a system known as the Seguro Integral de Salud that extended health-care services to rural areas. Social security hospitals, as well as national hospitals and clinics constructed by regional governments, have also expanded (Crabtree and Durand 2017). At the same time, wages for doctors and nurses remain low, and therefore service quality has not always improved, particularly in rural areas, as Alex noted in Oronccoy:[31]

Right now, we have a health center that we ourselves built, but we do not have a doctor, only a technician that works there. It is a technician that does not work as a doctor or nurse. When we are sick, we treat and cure [ourselves]. As I told you, the Peruvian state has forgotten Oronccoy. We need all these things of a new district. Each person should have their own basic sanitation like a toilet, potable water, drain system, but we do not have anything. We do not have anything in this pueblo, this district. We need a lot of support from the central government or a private institution that can help.

Feeling forgotten by the state is not unique in postwar life. In an interview with the CVR, a woman from the community of Huallhua-Belén Chapi in the Oreja de Perro pleaded that the state does not forget them: "We ask *Señor* President Alejandro Toledo to listen and support us, do not leave us, help us educate our children, help us go ahead, we have told the truth to the commission: we also ask that you do not forget about us until the moment you leave your government, that's our life" (CVR 2003, 9:33). According to Ashley Greenwood (2019), Asháninka leaders repeatedly lamented feeling forgotten by the state before and during the period of unrest and pushed for "recognition by the state for their own security" (753). Nevertheless, the Asháninka, like those in the Oreja de Perro, struggle with "conditional recognition" in which Indigenous or subaltern peoples must submit to an external definition to access rights (753). In other words, they must be distinct enough in their experience to merit attention but not so different that they are too alien to be recognized. While Oronccoy has been distinguished as a region most acutely affected by the violence, its continued association with terrorism and the drug trade has also alienated the community.

To further complicate matters, those most impacted by the violence often must co-opt identities that further cement their position within the social hierarchy. According to Nathalie Koc-Menard (2015), individuals in Chungui and Chapi have subscribed to an external definition to explain their position and discrimination in society—that of being marginal. Marginality is a condition understood as being physically isolated, hidden away, or forgotten while being simultaneously despised and subject to years of state neglect and abuse that necessitates state intervention and aid. Marginality is both a place and a relationship leveraged to garner state attention and support. Similarly, Graciela and her comuneros have appropriated an identity as marginal in calling for the state to address past transgressions and present needs, yet by identifying as marginal, rural communities are further reinforcing their inferior and dependent position in relationship to the state and society writ large, which risks fostering even more discrimination and isolation. That said, due to Oronccoy's marginal and alien status that has resulted in a lack of government recognition, limited resources, and sparse population, the community is particularly vulnerable to not only continued neglect and discrimination, but also further exploitation.

Mining Potential in Oronccoy

Peru's booming postwar economy was largely supported through expanded mining and oil concessions in the rural Andes and Amazon basin—areas with the highest rates of poverty, Indigenous populations, and political neglect—which has sparked intense social protest.[32] According to Graciela, engineers and other prospectors have come to Oronccoy seeking potential gold-mining opportunities, which the local community largely rejects: "They say there is a mine close to Oronccoy that is pure gold. They have seen it, the engineers who have come from Lima, Arequipa, from Cusco; the engineers are positioning to begin work." Graciela claimed that her paisanos in Oronccoy oppose the mine:

> Therefore, us, the community, do not want the mine to enter. It would cause a lot of contamination, and we could not have animals either. The land would return poor. For this, more do not want the road. Us from our community eat all clean, we do not use one gram of fertilizer, nothing. [In other places] they bring sacks and sacks and sacks of chemicals. There in my community, we do not know how to use this.

I asked Graciela about the views of individuals from pueblos surrounding Oronccoy, and she claimed that others also do not want a mine: "They do not want it. The young do not want it. Until here to Huancabamba, we see with our own eyes when [miners] come." In mentioning Huancabamba, Graciela was referencing reactions against a proposed iron ore mine outside of Andahuaylas. In 2011, the proposed mine incited intense backlash, with public protests in the city of Andahuaylas wherein upward of forty people were injured. Protesters called for a ban on mining and a cancellation of contracts with the Apurímac Ferrum Company.[33] The protests in Andahuaylas represent one of many pushbacks against mining development throughout Peru.[34]

Aware of the negative social, economic, and environmental impacts of mining and the social protests across the country, Graciela and her community did not want mining to take place in Oronccoy:[35] "Yes, but we think now all the communities think the same. None of us wants the mine. For a little bit we will have money, but when our animals die, when our land is impoverished, what will we eat? We will need money to eat, we say." Graciela then mentioned that she viewed some people who were beginning to support the mine as lazy and just wanting to earn easy money:

> Some lazy people [support the mine] who only want easy money. However, the money ends quickly, but the land when you care for it does not wear out rapidly, right? When you work clean and healthy, nothing happens. We do not want it. . . . Because us in the community think others want the mine, others no, but the mine would destroy everything that we eat. Our land would be impoverished. So it is better that we leave our land to care for it. We could earn money with the mine, but it would pollute our pueblo.

Graciela described contamination in the neighboring department of Huancavelica, the poorest department in Peru with a long history of mining.[36] "Like in Huancavelica, all are in poverty and there is no land, and they cannot grow anything when it is contaminated. . . . So, our future with this gold is nothing." Alex contended that people from Oronccoy do not want a mine but rather agricultural opportunities:[37]

> Right now, they do not want the mine. They more want a livestock farm. The livestock, that is agricultural, that is all natural. Maybe products that are ecological, natural, that we can sell. However, if the mine enters when it is a small pueblo, they will exploit and contaminate all. The cows and animals that live there will die. There will not be agricultural production, and the people do not want this.

Silenced Voices

Although those from Oronccoy and surrounding communities opposed the mine, Graciela believed their voices were not being heard. I asked if the government supported residents' wishes not to build the mine.

> No, only the people [listen]. Maybe the government wants to sell the land, I do not know. They say to the community, "This land has been sold to the mine," but what is the reality? I do not know. However, no one is working there still. We do not want it. When we are few people, we want to preserve the land. We want to keep it natural.

Alex described the Consultation Law that was signed under the administration of Ollanta Humala, which requires government consultation with Indigenous people directly affected by oil and mining investments (Oxfam 2011).[38] While the law promises honest dialogue with affected communities, it was followed by an attempt to prevent campesinos from being considered Indigenous peoples. Ollanta Humala claimed that the only populations considered to be Indigenous, and thus subject to the Consultation Law, are Amazonian ones, effectively excluding all campesino communities in the Andes. As Benjamin Hoffman (2013) of EarthRights International argues, after hundreds of years of discrimination and exploitation for being considered "Indians," denying

Figure 19. Men walking along the road from Ninabamba to Yerbabuena by the face of the Pampas. There are two roads along the Apurímac side of the river; one is extremely long and the other is incredibly dangerous because it crosses cliffs and mountains in the jungle. Photo by Max Altamirano Molero.

campesino communities the right to consultation for taking steps to overcome oppressive treatment proves to be a double injustice.[39] Moreover, time has proven that this law was merely a mechanism to gain trust and secure stability for private investment, as the government has not consulted even recognized Indigenous Amazonian populations.[40] Not surprisingly, the government of Peru continues to privatize and sell mining concessions without input from campesino communities.[41] By 2012, Peru had awarded twenty-three million hectares in concession to mining companies, 17 percent of the country's entire land surface (Crabtree and Durand 2017).[42]

Alex reflected on this process occurring throughout Peru: "I think in the time of the president Ollanta, the mines without a consultation were privatized, the concessions [were given], and now the owners are selling what the communities have." Echoing Graciela's and Alex's sentiments, a lawyer who works in human rights cases in the highland provinces, Sally Ccotarma, claims, "Rural and indigenous communities don't feel protected by the state. Then it was the armed conflict; now it's the mining companies" (Martínez

2013).[43] However, while mining lobby groups have continued to oppose the extension of the Consultation Law to Andean highland communities, arguing they are not sufficiently Indigenous, communities have actively protested mining operations and rendered unviable major projects (Crabtree and Durand 2017).[44] Although Indigenous mobilization has been understood as "marginal" (Albó 1991), "largely nonexistent" (Yashar 1998), and poorly articulated at the national level and in the highlands in Peru (García and Lucero 2011) as compared to Ecuador and Bolivia, the recent developments surrounding the Consultation Law have galvanized Indigenous mobilization and fostered collaboration between Amazon and highland organizations (Rousseau and Hudon 2015).[45]

Both Alex and Graciela believed the government was forging ahead with plans for the mine in Oronccoy, evidenced through building a road. Graciela stated, "Now they want to commence work, but there is no road. A horse can only carry a little, right? The mules can only carry a little. Maybe they will quickly build a road." Alex conferred that the mine was an impetus to build a road to Oronccoy: "Maybe with this road, maybe the mine is the motive. With this mining concession, maybe with this finalization of exploiting this mine, they are constructing this road because they say this gold is the purest in all of Peru, and how can they export or transport it?" In addition to opposing the mine, Graciela did not support construction of a road:

> I hope they do not build a road either. If they build a road, thieves will come to steal our cows, our sheep, and our animals. We are used to walking by foot, carrying things by horse, walking peacefully. Yes, for this, I do not want a road. When a road comes, there is poverty. No more will we eat naturally in our pueblo, not potato, not maize, [it will] all be with fertilizer. [Now it is] with organics only.[46]

Alex partly supported construction of a road to be able to access markets for their produce and perhaps to make people aware of this region of Peru.

> Thanks to God, now it is a district, because before it was just an annex, and they are building a road and hopefully it arrives [to Oronccoy]. Maybe with this Peru will know where Oreja de Perro is. For the other part, the road is a development for the pueblo for communication, for financing of our products.

However, much like Graciela, Alex feared additional consequences of road construction:

> However, for the other part, it is bad, because at times the road brings development, for the other part it is a destruction. There are people who say not to exploit the mine, that they will rob the livestock. Many things. It appears there will be assaults that happen in other sites like in Chimbote, Trujillo, in these parts where there are assaults daily. Many things appear with this, right? I could think good things that it will bring development or for the other part, it could bring destruction. I do not know. If only to know our destiny, right?

With sparse population and little political or economic power or support, Graciela and her family feared that the government will forge ahead, effectively exploiting their land and resources without recourse.

Ongoing Political Corruption

Continued corruption and scandal have enveloped much of Peru's recent political history, making reparations and the acknowledgment of Indigenous rights a far-flung dream. In November of 2005, Alberto Fujimori was arrested while visiting Chile and was subsequently extradited to Peru (*BBC News* 2006). Fujimori was convicted of violating human rights associated with the Grupo Colina death squad—particularly murder, bodily harm, and two cases of kidnapping, as well as embezzlement and bribery.[47] Four subsequent Peruvian presidents have been investigated for money laundering, corruption, and human rights abuses.[48] Most recently, in November of 2020, Peru faced great turnover and disruption, with three presidents taking office within one week (Taylor 2020).[49] Moreover, leading up to the 2021 presidential election, eighteen individuals, including two children, were massacred in the remote VRAEM region on May 23, 2021, which the government credited to the Militarized Communist Party of Peru, successor of Sendero Luminoso, while others cited drug traffickers (*Economist* 2021). Public outcry against violence and fraud has grown steadily in postwar Peru, and investigations have unveiled entrenched corruption among all branches of Peruvian government.[50]

Continued corruption and scandal have impeded the enactment of justice and reconciliation in Peru. The National Penal Chamber of Peru sentenced Sendero

Luminoso leaders, including Abimael Guzmán, to life imprisonment (Human Rights Watch 2019). Guzmán died on September 11, 2021, at the age of eighty-six, after serving twenty-nine years in prison (Alarcón 2021). Nevertheless, there has been little headway in enacting justice of military personnel responsible for torture, death, and disappearances throughout Peru during the war. This is largely due to a lack of collaboration with the Defense Ministry, as they refuse to share evidence (Human Rights Watch 2019; Laplante and Theidon 2007).[51] Additionally, the Instituto Nacional Penitenciario, which operates the prison system, continues to be one of the most corrupt institutions in Peru.[52] According to Peruvian human rights groups, as of May 2017, prosecutors had achieved rulings in only seventy-eight cases and only seventeen convictions related to abuses committed during the armed conflict (Human Rights Watch 2019).[53] In addition, the CVR documented 554 cases of wartime rape, including 16 cases with evidence, yet none has proceeded to trial (Boesten 2014, 5).[54] The Human Rights Trials in Peru project, led by political scientist Jo-Marie Burt, found that from 2006 to 2012, 187 state agents had been prosecuted, yet of these 187 state agents, only 66 were convicted, while 121 were acquitted.[55]

In questioning what led to such a high rate of acquittals following solid sentencing practice, Burt concludes that this shift was due to "political winds [that] narrowed the space for accountability efforts" that raises important questions about the independence of the judiciary with relation to the executive and armed forces (quoted in Milton 2018, 24). According to Burt, the powerful actors formed an "impunity bloc" that began under the leadership of Alan García and solidified with Ollanta Humala, whose governments both made public statements "that absolved the Armed Forces of wrongdoing or lessened their culpability" (24). In addition to political obstruction, seeking justice in Peru is particularly challenging, as most victims do not pursue criminal investigations because they cannot identify the perpetrator, judicial systems in Peru are barely functional, and jurisdiction for crimes against humanity are held in Lima (hours away from evidence and witnesses). Moreover, there is a tendency among poor and marginalized populations to distrust the national legal system that failed to protect them during the years of civil unrest (Laplante and Theidon 2007, 243–44). As a result of the scarcity of resources applied to reparations, the limited scope of victims, and the dearth of judicial accountability, "Peru is one of the States with more cases in the Inter-American System of Human Rights" with "29 judgements issued against the Peruvian

State related to the internal armed conflict" (Guillerot 2019, 49). By excluding members of subversive organizations from victim status, Peru violates various treaties on human rights of which Peru is a part of as well as the Peruvian constitution. As Julie Guillerot (2019) argues, "If the real concern behind the exclusion of the victim's quality was participation in human rights violations, the recognition of the victim's status to some members of the Armed Forces and the National Police should have been questioned as well, given that, according to the figures of the CVR, they are responsible for 37% of the deaths and disappearances," reflecting the refusal of the political class to recognize state abuses (51). Without providing due reparations or holding the government or armed forces accountable for injustices committed during the war, Peru is far from reaching reconciliation as outlined in the initial CVR report indicating that "the past is not far from the surface" (Guillerot 2019, 54).

While an egalitarian horizon has appeared in Peru postwar, with a multicultural discourse that expects equality and demands spaces of recognition for the Andean world and cultures of the Amazon, such demands coincide with continued corruption in Peruvian society (Portocarrero and Vich 2012, 147). The increased privatization of public goods and political clientelism, as well as neoliberal economic growth, have excluded vast social sectors, particularly rural Andean communities and migrants to the cities, reinforcing racial divisions throughout the country.

———

Lost opportunities because of the war have acutely shaped Graciela's current reality and her family's prospects. Upon losing their land, livelihoods, and loved ones in the Oreja de Perro, Graciela and her family continued to persevere while contending with ongoing discrimination and persistent inequality as depeasantized workers. Ironically, securing land in a danger zone represented a form of stability for Graciela, yet it also illustrates how displaced survivors of the war face persistent discrimination by citizens, landowners, and the government. The state's inability to follow through on promised reconciliation efforts and reparation for war survivors further demonstrates the underlying discrimination toward campesinos. Any chance for education and securing a "professional" position in society for most survivors and their children has been largely shattered through nearly two decades of war and disruption. Moreover, the state has largely neglected areas particularly brutalized by the war, such as Oronccoy, making these regions acutely susceptible to exploitation. Growing awareness of the harmful impacts of mining throughout the Andes has fostered rejection of such prospects yet underscores how the continued exploitation of Indigenous lands and bodies continues largely unabated throughout Peru. The continued corruption enveloping much of Peruvian political life further impedes accessing truth and reparations and embeds deep divisions in society. Consequently, the unequal social relations, which sparked the attempted revolution, continue to foster suffering and discontent among those originally targeted in need of liberation. Nevertheless, survivors were continuing to, as Graciela said, "triumph each with their own destiny."

Conclusion

Remapping Personhood Postconflict

Constructing and Deconstructing a Sense of Self

Graciela's story provides a deeply personal window into life amid the war and continued challenges navigating marginalization, the weight of memories, and the complexities of identity in postconflict Peru. The war, predicated on centuries of inequality and exploitation, upended Graciela's life and that of hundreds of thousands of the so-called lost generation of Peru. Graciela struggles every day as a survivor of political violence. She harbors traumatic memories and faces quotidian discrimination based on her ethnic identity and place of origin. She has lost opportunities for education and stability that continue to affect her ability to support her family financially. She has experienced tremendous violence, both directly and indirectly in her formative years, which has shaped who she is today. As Ponciano Del Pino and Eliana Otta Vildoso (2019) argue, for victims, violence is not something abstract, rather "it is a concrete reality, embodied in persons and villages with specific pasts, and it condenses their experiences of loss, pain, and suffering in the depths of their being. It is a rupture of the world that marks and defines their life paths" (357). In line with such insights, Graciela's history illustrates how the war distorted the primary tenets upon which highland residents base a sense of self, remember the war, and continue to navigate the complexities of identity in postconflict Peru. Consequently, one of the greatest challenges for Graciela, and other displaced survivors, is navigating a sense of self in the aftermath of war.

Before the violence began, Graciela's life was structured around festivals, communal labor-exchange practices, and caring for the land and animals. She defined her sense of self via relationships with others and the natural world. In relaying her life history, Graciela continually situated herself, and thereby her identity, in relationship with others and place, using terms such as *comunidad*, *paisano*, *comunero*, *compañero*, and *pueblo*. While having a physical sense of the place of her community, memories were dominated by experiences with the fields, eucalyptus trees that had been planted by her ancestors, archaeological sites, animals, sacred mountains, festivals, condors, food, and music, as well as people, many whom had been displaced or were deceased. In other words, memories of this place were layered with experiences and relationships with people, animals, and the environment and through time, which reflect a unique sense of self—all of which the conflict fundamentally altered.

Horizontal and Vertical Linkages

As illustrated in Graciela's story, throughout the Andes, horizontal ties of reciprocity serve to provide much-needed labor for survival and connection with one another for support. People form these horizontal ties through collective labor practices such as ayni, minka, and faena, as well as through festivals and other events that connect kinship groups, neighbors, and communities. We can see this focus linguistically as the Quechua term *runa masinchik* refers to people with whom we work, underscoring how people relate one's identity to reciprocity and collective labor in the Andes (Theidon 2006, 452). Graciela relayed early memories working in ayni and minka and celebrating festivals in which individuals fulfilled cargos, shared resources, cemented ties with one another, and gained social prestige. Once the violence began and Graciela fled, these practices ceased.

Sendero actively disrupted horizontal ties between and within communities by preventing the celebration of festivals and regional markets that brought communities together. Sendero did not respect funeral rites or other rituals that communities conducted to guarantee a successful harvest and tied people to one another. The war also sparked conflict within and between communities, as individuals often did not know who supported whom and potential enemies resided in proximity, leading to overall distrust (Theidon 2013). This disruption is apparent, as Graciela expressed confusion about her own paisanos from a neighboring community who had turned into enemies during the conflict. Furthermore, as individuals sought refuge in nearby towns and cities, families were separated from their ayllus.

While ayllus are oftentimes defined around human relationships, de la Cadena (2015) describes ayllus as a weaving in which the entities—including people, plants, animals, and landscapes—are threads of the weaving: "they are part of it as much as the weaving is part of them" (101). One is inextricably "*in-ayllu*" wherein humans and other-than-human beings "emerge within *ayllus* as relationship, and from this condition they, literally, take-place" (102). The substance of an individual and "other-than-humans that make an *ayllu* is the coemergence of each *with* the others," including land (102). Accordingly, people are not *from* Oronccoy, they *are* Oronccoy. Therefore, the forced displacement of people from their lands not only disturbed seasonal migration, impaired production, and seriously disrupted reciprocal labor practices and social support networks with devastating economic consequences (Pedersen, Kienzler, and Gamarra 2010, 287), it also fundamentally altered personhood.

Graciela continued to make connections with others while fleeing violence. While living in the Amazon, she built friendships with neighbors who she viewed as kin. They relied on one another during the birth of children, to provide guidance and support with work, and comradery when once again fleeing violence. Upon resettling in the city of Andahuaylas, Graciela developed relationships with those in her neighborhood, which was largely populated by others displaced from the Oreja de Perro region, whom she referenced as *comuneros*, a term typically used for someone from the same community. They banded together to form an association that successfully resisted eviction by the municipal government and provided support to Graciela's family after she was in an automobile accident, assuring they had food to eat. Much like other displaced individuals residing within transnational networks, Graciela defined a sense of place and self through connections with individuals, reallocating terms of community and kinship accordingly. Nevertheless, these networks do not continue to serve her to the same degree.

Given her residence in the city, Graciela can no longer engage in enduring ties of labor reciprocity or hold a leadership position in her natal community. However, she also cannot access services such as reputable microfinance savings and loans programs in the city, which typically would serve economically poor, disenfranchised, and illiterate women. For instance, Graciela tried to access loans from several reputable microfinance organizations in the city of Andahuaylas; however, the lenders repeatedly denied her loans due to a lack of collateral in the form of land and animals or a well-established local network of women. Years later, Graciela needed to access a savings account and was subject to a less reputable microfinance program. When she tried to withdraw part of her savings (US$600.00) less than a year later, the agency told her the funds were no longer available, as they had spent the money on land and had been unable to recuperate their costs. Graciela said others in Pochocota were unable to access money they deposited with this microfinance agency as well. Within the following year, the agency shuttered their doors and the business had disappeared, taking along Graciela's savings. In lieu of reliable banking and social support agencies, Graciela must depend on other displaced individuals who face similar impediments to accessing resources, thereby exacerbating barriers to economic advancement and stability.

In addition to Sendero's severing of horizontal ties among individuals in the Andes, they also actively sought to break vertical connections. The ways in which individuals are vertically tied to one another has a long history in the Andes. Miguel La Serna (2012) describes how campesinos accepted a certain level of inequality with, or even abuse by, hacendados with the recognition of their interdependence. When excessive liberties were taken and hacendados abused their power, those reciprocal ties were viewed as effectively broken and there was reason to revolt. However, campesinos perceived hacendados who had greater resources and power but did not overly exploit as points of stability that were in some cases worth protecting. Campesinos often sought out compadrazgo relationships with hacendados or with those of higher social status to ensure a level of reciprocity (Starn and La Serna 2019). Therefore, while some level of inequality and power differentiation was accepted, both parties were expected to foster reciprocal relations.[1] In their quest to create an egalitarian utopia, Sendero targeted individuals who had abused their power or had greater resources than others had. When Sendero began to kill individuals for cattle theft or other wrongdoings, their actions were acceptable when campesinos viewed the targeted individuals as abusing their position of power and effectively breaking any form of reciprocity. However, in their ignorant pursuit of pure equality, Sendero began to target anyone who represented inequality, ignoring the vertical ties of reciprocity that bound people together. Sendero severed not only horizontal ties but also vertical connections upon which people depended for their well-being. When Sendero enacted justice that cut reciprocal, even if unequal, relations upon which people depended, they diminished mutual interests, and support for Sendero waned.

Such vertical connections were a part of Graciela's early memories regarding godparent relationships and served as a key means of survival while on the run. Throughout Graciela's experience escaping violence, she found herself dependent on, and at the salvation of, various middle- to upper-class mestizos, accessing vertical ties of reciprocity. For example, certain individuals relied on Graciela to care for their animals and fields, and she needed them for shelter, as well as to provide her children with quality education. While she provided much sought-after domestic labor, her employers also helped her escape violence. While some of these relationships were exploitative, and in some cases akin to slavery, she perceived others with deep affection. Without a strong established and stable horizontal network of support, Graciela was in a vulnerable position, often unable to resist exploitative circumstances. She did not have a community to band together and denounce an abuse of power and was subject to relying on others with more resources and power for survival. Ironically, even though Sendero aimed to create an equal society, the conflict effectively strengthened vertical linkages while weakening horizontal ties of the most vulnerable, ultimately exacerbating inequality.

In disrupting vertical and horizontal systems that provided vital financial and social support, the war also upset gender relations and exacerbated gender-based violence. While the Agrarian Reform dislocated varayocc leadership, the war further severed this social structure, with impacts on violence against women. According to Jelke Boesten (2010a), women from the community of Llusita argued that violence did not occur against women before the war, as the varayocc would not allow it. While difficult to discern prewar reality, conversely, in postwar life there was little institutional support regarding family violence (126).[2] The disappearances, death, and displacement from the war tore communities apart and "led to the loss of family ties that otherwise could provide women with social resources such as protection and support" (Boesten 2006, 365). Moreover, the war exacerbated violence against women, as men reportedly learned how to rape during the war. Women were often blamed for rape that resulted in children, and women and children continue to suffer abuse to the present day because of the exacerbated violence against women during the conflict (Boesten 2010a, 126).[3]

On the other hand, postwar influences altered gender relations in rural communities in ways that provide space for women to disavow abuse and renegotiate their reproductive and domestic rights. According to Caroline Yezer (2013), for men in the Ayacucho community of Wiracocha (a pseudonym) the war disrupted the varayocc leadership, which was largely subsumed within the rondas campesinas. At the end of the war the disbandment of the rondas along with the infiltration of a foreign human-rights framework threatened men's authority. Men felt that their ability to bring order and cohesion to the community had been lost. Conversely, women welcomed the presence of organizations that introduced a human-rights discourse that provided an opportunity to challenge gender-based violence and demand more equality in domestic affairs and reproductive rights (Yezer 2013; see also Oliart 2008). Although men and women had divergent responses to outside influences and the shift in leadership structures, they both strongly rejected attempts by human-rights organizations to implement their own means of restitution and punishment, which they found often did not fit the realities of life in the campo and threatened their communal autonomy (Yezer 2013).

Prior to the war, Graciela's community of Oronccoy addressed issues of marital dispute and domestic violence collectively, with the varayocc leadership enforcing a fine for offenders that would then be used to help community members in need, which the war completely obliterated. That said, I do not know to what degree women's calls for domestic equality and justice were represented and respected by community leadership before the violence began. Moreover, while on the run, Graciela was subject to male authority members who largely discredited her call for sexual rights. Even with such limitations, conversely, there was no social structure available for Graciela to prevent or address sexual harassment and assault during her capture and incarceration, and within work environments. As a displaced resident of Andahuaylas, her recourse to any form of gender-based violence is organizations and agencies (e.g., police departments, legal firms, nongovernmental organizations, and government agencies) largely dominated by mestizo men operating within particular gendered regimes, thereby not offering the level of support and justice available to her prior to the war.[4] According to Boesten (2006), "discrimination and corruption are huge problems in many of the institutions set up to combat domestic violence and their existence reveals the prejudices and inequalities that contribute to and sustain violence against women" (365). Therefore, while Graciela has established reciprocal relationships with others in various settings in postwar life, given her lack of connection to place and established kinship networks, those displaced bonds are not adequate to access resources and are thus unable to provide the same level of security, support, and corresponding sense of self that she experienced before the war.

Sociocentric Self

Moving beyond vertical and horizontal ties of reciprocity, Graciela expressed a sociocentric orientation, in which one defines oneself by social relationships (Shweder and Bourne 1984), which the war severely upended. Olga González (2011) discovered that a "sociocentric" orientation in the Andean community of Sarhua created a sense of collective blame in which "no one was alone in carrying the blame for his or her misdeeds" (202). For example, González learned that a mother of a thieving son asked that she also be whipped, arguing that she should have raised her son better. This collective sense of blame has also been displayed in cases in which higher-ranking individuals were whipped alongside their misbehaving lower-ranking individuals in the *varayoqkuna* system following the belief "When one of us fails, we all fail" (202).[5] Similarly, Graciela relayed a collective sense of responsibility and justice, always situating her own suffering and accountability in relation to others.

While Sendero held a communist ideology of revolution with the aim of collective equality when faced with taking responsibility for actions or banding together in the face of danger, Sendero shattered any sociocentric orientation. Sendero directly countered a sociocentric view of self by targeting specific individuals for misdeeds and failing to take responsibility for any of their own wrongdoings, let alone those of their fellow guerrillas. Instead of collectively standing their ground in the face of the enemy, Sendero took the approach of fleeing in the face of threat, which confused agriculturalists and led to distrust. Later both Sendero and the military countered a sociocentric orientation by stealing from, raping, and killing scores of innocent people with no regard for determining blame or responsibility.

For Graciela, the natural world is also a part of a sociocentric understanding of self. For instance, for rural highland residents, natural entities such as mountains, fields, and pasturelands are integral players in a complex reciprocal relationship within which humans are a part (see Salas Carreño 2016). All beings (e.g., lakes, fields, mountains, pastures) count as individuals in society and are thereby referred to with the Quechua third-person pronouns ("he" or "she," not "it"). Such entities are thus treated as "persons of a special kind, who have powers that humans lack, and who therefore deserve special propitiation" (Salomon 2018, 38). They have power because pachamama (Mother Earth) and sacred places (such as mountains) act upon people's lives (Allen 2011; Van Vleet 2008).[6] Some humans, much like sacred mountains (apus), are ascribed more power than others, yet the destiny of all is dependent on the relationships formed. Reciprocity is not merely a relationship between entities but rather "it is a relationship from where entities emerge, it makes them, they grow from it" (de la Cadena 2015, 103). People do not *have* relationships, they *are* relationships; and as Frank Salomon (2018) argues, the "Andean habit of thought extends society as a web of personal causation outward to include all parts of the world" (39). Animals are thereby a part of this integrated sense of self. As Graciela's history illustrates, animals represent a means through which people foster positive social relationships with others by offering animals as a gift, to use in community negotiations, and to sacrifice for a festival, thereby affording its owner a sense of prestige and connection within the community. They also serve as a primary source of economic stability for families, particularly women, thereby supporting the family and larger kinship networks.

Graciela also understood the individual body with a sociocentric lens as an integral part of the natural world as found throughout rural highland Peru. As Pedersen, Kienzler, and Gamarra (2010) state, in the Andes the human body is "an open system that is permeable to and engaged in constant reciprocal exchange with natural, social and cosmological forces" (294). Sickness represents an imbalance between these forces and the individual. Corporal vulnerabilities may increase or decrease depending on the position of the body in space and time, as well as on other factors, such as discord within the family or with neighbors, witnessing a traumatic event, or deliberately induced spell through witchcraft (Chiappe, Lemlij, and Millones 1985). Increased vulnerability commonly results in illnesses that people tend to treat with herbal remedies, ritual offerings (pagos) to pachamama, rituals of restitution (*shunqo*), or other means of restoration of the lost balance (Frisancho Pineda 1978; Pedersen 2009).

In other words, people continually actively cultivate interconnected relationships with one another and with places to assure their overall social, economic, and physical well-being.

The war disrupted ties that people had not only with one another but also with the environment, animals, and their own bodies, ultimately dislodging their sense of self. Through perpetual violence and displacement, individuals were not able to perform pagos or other rituals that would foster positive reciprocal relationships with sacred sites, fields, or other natural entities. Sendero and the military thoughtlessly slaughtered animals and stole produce from the fields. Individuals were no longer able to sacrifice animals for festivals as part of a cargo to foster social relationships and secure status within the community. Displacement and death upended the balance of relationships between people and place, making people vulnerable to sickness, yet they lacked a means of restitution or restoration. Moreover, the disappearance, torture, and dismemberment of bodies during this sasachakuy tiempo (the difficult years) completely dehumanized individuals (Theidon 2013, 54). As Kimberly Theidon (2013) reports, the world was in disarray during the violence, which fostered an overall sense of collective madness, and because people were often unable to hold wakes or bury their loved ones, the fates of their souls were challenged and could become a danger to the living. Further, as Edward Chauca (2016) argues, the years of violence denied mourning to thousands of Peruvians, leading to a sense of alienation, confusion, and disorientation in which people felt they could no longer recognize themselves, "as if they were strangers in their own bodies" (70). The war effectively remapped the entire physical and social landscapes, as well as the human body, into places of trauma, violence, and danger. In effect, the war had turned upside-down all the relationships that had given individuals a sense of self and what it means to be human.

Memories, Emotions, and Time

Not only did the war threaten a sense of self by severing ties of reciprocity with others, natural entities, and the human body, it also invoked particular "idioms of distress" (Pedersen, Kienzler, and Gamarra 2010) or expressions of emotion tied to a sociocentric understanding of self.[7] In exploring survivors' own idioms of distress, Pedersen, Kienzler, and Gamarra (2010) found two primary emotional expressions: *ñakay* and *llaki*. The term *ñakay* conveys "the notion of collective suffering and distress stemming or inflicted from the outside or by external causes" and "entails a collective resignation, as little can be done to prevent or overcome *ñakary* as an individual" (290). Not only is the suffering itself perceived as a collective experience, but also the resignation is viewed as collective in the inability of individual agency to overcome it. Llaki, however, is an individual affliction that cannot be experienced by the collective. Llaki is framed by a life of worries and solitude in which material deprivations and insecurity prevail. Llaki is sorrow and sadness, feelings emerging from the inside that may well be induced by outside life events like poverty, daily life adversities, and violent events. In relating this to a sense of self, it is apparent that although llaki is experienced individually, it is precisely a lack of reciprocal ties with others that prompts the material deprivation that leads to the individual suffering. As Pedersen, Kienzler, and Gamarra state, llaki is related to the notion of an impoverished life, which is equivalent to "a life without family, roof, or shelter, and with no clothing and food" (291). It is often associated with single mothers and widows who are dependent on their own meager resources, as they "are unable to work in the *chakra* or exchange work in reciprocity with others," leading to material insecurity, as well as social isolation and discrimination (291).

In effect, the primary emotional expressions evoked in the postwar period represent collective experiences with and responses to external trauma (*ñakary*), as well as individual suffering stemming from a loss of collective belonging (llaki). Additionally, certain emotional expressions are not contained within an individual's body but can be passed from mother to child. According to Kimberly Theidon (2013), a mother can transmit suffering and susto to their child in utero or via breastmilk through *la teta asustada* (the frightened breast). This transferred emotional state embodied by susto can result in long-standing physical changes, causing a baby to have developmental delays or epilepsy (43–44). A sociocentric understanding of self is not only found through collective connections between one another and place but also experienced emotionally and transmitted intergenerationally.

These emotional expressions are apparent with Graciela. Although Graciela did not use the terms *ñakary* and *llaki*, the way in which she described the trauma and resulting impoverishment reflect such concepts. She described the war as a collective threat from outside inaccessible to individual resistance, which ultimately severed ties between herself, others, and the natural world, leading to material deprivation and suffering. She also framed her life as insecurities, sadness, poverty, and discrimination stemming from a loss of social belonging. While Graciela did not discuss la teta asustada specifically, a primary deprivation while on the run was the inability of her mother to nurse Graciela's siblings, due to malnutrition, resulting in intergenerational impacts. Graciela did discuss instances of susto and nervios stemming from the war, as well as physical characteristics of her children resulting from influences while in utero.

Alongside a sociocentric understanding of self and emotional response to the war is a particular sense of time that influences how memories of the violence and visions of the future are experienced. Throughout the Andes, temporality is more circular than linear, likely due to the prominence of agricultural cycles and related rituals. In such circular temporal structures, "memories of past events are infused into present realities and projected into the future, which is perceived as close and ominous, rather than remote and distant" (Pedersen, Kienzler, and Gamarra 2010, 294). Michelle Wibbelsman (2019) cites the Quichua term ñawpaman, which "connotes advancing forward in space while simultaneously moving backward in time" (132). Enrique Cachiguango, a Native Otavalan anthropologist, and Julián Pontón further describe an Andean cosmovision of time in which "the future is inscribed in the past and, at some point, the past actually becomes the future" (Cachiguango and Pontón 2010, 60, cited in Wibblesman 2019, 132). Conversely, a linear sense of time perceives past events as further distanced and less influential on future outcomes as time passes.

For war survivors with an Andean conception of time in which "the past and the future are inextricably linked" (Wibbelsman 2019, 132), recollections of past violence are infused into everyday lived reality in the present and actively shape visions of the future.[8] We can see this sense of time through Graciela's experiences, as memories of the war were not remote and distant. They were close and ominous as they continued to circulate, infusing her present reality with ongoing fear. Graciela's daily challenges of an impoverished life as a direct result of the war were also projected into the future via lost opportunities for her, her children, and her grandchildren. Moreover, for Graciela, to move toward the future, it was imperative for her to not lose sight of the past. It is not a history to be forgotten, as Graciela's memories actively shape her present person and future self, a self that is inextricably tied to her comuneros, land, animals, and all beings. To forget the past would mean losing oneself. To move forward, Graciela must simultaneously move backward in time. In other words, for Graciela, the knowledge acquired from hastening forward toward a tragic and fractured past is at the heart of transformation in becoming fully human (see Wibbelsman 2019).

In summary, the war disrupted the structures upon which Graciela, and countless others, fostered a sense of self. The violence disconnected horizontal and vertical systems of reciprocity that provided vital social, financial, and emotional support. It countered collective conceptions of responsibility and justice. The war also severed relationships between individuals, communities, animals, places, and natural entities upon which people gained sense of self and well-being. At the same time, the war enacted emotional responses embedded in a sociocentric understanding of self that people were no longer able to construct actively, thereby exacerbating suffering. Lastly, a circular sense of time and intergenerational transmission of emotional expressions continue to shape survivors' memories of the war that infuse daily reality, shape projections of the future, and directly affect subsequent generations.

Contending with the Past/Envisioning a Future

Peru as a country has increasingly grappled with how it engages with its violent history and how it will follow through with promised reparations within a politically heated and corrupt system dating back to the Spanish conquest and colonialization. Sendero emerged at a particular point in Peru's history that represents a rupture from the norm yet a continuation of trends that have sought to liberate Indigenous populations with little acknowledgment of their own conceptions of what they want or even who they are. As Jaymie Patricia Heilman (2010) argues, through a detailed analysis of eighty-five years of history leading up to the rise of Sendero Luminoso, the war "was a period of both historical continuity and historical rupture" (193). While drastic in its approach and tragic in its ultimate impact, the rise of Sendero and the military backlash represent a continuality of political efforts and actions that spanned the twentieth century, with historic roots that stretch back to the conquest. As Boesten (2010a) argues, in exploring a continuum of violence, the war does not ultimately represent a rupture and exceptionality within Peruvian society; rather, it illustrates a continuity that forces us to explore underlying values, norms, and institutional structures "that normalize certain violences and exceptionalize others" (113). One question that arises is whether the war will ultimately represent a continuity, a rupture, or a rite of passage in Peruvian society in which something transitional emerges.

Alexander Hinton (2010) points out that the symbolic-temporal work of transitional justice resembles a rite of passage. Like such rites of passage, truth commissions, museums, and memorials are highly symbolic and enact liberal ideals and subjectivities, as well as signifying "a purification of the social body," moving from a contaminated state of conflict to one of liberal democratic purity (8). Throughout this process, "new narratives are forged" that delineate the violent past in a way that "increases the social cohesion of the fractured society and legitimizes the post-conflict government initiating the transitional justice process" (8).

It is important not to overlook the socially transformative effects of symbolic rituals embedded in transitional justice efforts (Cole 2010) and the contributions of Peru's truth and reconciliation process overall.[9] Nevertheless, how can Peru purify the social body when certain bodies continue to be contaminated by association with terrorism and the social fabric is so widely divided? How can Peru address continuous gender-based violence through transformative justice without aiming to undo and remake the social relationships that lead to violence against women (see Boesten and Wilding 2015)? How can new narratives be forged that increase social cohesion when liberal democratic purity is only available to a minority of the citizenry and representations of the past are censored by the state? Lastly, how can the postconflict government be legitimized when it fails to enact promised reparations, attempts to exploit Indigenous lands, and is mired in corruption?[10] Even though Peru has held regular and reasonably democratic elections since 2001, "the power balance between different social sectors has tilted persistently in favour of elites, with the interests of other social sectors poorly or only intermittently articulated" (Crabtree and Durand 2017). As Edward Chauca (2016) argues, the CVR did make visible the causes of the violence, but without systematic engagement with reconciliation by the state, the psychological and social scars of historical violence cannot be healed. Yet Salomón Lerner points out how the state itself represents a divided society, stating, "Peru is a country where exclusion is so absolute that the disappearance of tens of thousands of citizens went unnoticed by the dominant society" (Lerner quoted in Chauca 2016, 69). While the state of Peru is arguably a long way from systematic social transformation, some evidence suggests that a revolution is occurring outside of the state system in which individuals and communities are redefining personhood.

Remapping Personhood

Graciela, Juan Pablo, Nayely, and I traveled to the city of Ayacucho together and visited the Museo de la Memoria ANFASEP (Asociación Nacional de Familiares de Secuestrados, Detenidos, y Desaparecido del Perú, or National Association of Relatives of Abductees, Detainees, and Disappeared from Peru). At one point in our short tour, Graciela was startled by a recreation of a torture scene. While Graciela was consoled by another war survivor who worked in the small gift shop, Juan Pablo and I sat on a bench together. He expressed how difficult it was for Graciela, given her tender age when the violence happened. "Not so young as to forget—rather the age when one forms into a person. That is why it is so hard on her and she is so sensitive. She was forever changed by the violence. She will never be the same." Juan Pablo's views of Graciela's personhood reflect Andean conceptions of identity and memory. Identity is understood as mutable, fluid, and something to be achieved, which can therefore be lost and regained. For example, older children are often referred to as *yuyaniyuq*. *Yuyay* in Quechua signifies "remembering," and the accumulation of memory makes individuals more fully human. In contrast, younger children are considered *sonsos* (senseless, witless) (Theidon 2006, 450). When the violence unfolded, Graciela was clearly at an age where she could remember, and the accumulation of memory made her more human. Yet she was also at a tender age wherein she was still becoming a person, which made her particularly vulnerable. Essentially, the war is part of Graciela. It forever shaped her in a way that cannot be undone. Yet Graciela is not only the war. Her sense of self is fluid and ever-changing, as certain memories and visions are lost and regained. Graciela, along with countless others who have lived through the violence, are continually changing and redefining what it means to be human in postwar Peru.

There is no denying the long-standing divisions within Peruvian society that the war unveiled and the devastation it left in its wake. The war destroyed landmarks upon which people built their identities, broke apart families and communities, and dissolved social organizations and groups (Cárdenas et al. 2005; CVR 2003). Nonetheless, the war also served to blend, recreate, transform, and invest new attributes in what it means to be a campesino/a from the Oreja de Perro in postwar Peru. As war survivors continue to build alliances with one another through associations and informal networks, rely on ayni, minka, and faena to meet individual and collective needs, host annual festivals, and navigate postwar life, the concept of self is evolving within and perhaps despite the state of Peru. Like Krista Van Vleet (2019), I resist an analysis that presents "an opposition between (a lost) indigenous sociality and (an acquired) modern" identity (28). Such a dichotomy obscures how Graciela and other survivors act upon and within complicated webs of relationships and "reproduces representations of (native Andean) women as either inextricably linked to traditional practices or ambivalently involved in contemporary social, and political economic worlds" (28). I also do not want to contribute to a myth of "a community stripped of its pastoral bliss and born into a world of pain" (Agüero 2021, 66). Graciela and others may see and revision themselves in relation not only to the war but also to the deep history preceding the violence and the long future that circles back behind us, as illustrated through Graciela's connection with a particular novel.

Graciela's two youngest children had been assigned Óscar Colchado Lucio's (1997) novel *Rosa Cuchillo* at school and read it to Graciela. All agreed that it accurately portrayed Andean life and the years of violence. In the novel, Rosa Cuchillo, although she has lived through and witnessed horrific times during the conflict, remembers herself as a happy child growing up in the Andes, and then as an Andean goddess who will never lose her connection with people on earth.[11] Throughout the novel, the internal conflict "comes almost as a parenthesis, a brief interruption in a long and continually evolving indigenous Andean history" (Lambright 2015, 132). Anne Lambright questions whether the national subject we are asked to consider represented by Rosa Cuchillo, "while marked by the war, is not someone whose fundamental identity is the victim of the conflict" (132).

Like Rosa Cuchillo, Graciela witnessed and directly experienced traumatic events yet has fond memories of her childhood in Oronccoy and maintains connections with others and places in postwar life. Maybe in finding truth in the novel, Graciela recognized the constantly changing identity of herself, her community, and those throughout the Andes more generally. The war disrupted structures upon which Graciela bases her sense of self, and although Graciela laments the violence, trauma, and loss from the war, she never expresses fear of losing connection with people or her community. Although the places, people, and networks have shifted, Graciela continues to identify herself in relation to others, deriving strength and support through collective and reciprocal relations of responsibility and justice. The war largely shattered the structures within which a sense of self is germinated but failed to eliminate the seed.

Graciela shared a testimony of horrible injustices that underscores her victimhood, yet by the act of telling her story, she has moved beyond "a defenseless, depoliticized individual" to embody the complexity of humanity (Agüero 2021, 82). Her sense of self is fluid and ever-changing, as Graciela along with countless others who have lived through the violence are "not only victims but also agents of diverse struggles for truth and justice, as well as processes of change and reconstruction" continually redefining what it means to be human in postwar Peru (Del Pino and Otta Vildoso 2019, 364). While being a victim of the internal conflict, that is not all Graciela is, and that is not all those from Oronccoy, or the hundreds of thousands of survivors throughout Peru, represent or will become.

Final Word: Graciela

This book began with Graciela's wishes for the text and a description of Graciela as an individual. To end, we offer Graciela's reflections on herself, which relay her ever-evolving wisdom, humility, and compassion for others.

One day after covering various intense subjects, I sought to lighten the focus and asked Graciela a series of random questions. When asked to describe herself, Graciela said, "I have patience, love, and care. I am not violent." She then began to laugh and continued, "I have patience to attend my children. I care for others like my family that I love, for my neighbors, always for those who show caring. This I have, nothing more." When asked how she has been able to maintain such a softened heart after all she has been through, Graciela described her faith and learning about the importance of forgiveness:

> Now I understand that all are pardoned with love. For example, you love me a lot, right, Nicole? [Yes.] I also love you very much. I love my children. Because of this, we go out to meet others from afar to give love to whoever. It is not important the race, nor the color, if they are little, if they are big. We help them, as we are parents, as if they are our children. This is what I carry in my mind. This is what I teach my children also. This is what they know. This is my word, Nicole.

I then asked what experiences she would like to have at some point in her life. With a confused expression on her face, she brought my own cultural bias into stark relief and replied, "All that we live is an experience. All that we do is an experience." She then described what she would like to do before she dies: provide service to her community. "Some cargos of the authorities that do good things for the community. That's what it would be." Graciela also wished for others to have positive memories of her family: "Before I die [to think] this family was good. To remember this in your hearts." When pressed about what exactly she would like people to remember about her and her family, she responded:

> That I did good things or when they came to my house, I served them water, that I gave them food; that I served them well. Of my community, when someone comes, that they were attended to. When someone comes, I can say, "Come to my house. You must eat. You must drink water." This I want them to remember.

I joked that she would be remembered as *hatun sonqo* (big heart) and Graciela laughed saying "Mucho hatun sonqo achkapaq bastante" (very much big heart).

In closing, I asked Graciela of all the places she had been, which place she favored and where she ultimately would like to live. Graciela said of all the places she had experienced, she preferred her pueblo of Oronccoy. "I miss my pueblo of Oronccoy. I miss it a lot. When I was little, I would play in the trees in the forest pasturing my sheep. These are the memories I have. Always I miss my pueblo. . . . When I am still living, I will go to my pueblo. I will return."

NOTES

Introduction

1. While conducting fieldwork in rural communities surrounding Andahuaylas, Peru, in 2005–2006, I heard on various occasions that you could assess the number of children a woman had by the number of missing teeth, with the belief that women typically lose one tooth per pregnancy due to malnutrition.

2. The process of concentrating resources among the elite continued postindependence. Peru gained independence from Spain in 1821 and began to export the nation's varied and vast resource base, with Peruvian elites aligning themselves with interests of foreign capital, "keeping its opponents divided and—when necessary—exercising repression" (Crabtree and Durand 2017, 29). To read more about the details of periods in Peru's history following independence and leading up to the Agrarian Reform of 1969, including the Guano Republic (1840–1880), the Aristocratic Republic (1896–1919), repression and populism (1919–1963), and the changing tide (1963–1968), see Crabtree and Durand (2017).

3. According to a Gini index of land distribution in fifty-seven countries, Peru had the highest index of inequality (Taylor and Hudson 1972).

4. The Amazon region did not remain largely intact for long, with exploitation of rubber, timber, gold, and, most recently, natural gas reserves throughout the Peruvian Amazon.

5. To read more about the racialized history of Peru, see Scarritt (2012).

6. According to Arguedas, the mistis were "annoying," "bad," and "corroded by envy and betrayal" of landowners and rulers who needed the Indian labor to survive. By contrast, Indians were "good," lived in rural communities, spoke Quechua, and silently suffered under misti domination (Arguedas 1983, cited in Flores Galindo 2010, 199). The term *Indian* can be translated in Spanish as *indio* and *indígena*, with the former typically considered a racial slur or appropriated by groups promoting Indian empowerment (García 2005). Krista Van Vleet notes, in much of Peru, the term *mestizo* may be substituted for *white* as *mestizo* represents the standard or unmarked hegemonic racial norm (Van Vleet 2019, 39; see also Weismantel 2001).

7. It is important to note that various ethnic associations shape identities within highland communities that can create conflict. For example, Miguel La Serna (2012) found that two distinct ethnic groups, the Aymaraes and the Canas, settled the community of Chuschi, in the Department of Ayacucho. Such distinct ancestries occasionally

fueled the use of racial slurs by neighbors, underscoring how Indigenous highlanders often enact ethnic and racial categories that move beyond the mestizo–campesino or Indigenous divide.

8. To read more about the debate on the role of creole identity in shaping modernity and a plural present by Mariátegui, Arguedas, Vargas Llosa, and Flores Galindo, see Portocarrero and Vich (2012).

9. While the criollo identity seeks ethnic purity, it is often associated with Indigenous and Black bodies, resulting in an undesired *mestizaje*. The Spanish Crown understood the criollos as an undesirable reality competing for the surplus produced by Indians without culture or will (Portocarrero 2008).

10. Portocarrero points out the malleability of racial identities as individuals move from rural to urban settings, they play the part of the "cholito" being maltreated, beaten, and swindled, and then become more criollo, shrewder and slyer (Portocarrero 2008). Race is therefore flexible as racial credentials can be acquired to become *gente decente* (literally "decent people" but figuratively "white") through social practice and comportment.

11. Modernization has also reinforced "Indianization of women," while expanding cultural mestizaje to men. Women are "oftentimes recognized around the globe for their 'traditional' lifestyles and as guardians of the natural environment" (Canessa 2005, 4). Radcliffe, Laurie, and Andolina (2004) argue that Indigenous organizations or NGO allies commonly produce indigenous "authenticity" by arguing that gender relations in indigenous communities are different from those in dominant society. Indigenous women are described as emblematic of indigenous culture, which can reproduce indigenous women's oppression while promoting their political participation. While Andean women are considered more "Indian" than their male counterparts are, they consequently suffer greater social inequalities (Babb 2012, 38). On the other hand, indigenous women and men often deploy notions of "traditional" or "authentic" cultural identities as an active strategy to attract tourists and consumers (Babb 2012, 38). To read more about indigenous women's movements in Peru, Mexico and Bolivia see Rousseau and Hudon 2015

12. Scholars have sometimes written about Sendero Luminoso in the tradition of eighteenth-century neo-Inca rebel Túpac Amaru II, but its leader, Abimael Guzmán, traced his lineage to Marx, Lenin, and Mao rather than Túpac Amaru II, Juan Santos Atahualpa, Manco Inca, or other well-known Indian rebels (Starn 1995b; see also Starn 1999). Manco Inca was a puppet Inca emperor who attempted a failed rebellion against the Spanish in 1536 (Stern 1982). Juan Santos Atahualpa launched an insurrection against the Spanish in 1742, driving colonizers to the subtropical region of the eastern slope of the Andes. José Gabriel Condorcanqui, later named Túpac Amaru II, led yet another insurrection against the colonizers in 1780–1782 and attempted to take over Tawantinsuyu (the Inca Empire) at the cost of over one hundred thousand lives, only to be later taken over by the Spanish (Stern 1987). Antonio Díaz Martínez, an agronomist turned revolutionary, greatly influenced Guzmán, who determined that state and international development efforts had failed. Díaz Martínez traveled to China in 1974 and discovered that Mao was successfully implementing many of his proposed programs. Díaz Martínez therefore

returned to Peru in 1977 and wrote *China: la revolución agraria*, which included the ideology and language for Sendero's "prolonged peasant war to liberate the semi feudal and semi colonial masses of Peru from bureaucratic capitalism" (Isbell 1992, 61).

13. Guzmán placed himself in the tradition of José Carlos Mariátegui, a self-educated child of a humble family from the southern Peruvian town of Moquegua and a leading Latin American Marxist (Starn 1995a, 412). Like Mariátegui's Marxist ideals, Guzmán largely ignored cultural practices, values, and organization in his vision of a political and economic revolution (see García 2005).

14. While Sendero offered opportunities for women, it did not lead to gender equality and was not a feminist movement, as it relied on classist principles, required women's bodily and mental submission, and actively reproduced patriarchal hierarchies (see Boesten 2010b). The CVR reported that the Sendero Luminoso's use of gender-based violence was founded on a different ideology than that of state entities. In the early years of the war, the Sendero Luminoso adulterers and rapists were publicly and violently punished, yet there is evidence the Sendero Luminoso activity led to forced pregnancies, sexual torture and slavery, and forced marriages (Boesten 2010b). To read more about the changing role of women in Peruvian society, see Henríquez (1996). To read more about the role of women in Sendero see Barrig (1993), Boesten (2010a), Coral Cordero (1998), Del Pino (1999), and Lázaro (1990).

15. Abimael Guzmán joined an envoy to Communist China in 1965 and took courses in theory and guerilla warfare. In 1969, while teaching at the university in Ayacucho, Guzmán and his wife, Augusta La Torre, mobilized a coalition of peasants, faculty, students, and workers to protest an effort to restrict free university education, which led to policy brutality and Guzmán's arrest. Once released from jail, Guzmán established the Sendero Luminoso, which some claimed was a Maoist splinter group of the Peruvian Community Party and others claimed were one and the same (La Serna 2019). By spreading their ideology through local schools, Sendero used the position of schoolteacher, a figure commonly vested with authority, with the goal of "bringing civilisation and eradicating superstition from the backward classes" (Wilson 2009, 57). However, in some rural communities, schoolteachers are criticized for being lazy and overdrinking.

16. Abimael Guzmán established the Guaman Poma School of Practicum, a teaching program at the university that later produced some of Sendero's first militants (La Serna 2019).

17. Many of these youth had migrated to cities in search of work and found themselves in a national setting that made them feel ambivalent about their natal homes and national culture (Degregori 1990, 114). For example, of those arrested for terrorism between 1983 and 1986, 79.8 percent were under thirty years of age. Moreover, 35.5 percent had some university or professional education (in comparison with 2.5 percent of those imprisoned for assault and robbery and 7.7 percent of all Peruvians over the age of fifteen), yet 85.8 percent had incomes below the poverty line (Chávez de Paz 1989, 55). Women also played key roles in Sendero, with 16.4 percent of women imprisoned for terrorism, as opposed to 3.4 percent in prison for assault and robbery. William Mitchell

argues that the strong role of women in Sendero Luminoso "may be rooted in strong traditions of female independence as peasant landowners, market vendors, small scale commercial entrepreneurs, and guardians of family finances" (Mitchell 1994, 8). The use of schools by Sendero has a deep history in Peru. Peruvian scholars argue that the authoritarian organization structure of Sendero copied the symbolic violence, authoritarianism, and ubiquitous humiliation present in Peruvian schools (Ansión 1989; Degregori 1991).

18. The MRTA acquired its name from the eighteenth-century rebel Túpac Amaru II, who traced his lineage to the last Indigenous Inca rebel, Túpac Amaru. Like Sendero, MRTA called for an end to imperialism; however, the MRTA differed from Sendero in its aim to create a socialist state, as opposed to Sendero's goal of destroying state presence altogether. The MRTA rebels worked with other Latin American insurgent groups such as Colombia's M-19 and Ecuador's Alfaro Vive Carajo (La Serna 2019). The movement attracted several hundred individuals, but its influence waned through conflicts with Sendero, as well as the incarceration and death of senior leaders. On June 9, 1992, the leader of MRTA, Víctor Polay Campos, was captured in the neighborhood of San Borja in Lima.

19. In 65 percent of the 4,500 reported cases of forced disappearances at the hands of state officials, the whereabouts of the victims are still unknown (CVR 2003, 6:113).

20. The CVR was inaugurated on July 13, 2001, and president-elect Alejandro Toledo appointed twelve council members: ten men and two women, who the Council of Ministers approved. Notably, none of the twelve commissioners were Indigenous, and only one, the previous rector of the Universidad Nacional San Cristóbal de Huamanga in Ayacucho, spoke Quechua (Lambright 2015, 10).

21. Over eight hundred people worked for the CVR and traveled to Peru's twenty-four departments to gather firsthand testimonies (CVR 2003). The CVR also conducted interviews with main actors in the internal conflict, such as members of various political parties, military personnel, and members of armed opposition groups.

22. Additionally, the CVR initiated a photography project entitled *Yuyanapaq: Para recordar* (to remember), which resulted in an exhibit in Lima's Museo de la Nación. While access to the exhibit is largely out of reach for many Peruvians, a visual representation of the war entitled in both Spanish and Quechua is notable, given that 15 percent of Peru's adult population is illiterate, and even higher for women and Indigenous populations, those most affected by the war (CVR 2003). To read more about the visual and artistic approaches of the CVR, see Milton (2007).

23. Over four hundred testimonies relating to over three hundred different cases of human rights violations were collected (CVR, n.d.).

24. The conflict covered a larger proportion of the national territory than previous conflicts since the country's founding. The number of people killed and disappeared during the conflict surpassed lives lost in all foreign or civil wars since independence.

25. The Peruvian journalist Ricardo Uceda describes in detail violence enacted by state security forces against citizens. Drawing from in-depth interviews with different state agents, he portrays the violence as endemic to the chain of command, and none of

his informants express remorse for what took place, couching their actions in the protection of democracy and the state (Milton 2018, 56).

26. The CVR concluded that 75 percent of the cases of torture were carried out by state officials and the police or people acting with their authorization or acquiescence (CVR 2003, 6:183) and were systematically inflicted in military bases, barracks, detention centers, police stations, and counterterrorism units.

27. Tens of thousands of innocent people were subjected to torture and inhumane treatment unjustly. For instance, of nearly thirty-four thousand cases of pretrial detention between 1983 and 2000, almost half of those detained had to be released due to lack of evidence (CVR 2003, 6:428). Moreover, almost 1,400 prisoners were found to have been unfairly convicted for terrorist-related offenses and were acquitted by the courts, released by presidential pardon, or granted clemency between 1996 and 2000 (6:428).

28. The report stated that Ayacucho, Huancavelica, Apurímac, Junín, Huánuco, and San Martín were the most affected departments in Peru. One in every two victims came from Ayacucho (CVR 2003, 6:53–55).

29. Consequently, women were often left to care for their families and land unsupported. They were also commonly scripted to serve armed opposition groups and security forces, being subjected to forced marriage, cohabitation, recruitment, and sexual violence.

30. To read more about the use of retablos, novels, songs, and cinema in postwar cultural production in Peru, see A'ness (2004), Gusterson (2007), Isbell (1998), Lambright (2015), Milton (2014), Ritter (2002), Rueda (2015), and Wissler (2009).

31. To read more about Peru's ongoing battles for memory and opposing interpretations of Peru's violent past as illustrated with the monument the Eye That Cries (El ojo que llora), see Drinot (2009).

32. It is notable that the Lugar de la Memoria is the first and only state-sponsored museum to commemorate the past for the entire country; however, it is located on a former garbage dump in a middle-class neighborhood of Lima that has no direct connection to the war (Milton 2018). Conservative sectors originally opposed the museum and President Alan García initially turned down the German government's donation to build the museum. In 2009, the Minister of Defense, Ántero Flores Aráoz, criticized the museum, claiming the money would be better spent on aid to the poor, which sparked a polemical public debate with fears the museum would not be objective, would honor subversives, and would tarnish the military's image. Mario Vargas Llosa ultimately saved the museum by persuading President García of its value (Henríquez and Ewig 2013, 276). The original aim of the museum was to house an exhibit produced by the Peruvian CVR, *Yuyanapaq* (to remember), yet disagreements ensued over the museum's physical construction, content, and representation of the conflict. *Yuyanapaq* was never installed in the Lugar de la Memoria and has a lease to be displayed in Lima's Museo de la Nación until 2026 (Feldman 2018).

33. The *Tablas de Sarhua* includes thirty-one paintings made by the Asociación de Artistas Populares de Sarhua, a nonprofit organization comprised of artists from the community of Sarhua in Ayacucho who migrated to Lima (González 2011). Before making a

public appearance, the Counter-Terrorism Directorate and the public prosecutor's office confiscated the artwork for its alleged defense of terrorism under Law 25475, which was created in 1992 under the administration of Alberto Fujimori. The law was modified in July 2017 with Article 316-A, which mandates fifteen-year prison sentences for the use of books, texts, recordings, or visual images that justify, glorify, or exalt terrorism.

34. Edwin Donayre even disguised himself as a tourist and recorded a tour at the Lugar de la Memoria, la Tolerancia, y la Inclusión Social (Place of Memory, Tolerance, and Social Inclusion) with the goal of proving that the museum was promoting terrorism.

35. The active silencing of various interpretations of the past is also apparent in the difficulty of accessing retablos that depict the war. A small sampling of retablos is on display at the Universidad Nacional San Cristóbal de Huamanga, but as of June 2013, not one referenced the internal conflict. Jiménez's works are also housed behind guarded doors at the Instituto de Estudios Peruanos office in Lima (Lambright 2015, 161). Moreover, several national art contests in the 1980s disqualified entries for "depicting violence or social commentary" (Ulfe 2011, 111). To read more about additional acts of censorship in Peru, see Milton (2018).

36. I worked in a community called Sacclaya a couple of hours south of Andahuaylas and my spouse conducted fieldwork in communities a couple of hours north of the city. We both lived with host families. Therefore, to meet periodically, we rented a house on the edge of the city of Andahuaylas for approximately US$30.00 a month.

37. I later learned that Graciela did not receive the cards because she was no longer living in the home and the homeowner did not know her whereabouts.

38. I obtained permission from the University of Maine at Farmington Institutional Review Board for this project before returning to Peru in 2014.

39. To protect participants' confidentiality, we have used pseudonyms for Graciela's family members, most of them chosen by the individuals themselves. Given the sometimes sensitive nature of material shared, we have also used pseudonyms for all other individuals mentioned. After extensive consultation with Graciela and her family members, colleagues, and friends, Graciela explicitly requested that we retain her full name, as well as that of her community.

40. People throughout the Andes have traditionally chewed coca leaves to ward off hunger and protect against altitude sickness. People commonly share coca with others to forge personal relationships and use coca in spiritual or religious ceremonies such as giving offerings (*pagos*) to a mountain god (*apu*) or one's fields. For more information on the myriad meaning and uses of coca, see Allen (2002).

41. Because testimonials often stem from those whose experiences have been misrepresented or neglected, they offer a unique authority, authenticity, and truth, yet their production and consumption can be a political process, as it connects a wide range of people across ethnic, class, national, and other boundaries (Tula and Stephen 1994, 223).

42. The testimonial discourse in Latin America has been closely associated with revolutionary developments, as a central theme is the violation of human rights by state agents. It can be traced to Cuba in the mid- and late 1960s with Cuban Miguel Barnet's

autobiography, which serves as a corrective to Oscar Lewis's ethnographic-oriented life histories (Gugelberger and Kearney 1991, 5–6). In responding to revolutionary movements, testimonio represents a new form of discursive authority that challenges previous accepted notions of the "great writer" to represent Latin American development and culture (Beverley 2004, 77).

43. The genre of testimonials continues to evolve in response to differing threats to human rights, including recent testimonial and ethnographic work surrounding the US–Mexico border (see Cruz and Collazo 2020; Getrich 2019; Mayers and Freedman 2019; Slack 2019).

44. In relaying her experiences as a wife of a Bolivian miner, Domitila Barrios de Chungara states, "I don't want anyone at any moment to interpret the story I'm about to tell as something that is only personal. Because I think that my life is related to my people. What happened to me could have happened to hundreds of people in my country" (Barrios de Chungara, Viezzer, and Ortiz 1978, 15).

45. This argument highlights the privileged position of scholar, which is ensconced in broader hierarchical relationships and fields of power, that has historically been tasked with creating representations of other marginalized places and individuals for audiences back home (e.g., Asad 1973; Goldstein 2009; Kovats-Bernat 2002).

46. Like Krista E. Van Vleet's research with young mothers in Cusco, my fieldwork with Graciela "relied on and reinforces particular structures and relationships of privilege even as it illuminates the lives of individuals who are often marginalized" (2019, 25–26).

47. As John Beverley (2004) notes, "The complicity a testimonio establishes with its readers involves their identification—by engaging their sense of ethics and justice—with a popular cause normally distant, not to say alien, from their immediate experience" (37).

48. Rather than evaluating testimonials from a social science or journalist perspective, "they should be valued for the vision and experience they represent and respected for the survival strategies that their tellers have woven into them. Without these characteristics, testimonials may not exist" (Tula and Stephen 1994, 230).

49. To read more about how memory has been shaped postconflict in Peru, see Jeffrey Gamarra's (2002) study on the creation of "hegemonic memory" that became "communal" in communities throughout Ayacucho, which has given rise to "hidden memory." To read more on the role of secrecy in engaging with memory, see Kimberly Theidon's (2004) call to confront the "secretly familiar" to adequately engage in reconciliation.

50. I seek to relay how Graciela constructs her world stemming from her historical memory situated within particular forms of gender and ethnic relations, class inequality, exploitation, repression, and opportunity (see Beverley 2004, 86). As John Beverley notes, "There is not, outside of discourse, a level of social facticity that can guarantee the truth of this or that representation, given that what we call 'society' itself is not an essence prior to representation but precisely the consequence of struggles to represent and over representation" (73).

51. While much of the scholarship on the pornography of violence focuses on visual imagery, it is a useful metaphor through which objectification of violence in general can

be framed. From one perspective, horror and violence is presented to "make a moral claim on its audience, whereby looking at such imagery is to bear witness to atrocity" and to ensure acts are not repeated (Tait 2008, 94). However, images of horror may be unable to sustain a moral dimension if they produce "compassion fatigue" or involve pleasure and thus become pornographic. Compassion fatigue also decontextualizes and objectifies, ultimately producing an "other" (William Mitchell, pers. comm., October 4, 2021).

52. Drawing from Megan Boler (1997), it is our hope that the reader engages in an in-depth introspection that does not entail "an ability to empathize with the very distant other but to recognize oneself as implicated in the social forces that create the climate of obstacles the other must confront" (263).

53. As Halbwachs (1992) argues, Graciela took memory out of the confines of linear time to reconstruct the past from the perspective of the present.

54. I found that Graciela's experiences with memory and cyclical sense of time resonated with Walter Benjamin's philosophy of historicism as described by Brand 2020.

Chapter 1

1. While the poverty rate improved for much of Peru between 2013 and 2018, the La Mar province of the Department of Ayacucho remained at the highest percentile (Instituto Nacional de Estadística e Informática 2020).

2. In the early 1980s, Oronccoy lay within the district of Chungui, but the government of Peru declared Oronccoy the district capital on June 15, 2016, under Law No. 30457. (*El Peruano*, n.d.). The first elected mayor to the district of Oronccoy, Yuri Eusebio García Orihuela, was shot and killed on February 27, 2018 (*El Comercio* 2018).

3. When possible, I have included scientific names for all plants Graciela identified; nevertheless, I have been unable to locate the scientific terms for all the products mentioned. I worked closely with Graciela's family members to assure the correct spelling of the Quechua terms and plant names Graciela identified.

4. While some communities continue to use the chaki taklla, other communities utilize the labor of two cows with a *yuhoo taklla*. The *yuhoo* is a yoke that goes across the cows' heads and the *taklla* is a wooden beam that is dragged between the cows. The blade at the end of the taklla is called a *recca* and the piece of wood that fits the yuhoo with the taklla is a *yavecca*.

5. As Orin Starn argues, a sense of Andeanism creates "an imagined geography that presents the coast, and especially Spanish-settled Lima, as 'modern,' 'official,' and 'Western' in contrast with the 'premodern,' 'deep,' and 'non-Western' Andes" (Starn 1995b, 549–50). While communal labor dates to pre-Inca times and was prohibited by Spanish rule in 1810 (Fuenzalida 1970, 71), it continues to function throughout the Andes and has even become an integral part of urban squatter settlements throughout Peru (Isbell 1978).

6. *Huatia* is a general term for earth oven. Oftentimes people make a small aboveground huatia when working in the fields to cook a few potatoes to eat. To prepare

pachamanka, you typically dig a hole in the ground to create a large huatia to cook a greater quantity and variety of food.

7.   The charango reportedly originated in the eighteenth century in the Andes, likely around modern-day Potosí, Bolivia. There are many beliefs of how the charango came into existence. One idea is that native musicians in the Andes liked the sound of the vihuela (a precursor to modern guitars) but lacked the technology to shape wood in that manner. Others claim that the charango was adapted as people could hide it under clothing when the Spanish prohibited natives from playing their traditional music.

8.   Llaqta Maqta is a traditional local style of song originally associated with courtship rituals, yet during the internal war, residents of Chungui transformed it to express social and political critiques (Lambright 2015, 140).

9.   Graciela's use of the term *camayuc* likely stems from its historic roots, which indicated a person of authority. For example, during the colonial era, the governor of a pueblo was referred to as *llacta camayuc* (*llacta* is "town" in Quechua) and a superintendent of bridges was referenced as *chaca camayuc* (*chaca* is "bridge" in Quechua). Likely, this individual is a *vaca camayuc* (Velasco 1841–1844).

10.   People dye the threads spun from the puscha and intertwine two of the threads to make a final strong thread for weaving. Men whip one another with a huaraca in staged fighting during festivals. Ritual fighting in the Andes extends back at least two hundred years to regularly scheduled intracommunity and intercommunity ritualized conflicts called *tinku*. To read more about ritualized fighting in the Andes, see Gorbak, Lischetti, and Muñoz (1962), Hopkins (1982), Orlove (1994), Platt (1986), and Skar (1982).

11.   Scholars note the Andean intersection of space and time through the concept of *pacha*. In general, the Andean universe is divided into *hanaq pacha*, or the upper world that contains the celestial beings and heavens; *kay pacha*, which is the physical world and current time inhabited by humans; and *ukhu* (or *hurin*) *pacha*, which is the inner earth or under world (Lambright 2015, 112).

12.   Todos los Santos correlates with other festivals throughout Latin America, such as Dia de los Muertos (Day of the Dead), in which ancestors are given tribute and the boundaries between the living and the dead are blurred.

13.   *Mazamorra* is a general term for traditional dishes in Córdova, Andalusia, and Latin America. The recipes vary and typically include ingredients such as milk, maize, sweet potato, and sugar. In rural Peru, mazamorra is generally a side dish or dessert and has a custard- or jelly-like consistency.

14.   The central role of food in festivals also underscores the dearth of variety, as well as lack of meat, in diurnal rural Andean diets. For example, while living in the highland community of Sacclaya in the Department of Apurímac in 2005–2006, I only ate meat during community festivals or godparent events. Personal wealth was determined via quantity of livestock, particularly for women, and the well-being of one's family was often dependent on whether their cattle were producing milk and their hens were laying eggs, without which the family diet was limited primarily to tubers. It is also worth noting that

every piece of the animal is used and consumed, including the bladder, stomach, brains, bone marrow, and of course intestines (Kellett 2009).

15. Taking a historic view, the Andean cargo system of religious and civil posts has been understood as an institution of "ritual impoverishment" within a "prestige economy" utilized to redistribute wealth accumulated through the market economy (Saignes 1995). Many times, the cargo-carrying festivals have ties to Catholic celebrations. To avoid the high costs of supporting such events, some anthropologists have found that individuals have turned to other religions (Sanabria 2016). For more information on the cargo system in the Andes, see Heilman (2010).

16. Although it could appear that Graciela was referring to a bull (*toro*) when she references a cow (*vaca*), I translated Graciela's words as spoken, in which she interchanged the two terms.

17. In 2018, Graciela explained that they continue to commemorate Easter in this manner, and she was in Oronccoy for the celebration three years prior. Graciela stated that Oronccoy had not observed Easter in this fashion for two years, which she attributed to the limited economy, yet the community planned to reinstate the festival the following year.

18. To read more about the relationship between Andean dance, music, and cosmology, including the role of dancing in circular rotations, see Wibbelsman (2019). To read more about the role of drinking in Andean life and how it relates to Andean cosmology, colonial influences, and contemporary practices, see Jennings (2019).

19. People continue to celebrate carnival in a similar fashion throughout the Andahuaylas valley. Sacclaya hosts a large carnival celebration and in addition to the dancing, singing, and yunsa, people ride horses throughout the open pampas. People decorate the horses with newly woven mantas and women decorate their hats with peacock feathers. A swirl of bright colors moves from one village to another for a full week. Typically, local huayno bands play traditional harp music blasted through a series of oversized speakers precariously balanced on top of one another.

20. While working with a microfinance organization in Andahuaylas in 2005–2006, I learned that the primary time people sought loans was the few months leading up to carnival celebrations. While the loans were designed for business, agricultural, or pastoral investments, everyone was aware those funds were also channeled to new wardrobes for carnival (see Kellett 2011).

21. The *Juglans neotropica*, or nogal, tree is found in Colombia, Ecuador, and Peru and is threatened by habitat loss.

22. When I was staying with friends in the rural community of Churrubamba outside of Andahuaylas, I witnessed this practice. Following the death of an individual in the community, the family had a multiple-day wake. On the final day of the wake in which the burial would take place, a group of four older women dressed in black huddled together singing a high-pitched wailing song. The women were weeping and howling as they sang in unison. The other community members did not join the singing or give it sustained attention but rather prayed and continued the process of preparing the body for burial.

23. This can contrast with immaterial but immediate and intense expressions of parental grief, such as gestures and vocalizations (Baitzel 2018).

24. The symptoms of nervios are far-reaching, including crying fits, shaking, or trembling and feelings of hopelessness and depression. It is not considered a mental illness but rather nervous attacks following a stressful event or a way to express everyday anxieties. The causes of nervios can range from financial difficulties, family feuds, food and work problems, accidents, not eating well, or drinking too much. Nervios varies greatly across different Latin American regions; however, research has shown a similar shared understanding of the causes, symptoms, and treatments of nervios (Baer et al. 2003). Nervios is distinct from, but related to, *susto*. Susto can entail similar symptoms to nervios and often stems from some form of intense fear that can cause the soul to separate from a person's body (see Rubel, O'Neill, and Collado 1984). During the war, people commonly believed that children were always getting sick with susto because of the violence (Theidon 2007, 461).

25. Through the years, I have found a focus on the cost of Western medicine and confidence in herbs to be widespread throughout the Andahuaylas valley, among both rural and urban inhabitants. Shortly after the conversation with Graciela about marqarinqa, a taxi driver pointed out the herb to me on the side of the road, explaining that it was effective in healing gastritis and other stomach maladies.

Chapter 2

1. Velasco's land reform limited ownership to 375 acres to prevent the rise of new haciendas at the expense of small farmers. Decades later, Alberto Fujimori's land law removed all limits on landownership and overturned legal norms created to protect campesino community lands from being divided and sold (Manrique 1996).

2. Marisol de la Cadena claims that through this move, Velasco appropriated the language that leftist politics had promoted since the 1930s, thereby dealing the final blow to Indigenismo and the racial-cultural rhetoric, which had served as vocabulary to discuss rural problems and development (de la Cadena 1998). Indigenismo emerged as an urban literary movement in the mid-1800s that underscored the marginalization and exploitation of Indigenous peoples in Peru (García 2005) and evolved into a frame with which to address Indigenous rights. Robin M. DeLugan notes the contradictory meanings and elasticity of Indigenismo. For example, on one hand, Indigenismo entails "the defense of indigenous communities, the promotion of their cultural practices, and support for policies ranging from increased participation in national society to degrees of autonomous self-determination" (DeLugan 2000, 1). On the other hand, Indigenismo often stems from a view of Indigenous culture as "anti-modern, an obstacle to progress for both the indigenous communities as well as for national society, leading to a prescription for assimilation to an imagined national norm" (DeLugan 2000, 1). While Velasco solved "the Indian question" by referring to them as peasants, in 1975 he also made Quechua an official language of Peru and created programs with names such as Plan Inca and Plan de Gobierno Tupac Amaru (Barre 1985, 56).

3. While some individuals throughout the Andes currently identify as campesino, others can find it condescending and prefer to be referenced as producer or agriculturalist (*agrikulturya kayku*, "we are agriculturalists/farmers") to highlight the expertise and skills necessary to successfully cultivate and manage a means of production (Huayhua 2019, 420). Graciela and her family members openly identified themselves as campesinos, but often regarding their marginalized status in society. Throughout the text, I have attempted to avoid the term *campesino* except when it is referenced directly to highlight the power dynamics between agriculturalists and the rest of Peruvian society.

4. The Varayocc is also often referred to as the *Umachac*, which literally means "head" (*uma*) in Quechua (*chac* serves as a possessive). *Varayocc* generally refers to a community's leadership. The main leader of the community is the Varayocc, a Quechua term that translates to the holder of the *vara*, a decorative staff passed down along the lineage of community leaders. For more information on the Varayocc system, see Heilman (2010).

5. Although scholars describe them in various ways, ayllus can be understood as malleable social formations consisting of individuals joined together by real and imagined kinship, individuals who share the same origin place and ancestor, and groups of people with rights to communal landholdings (Hyland 2016, 12). Within ayllus, these moieties "existed in a complementary, hierarchical relationship to one another" and their status depended on the resources they controlled, if they were original inhabitants of the region, and their alliances with the Incas (Seligman 1995, 109). With disregard to the existing moiety system in communities, oftentimes the lower (*Uray*) moiety benefited from the reform, while the upper (*Hanay*) moiety became isolated from the formation of cooperatives (Isbell 1978; Skar 1982; Zuidema 1990), instigating conflict and inequality.

6. In fact, in response to the failure of the agrarian reform to turn over land, haciendas in Andahuaylas were taken over by land seizures well after the enactment of the Agrarian Reform of 1969. The government only agreed to recognize campesinos' legitimate claim to the invaded lands in exchange for campesinos' acquisition of the "agrarian debt," thereby paying for the seized lands over a period of time to compensate the aggrieved hacendados (Llamojha Mitma and Heilman 2016, 143). From the beginning, the cooperatives also ran into difficulties due to deficient capital and administrative experience. Additionally, in regions that the government divided into cooperatives, before losing their land hacendados typically dismantled their estates, taking and selling moveable property (livestock, machinery, etc.) (McClintock 1984). As many of the collectively owned cooperatives proved to be economically unviable, they were gradually dismantled through a process called parcelization (Manrique 1996). In many areas of Peru in the 1980s, campesino communities enacted massive invasions of Sociedades Agrarias de Interés Social lands to accelerate the parcelization process.

7. In 2018, Huancavelica, Apurímac, and Ayacucho Departments had poverty rates ranging from 33.3 to 36.8 percent. However, as recently as 2007, Huancavelica had poverty rates from 80.9 to 89.1 percent and Apurímac and Ayacucho had poverty rates ranging from 65.2 to 71.1 percent (Instituto Nacional de Estadistica e Informatica 2018).

To read more about the role of Andean peasants in the southern Andes in the national resistance during the War of the Pacific (1879–1883), see Stern (1982, 1987). To read more about the rebellions that directly led up to the rise of the Sendero Luminoso in Ayacucho, see Heilman (2010).

8. La Hacienda Chapi was converted into the Comunidad Campesina de Chapi until 1987 when it changed its name to Comunidad Campesina Belén Chapi. Payments went to the communities of Chupón, Chapi, Chillihua, Pallqa, Huallhua, Yerbabuena, Occoro, and Oronccoy (CVR 2003).

9. Alberto Flores Galindo (2010) notes that the possibility of a revolutionary project began to circulate in Andahuaylas around 1974, as evidenced in fliers, agreements signed by political leaders, and huaynos (a local music genre) of the period, whose lyrics were sprinkled with violence and rage and called for a desire to end servitude and personal dependency.

10. Adam Webb was curious how literacy and education influenced support for Sendero. He ran a simple statistical test in 1995 in the community of Pomatambo to explore the relationship between early levels of support and years of education. He found the threshold lay between two and three years of primary education, generally the level that would allow one to read a newspaper and comprehend radio broadcasts in Spanish (Webb 2009, 58).

11. Subsequent Sendero activities in Lima included numerous car bombings, assassinations of political leaders, and the recruitment of young urban youth in the growing *pueblos jóvenes* (literally "young towns" but signifying slums or shantytowns) mushrooming around the city.

12. Bourque and Warren (1989) argue that Belaúnde was hesitant to call in the army in 1981–1982 because the military had overthrown him in 1968 and he did not want to increase its power out of fear of another coup (12).

13. In the museum Lugar de la Memoria, there was a map of affected areas in Peru with the number of deaths in the Department of Ayacucho by year, which broke down to the following: 1980, 324; 1981, 412; 1982, 1,072; 1983, 2,232; 1984, 4,453; 1985, 2,083; 1986, 1,206; 1987, 942; 1988, 950; and 1989, 986.

14. In the community of Huaychao, peasants attacked a group of Senderistas with stones and knives and ended up strangling seven of them to death (La Serna 2012).

15. For example, during an assault on a Cangallo hacienda in 1980, the insurgents "first blindfolded their victims and then with a razor blade cut the ears off the farmer and owner of the hacienda house, Benigno Medina del Carpio, who then was beaten to death along with Ricardo Lizarbe" (Flores Galindo 2010, 226).

16. A friend of mine, Carlos, who lived in Ayacucho during the height of the violence, relayed a gruesome story that demonstrates this literal dehumanization. He explained how when he and some friends walked to the local market in the city of Ayacucho to buy some tunas (prickly pear cactus), they suddenly smelled a wretched stench. They looked around the corner of a makeshift stand to find a pig feeding on a dead human body.

17. According to Isbell (1992), it was apparent that Sendero had no knowledge of or interest in campesino/Indigenous life and did not consult the extensive anthropological

fieldwork conducted in the Río Pampas region in the 1960s and 1970s (66). As opposed to an omission, Deborah Poole and Gerardo Rénique argue that Sendero militants' Maoist ideology and class-based political vision contributed to their direct scorn for all things Indigenous (Poole and Rénique 1991, 144).

18. On August 14, 1985, the military killed sixty-nine unarmed agriculturalists in the community of Accomarca (Center for Justice and Accountability 2016). The Center for Justice and Accountability sought to bring two lieutenants in charge of the Accomarca massacre to justice, Lieutenant Telmo Hurtado and Lieutenant Juan Rivera Rondón. After years of hearings in both the United States and Peru, in 2016 Hurtado and Rondón were sentenced to twenty-four and twenty-three years in jail, respectively. Other crimes went unreported at the time, including a massacre in Qechawa in August of 1984 in which the military crowded villagers into a shack and set it on fire (González 2011). Those who attempted to escape were shot, and the military forced villagers of Qechawa to dig a hole and bury the bodies to hide evidence of the crime. Two girls were also taken to Sarhua and were raped, tortured, and killed (46).

19. A belief in *pishtacos* began when Spanish conquistadores sought rural agriculturalists to work off their mita, or required labor to the Spanish Crown, in the silver and gold mines. In the late 1500s, light-skinned, often bearded Spanish men scoured the highland villages for able-bodied men and forced them to work in the high-altitude mines. If the men survived, they often returned to their villages as walking skeletons. A belief soon arose that these men were taken for their fat (*unto* in Quechua), which was used to lubricate the machines in the mines. Soon, ideas abounded that fat was also collected for sale in the growing pharmaceutical companies in Europe. The men in search of these bodies became known as pishtacos (Spanish) or *ñanaq* (Quechua): a supernatural being, "often a white man who carries a bloody knife used for dismembering people," who likes to drink their victims' blood and suck their fat (Liffman 1977). Belief in pishtacos has persisted for hundreds of years and is found in national literatures and daily narratives of Ecuador, Peru, and Bolivia, with variations in its meaning. To read more about pishtacos, see Morote Best (1952), Oliver-Smith (1968), Salazar-Soler (1991), and Weismantel (2001).

20. For example, in 1982 when authorities in the communities of Chiquintirca and Anchihuay in Chungui refused to collaborate or hand over their communities to commanding Senderistas, the guerillas began to assassinate them and the people fled. "In the Chungui district the PCP-SL killed at least one *gamonal* [peasants of more than average position] in each of the annexes and communities" (CVR 2003, 1:108). Moreover, in November or December of 1984, military forces burned and assassinated twenty-nine comuneros from Oronccoy accused of being subversives (CVR 2003, vol. 5).

21. The counterinsurgency police, called Los Sinchis, had been trained and financially supported by the US military and the CIA as a special antiterrorist unit of the Peruvian Civil Guard in response to guerilla activity in the 1960s and were notorious for their brutal repression of demonstrations and strikes (García 2005; González 2011). The government initially sent Los Sinchis to Ayacucho, and various communities throughout Peru remember their indiscriminate violence.

22. The base in Chungui was under the jurisdiction of the Department of Ayacucho and the base in Mollebamba was operated out of the Department of Apurímac (CVR 2003, vol. 4).

23. The rondas campesinas first began in northern departments of Peru, such as Cajamarca and Piura, following President Juan Velasco's reforms, which consisted of vigilante patrols to capture, interrogate, and punish suspected thieves or vandals in the absence of an effective police force (La Serna 2012, 23). The rondas campesinas soon expanded to disciplining any wrongdoer, and by the 1980s some form of rondas campesinas or grassroots mechanism of communal justice spread throughout much of rural highland Peru.

24. As agriculturalists began to reject Sendero, they often did so through the rondas, relying on "knives, rocks, slings, spears and other makeshift weapons to defend themselves against rebel incursions" (La Serna 2012, 198). Postwar narratives have emerged that tend to be masculinized wherein ronderos are portrayed as defending their villages, defeating Sendero, and establishing new ideas for citizenship. Miriam Cooke argues that the homogenizing of such narratives has obscured alternative understandings of the civil war (Cooke 1996). Kimberly Theidon asserts that such disjunctions reflect axes of differentiation surrounding gender, generation, and ethnicity that operate within these villages (Theidon 2003, 68).

25. The number of deaths and disappeared in the district of Chungui as reported to the CVR are as follows: 1982, 47; 1983, 102; 1984, 273; 1985, 78; 1986, 76; 1987, 110; 1988, 21; 1989, 30; 1990, 5; 1991, 1; and 1992, 3 (CVR 2003, vol. 4).

26. The term *guerra fratricida* was used in the book *En Honor a la Verdad* (In Honor of the Truth) produced by La Comisión Permanente de Historia del Ejército del Perú (The Standing Committee on the History of the Peruvian Army) (Milton 2018, 101).

27. Similarly, in the community of Chungui a communal assembly concluded that they had to organize an escape, otherwise the strangers were going to exterminate them (CVR 2003, vol. 3).

Chapter 3

1. Even though it is apparent the torture and killing of animals directly affronted moral and cultural values and was clearly another form of torture, in the Comisión de la Verdad y Reconciliación final report, the destruction of animals was considered simply a "material loss" no different than pottery, tools, or produce (Lambright 2015, 147).

2. While urban migration had been occurring since the mid-1940s, the depopulation of certain regions of the highlands, especially in the Ayacucho and Huanta regions, was a new phenomenon (Bourque and Warren 1989).

3. The change in percentage of rural to urban dwellers in Peru illustrates such processes. In 1940, 35 percent of Peruvians were urban and 65 percent were rural. By 1989, there were an estimated 69 percent urban to 31 percent rural residents. Moreover, Guzmán sought to capture Lima by taking control over the enormous *barriadas* (barrios) that ringed the city and housed almost half of the capital's population (Burt 1998). To

read more about demographic changes at this time, see Mitchell (1994) and Webb and Fernández Baca (1990).

4. While living in the community of Sacclaya, I found that people described times of severe scarcity due to theft or ruined crops as a time without sugar or salt, a year without salt necessary to cure meat, retain fluids, and balance overall health. This is not surprising, given that in impoverished rural Andean communities in the Andahuaylas area, salt and sugar are often the only purchased food items; all other consumables are grown on one's land.

5. Although this book is based on the experiences of one survivor, Graciela, I have heard numerous other firsthand accounts of the ever presence of death during this violent era. My friend Carlos has been particularly open about his experiences while attending the Universidad Nacional San Cristóbal de Huamanga in Ayacucho. While having dinner one night with Carlos, he described various traumatic memories from his time in Ayacucho in the mid-1980s. He stated, "I went for a walk at one time and saw three or four corpses during my walk around the neighborhood, just lying in the grass, on the street. . . . One time there were a lot of people in the plaza and bombs exploded in different corners of the plaza. Everyone ran to another area, another bomb would go off, people were killed. Others ran to the other end, another bomb would explode, people killed."

6. My friend Carlos who studied in Ayacucho relayed a massacre that occurred in a community on the border of the Departments of Ayacucho and Apurímac during this period. One night a group of individuals suspected of being Senderistas, because they did not speak solid Spanish, slaughtered people with knives, machetes, and axes. In the aftermath of this massacre, they found a live baby nursing from her dead mother's body.

7. Such assumptions underscore dominant regimes of male power, while also ignoring how rapes were performed as "entertainment or spectacle, and certainly promoted male bonding" (Boesten 2014, 32). With the identification of the woman as "*gringa*," the soldier's narrative also demonstrates how "raping women perceived as higher on the social ladder through race and class may give the perpetrator a sense of domination toward the ruling classes, while raping a woman perceived as *chola* or indigenous, may create de-identification with that social group" (56).

8. In referencing pumas, tigers, and lions, Graciela is most likely discussing cougars or mountain lions (*Puma concolor*), jaguars (*Panthera onca*), or oncillas (*Leopardus tigrinus*), all found in the Peruvian Andes.

9. Although it is difficult to know if the individuals Graciela mentioned had leprosy, or Hansen's disease, primary risk factors for the disease are malnutrition and poverty. Graciela did mention individuals experienced limb numbness and paralysis, which are symptoms of leprosy.

10. According to Graciela, Paulina's house was unfortunately not a haven from abuse. Graciela described how Paulina would hit Graciela's mother if she lost a sheep or committed other misconducts. Graciela said her mother faced much abuse because she was an orphan and was quite afraid of her own sister; she still cries about the abuse she experienced as a child.

Chapter 4

1. Being considered an orphan is a particularly drastic social situation in the rural Andes, as it signifies someone who has lost ties to family and land, preventing their ability to participate reciprocally in the community (Lambright 2015, 75). As Jessaca Leinaweaver (2008) discusses, *wakcha* is typically used to describe an individual whose parents have died, but it is often used in a wider sense to describe physical separation from living parents and homeland, or more poignantly to identify someone who has lost all support from his or her family. According to Kimberly Theidon, *waqcha* means both "orphan" and "poor," as to live without family is to live in affective and material destitution (Theidon 2006, 443).

2. It is unknown if the site that Graciela describes, Llamayoq, is indeed an Inca site. By exploring the area through Google Earth, it appears that there are numerous Chanka (1000–1400 CE) sites on hilltops surrounding Oronccoy. Regardless of previous occupation, the mountain and archaeological site had sacred significance to Graciela.

3. These are similar flowers and hummingbirds as represented on the cover of this book. Graciela embroidered a blanket with brightly colored flowers and birds and gifted it to me the last time I saw her, which where recreated for the book cover.

4. This term could be indicative of the racialized geography of Peru wherein certain people are relegated to environments, which has played a decisive role in the highland/Indigenous coastal/mestizo split in Peru.

5. Reliable statistical data regarding sexual violence is particularly challenging to acquire, due to a lack of reporting to first-line service providers, biased surveys, and other factors in peaceful democratic countries, let alone in conflict settings (see Boesten 2017).

6. La Serna argues that virgin women epitomized community integrity and identity and the physical defense of virgin women against rape by nonvillagers was a key cultural value that in some cases even trumped protections that extended kinship could offer (La Serna 2012).

7. Theidon (2013) describes a woman who was raped by five soldiers to prevent the rape of her own daughter, then her husband left her: "He left me because people say that the women in Hualla are the soldiers' leftovers. There was a lot of gossip because the soldiers took the women away—married women, young women; they took them away to the base" (123).

8. It is also valuable to distinguish between peacetime and wartime sexual violence as it allows for prosecution under international law as survivors of wartime sexual violence seek accountability and reparation. However, such a distinction can also send the message that systematic wartime sexual violence is a crime, while domestic or private sexual violence is not (Boesten 2017).

9. For instance, according to the Centro de Promoción y Desarrollo Poblacional in Ayacucho, domestic violence was higher during the years of pacification (roughly 1993–1997), attributable to unstable mental health and rise in alcoholism because of war traumas (Boesten 2006). The study, however, also found that by 1997 the situation had stabilized and domestic violence rates in Ayacucho are no longer higher than average. At the same time, in 2000, 41 percent of Peruvian women reported having been beaten once or more in their life by their partners.

10.   Marriage was often used to protect a rape victim from dishonor and exempt a perpetrator from prosecution, which is written into Peru's penal code (Article 178, enacted in 1991). To read more about how the ways in which this statute was enacted were class- and ethnically biased, see Boesten (2008).

11.   As men verbally assaulted the women with ethnic insults while raping them, they effectively "whitened" themselves by transferring racist humiliation to their victims (Theidon 2013, 134).

12.   The effectiveness of the counterinsurgency came into question when Sendero attacked the police post in Uchiza on March 27, 1989, killing ten police officers. The event became a symbol of the inability of the military to contain Sendero in the Upper Huallaga region (Burt 2007, 54–54) and consequently, the Upper Huallaga became known as the Huallaga Republic (van Dun 2009). After nearly a decade of civil war, people took to the streets on November 3, 1989, in a march for peace (Perez 1989; see also *La République* 2003).

13.   Fuel costs rose from $0.25 a liter to $3.00 overnight, and the numbers of those living in poverty rose to nearly half the population. Peasant land was also privatized, and private property prevailed in all parts of Peru, replacing communal forms of property that had been in place for millennia (Crabtree and Durand 2017). Nevertheless, the Fujimori regime did gain support by targeting small-scale projects to select communities in return for political support and purging contacts with local municipalities, community organizations, and NGOs, "creating a direct dependency of vulnerable communities on the benevolence of the presidency" (133).

14.   Fujimori's administration was known for its use of repression and authoritarian tactics. According to Burt (2006, 33), Fujimori's regime used state power to keep civil society disorganized and unable to articulate an opposing discourse or politics with patronage as an instrumentalization of fear. The Fujimori government has been described as neopopulist, a "plebiscitarian" democracy, a delegative democracy, and a *democradura*, while some scholars question if it can be considered a democracy at all. John Crabtree argues it was a personalist regime that was never fully authoritarian or properly democratic (Crabtree 2010, 365–66).

15.   In 2018, Graciela, her husband, her youngest daughter, and I visited El Museo de la Memoria de ANFASEP in Ayacucho. On display was a dented silver bowl with a description explaining that the military used them to feed inmates as if they were animals. When Graciela and Juan Pablo saw this, they described their memories of their time in jail eating from the exact same kind of bowl.

16.   Gavilán Sánchez (2015) also describes the sex workers referred to as "charlis" who would come to the military barracks before the soldiers received their stipends. While they worked for money, soldiers would sometimes try to get the charlis drunk and rape them.

Chapter 5

1.   An *acta* is an official record or certificate, and in stating *capitalización* I believe Juan Pablo is referencing the word *capacidad* (capability, aptitude). In Peru, there is an official

notebook you can purchase with a hard blue cover known as an acta. Official minutes and other community records are often recorded in an acta. There were various actas on display at the Museo de la Lugar in Lima with names and dates of those who had been killed in the violence from research conducted through the Comisión de la Verdad y Reconciliación.

2.   I have found Graciela to be a particularly protective mother of her daughters. When visiting Andahuaylas in the summer of 2016, her daughter Rous was attending school in another town. Graciela was visibly preoccupied with the status of her daughter, who was at that time nearly seventeen years old. Although she had spoken on the phone with Rous and others had told Graciela her daughter was doing well, Graciela insisted that she needed to visit her personally to assure that she was indeed safe. Although Graciela maintained her mother never knew what happened to her, Graciela felt she would know if something was amiss with her own children, given her personal history with sexual assault and rape.

3.   Lima had a population of just over five million people in the mid-1980s (Sanders 1984). By 2018, Lima had a population of approximately eleven million inhabitants. Much of this population growth was instigated by the political violence in the southcentral highlands, wherein hundreds of thousands of people fled to the city.

4.   Graciela discussed the need to have a DNI to pass checkpoints on the way to the jungle. Although Graciela did not clarify, I assume her dueña was going to provide identification for her to fly to Lima.

5.   Mere weeks before Graciela and I had this conversation, she ran into this woman in the market. She invited Graciela and her daughter to her house for lunch to meet her son who Graciela was slated to work for so many years prior. The woman invited Graciela and her daughter inside and said, "Graciela, *achilita*, serve us the lunch." In calling Graciela "achilita," they were invoking the word *achinado*, which means "slanting" or "Indian-looking." Whereas *achilita* is often used as a term of endearment, the racial connotations and associated power relations are notable, given the context in which it was spoken. When Graciela grabbed the plates to serve the food, the son insisted she not serve them but rather eat with them, which made the dueña extremely angry. He shared stories about missing his family while living in Spain and about his heart surgery and asked Graciela about her childhood. Graciela described their connection, "Much suffering in other places, for this reason I think he understood our suffering." Graciela described how their warm conversation infuriated the man's mother. "We were conversing, and the mother was standing there *renegando* [loathing, hating]. . . . When he was inviting me to eat the fruit, I think that made the señora even more hateful."

Chapter 6

1.   Uncucha (*Xanthosoma sagittifolium*)—also called yautia, malanga, *macal, quicamote,* and *okomu*—is a vitamin-rich tuber grown in the Andes.

2.   A friend of mine, who grew up in a middle- to upper-class family in the city of Andahuaylas and worked as a schoolteacher throughout her career, also described this process of midwives shaking pregnant mothers to move the baby into the correct position for

birth, claiming it always worked effectively. While living in Sacclaya I became pregnant and visited a traditional midwife. By manipulating my abdomen with her hands, she determined the fetus's sex and exact week of gestation, which an ultrasound verified a few weeks later.

3. About twelve years before Graciela and I were having this discussion, the señora's husband told Graciela that the señora and her young daughter had died in a car accident. With tears in her eyes, Graciela told me about their death. Her husband had been transporting fruit for sale in his truck. "He was traveling to the campo, so the people said that the car weighed too much with all the fruit that was too much for the brakes." The brakes failed and his daughter was thrown from the car. The wife ran from the car in search of the daughter "and then the car smashed her." I assume this daughter was born after Graciela lived with the señora, since she previously only had sons.

4. Congress began an investigation of the attack, which Alberto Fujimori stopped short with his "palace coup" on April 5, 1992, in which he dissolved congress. The following Democratic Constitutional Congress did not review or complete the investigation (CVR 2003).

5. The university was located on the outskirts of Lima, attracted impoverished agriculturalists from rural communities, and had a reputation of fostering radical politics with the presence of Sendero and MRTA.

6. Abimael Guzman was first married to Augusta La Torre (1964–1988) and then married Elena Iparraguirre in 2010. He was located when DINCOTE began casing households in upscale Lima neighborhoods and traced Abimael Guzmán to a ballet studio. Reportedly, the DINCOTE found that the trash can below the ballet studio was producing far more garbage than expected for the residence, and they found discarded tubes of a cream used to treat psoriasis, a skin affliction of Abimael Guzmán. For more details on the behind-the-scenes life of Abimael Guzmán, see Starn and La Serna (2019).

7. Following further questioning by congress, the group claimed that the victims' bodies had been exhumed, incinerated, and reburied in a different location. In 2008, "former head of the SIN and Army general Julio Salazar Monroe and eleven other army officers were convicted in the disappearance and murder of nine students and one professor from La Cantuta University" (Milton 2018, 37).

8. I have tried my best to correctly recount the series of events that occurred during this first two years in the Amazon by reviewing transcripts and asking Graciela and other family members for verification at various times; however, given this tumultuous period, some details regarding the timeline of events may be inaccurate.

9. Sendero took an anti-imperialist and anticapitalist stance and often hung dead dogs from lamp posts. The dogs were supposed to represent the notion of "running dogs of capitalism," referring to people who served the interests of exploiting capitalists (La Serna 2019; Stern 1998).

Chapter 7

1. According to Richard Kernaghan, the repentance law combined mass propaganda and military and police reconnaissance with reduced prison sentences and a

witness-protection program. The approach borrowed from antiterrorist laws Italy used in the late 1970s and early 1980s against the Red Brigades and had roots in approaches taken by the British in post–World War II Malaysia and the United States in Vietnam (Kernaghan 2009, 53).

2. The law provided amnesty to any military, police, or civilian who were reported, investigated, indicted, prosecuted, or convicted of acts derived from or originated on occasion of or because of the fight against terrorism since 1980 (Coordinadora Nacional de Derechos Humanos 1995).

3. On December 17, 1996, members of the MRTA blasted a hole in the garden wall as the Japanese ambassador was hosting a party for high-level diplomats, government officials, military personnel, and business executives, who the MRTA took hostage. Once the chaos settled later that evening, the MRTA militants released the foreign female hostages but held the remaining individuals for 126 days. On April 22, 1997, the Peruvian Armed Forces invaded the residence to free the hostages, killing one hostage, two commandos, and all MRTA militants in the process.

4. This was not the first time I had heard of Marcos Williams. He had acquired a sort of celebrity status with much lore surrounding the work he had done in and around Andahuaylas before my husband and I settled in the area for our research in 2005.

5. In describing throwing flowers at Marcos Williams, Graciela is reflecting a traditional Andean gesture of throwing rose petals in adoration or purification (Lambright 2015, 102).

6. It was challenging to verify numbers of individuals in Oronccoy before and after the violence. From living in Sacclaya, I found population was determined by number of families versus individuals, which appeared to also be the case in Oronccoy. Asking such details always provoked lively discussion between Graciela, her brother, and Juan Pablo. In the end, they agreed that before the violence there were three hundred to four hundred families in Oronccoy and four thousand to five thousand in the greater region. After the violence, initially about twenty families returned to Oronccoy, and as of 2018, there were about forty-five families living in Oronccoy. Overall, the region lost at least one-quarter to one-third of the overall population. As mentioned in chapter 3, the CVR determined that the population in the district of Chungui was halved between 1983 and 1991, going from a total population of 8,257 to 4,338 (CVR 2003, vol. 4).

7. Arequipa is constructed primarily of a white volcanic stone, giving it the name Ciudad Blanca (white city).

8. While traveling with friends in Lima in 2018, a visibly intoxicated man, apparently in his mid- to late 50s, on the streets of the wealthy neighborhood of Miraflores motioned toward my friend's five-year-old son. He stated that he wanted to take the boy and give him his last name. The comment struck me as a reference to past activity during the war.

9. I am in regular contact via social media with Graciela's brother in Argentina and he has continuously expressed concern about and longing for his biological family in Peru. Moreover, the physical similarities between her brother and the rest of the family are striking.

10. Individuals in Andahuaylas have long considered the Oreja de Perro region to consist of rich pastureland and families have historically contracted with comuneros to care for their cows in exchange for one calf a year (CVR 2003, vol. 5).

11. While living in the community of Ampi outside of Andahuaylas, my husband, Lucas, was chosen as a godfather of a quermi in which he ceremoniously baptized the ball before the game.

12. Jessaca Leinaweaver (2008) distinguishes propinas from *sueldo* (salary) or pago (payment) in that propinas relate to the home in the context of interpersonal relationships yet also symbolize and produce hierarchy, reminding children that they are subordinate.

13. During the first decade of the twenty-first century, two conservative Catholic health ministers dismantled Peru's reproductive health services. Women's and human rights groups successfully campaigned for available emergency contraception in 2006, but by 2009 authorities banned distribution of the birth control bill in the public health system. Some policies assuring access to emergency contraception have since been restored (Van Vleet 2019).

14. An arroba is a unit of measuring weight, mass, or volume used in Peru, which is the equivalent of about twenty-five pounds.

Chapter 8

1. It is difficult to discern the legality behind the sale of land, but even if there were legal grounds to demand their money, Graciela and Juan Pablo lacked funds to hire a lawyer. To read more about the history of inequitable land distribution and unlawful sale of property in Rio de Janeiro that relates to the development and commercialization of urban sprawl around cities in Peru, see Perlman (2010).

2. To read more about the "new urban class of depeasantized workers" and their lack of social and economic opportunities, see Chávez de Paz (1989), Degregori (1986), Favre (1984), Mitchell (1979), and Poole and Rénique (1992).

3. Being concerned about the cost of gas for the stove, I asked Graciela how it compared to firewood and found the cost of propane and purchasing firewood in Andahuaylas was comparable.

4. They earned about 10 to 20 soles on weekdays (US$3.30 to $6.00) and about 30 to 40 soles on Sunday market days ($9.00 to $12.00). They had to pay to store the cart in a garage at night (10 soles or $3.00 a week), fees to the municipality (3.5 soles or $1.00 a week), and for the actual sugarcane (35 soles or $10.60 a week). Graciela, much like countless informal entrepreneurs in Peru, also constantly searched for additional ways to earn money. In 2018, she was peeling habas (flat beans) for a woman in town, earning two soles a kilo of peeled habas. Four enormous costales filled with habas sat in the corner of the house, and the entire family constantly peeled habas when at home. Utilizing every resource, Graciela saved the shells of the habas to sell as pig food in the market.

5. The word *humilde* is challenging to translate without losing meaning. A direct

translation is "humble," yet it can also mean "meek" or "lowly" and often refers to "poor." Graciela and Juan Pablo frequently described themselves and their fellow comuneros with this term, always in relation to the discrimination and prejudice they faced from others.

6. While living with Graciela during my fieldwork, I witnessed city authorities and middle- to upper-class mestizos discriminate against Graciela. For instance, in response to one of the landowner's dogs biting an individual, a municipal authority chastised Graciela as if she was a misbehaving child, pointing his finger, yelling, and accusing her of the dog's behavior, right in front of me as if assuming I shared his sentiments. Graciela followed his cue, bowing her head and failing to look him in the eye, taking the blame, even when I tried to interject, illustrating the habitus of social divisions in Peru.

7. The avoidance of recognizing the ethnic dimensions of the conflict were also linguistically apparent as the CVR actively referenced terms such as "peasant," "humble," "poor," and "disenfranchised" and avoided any ethnic terms (e.g., Indigenous, Quechua, Asháninka) (Lambright 2015, 16). It should be noted that an ethnolinguistic map by the Peruvian Ministry of Culture lists seventy-seven ethnic groups and sixty-eight languages (INDEPA 2010) and there are also Afro-Peruvians and communities of Asian heritage living in Peru.

8. Moreover, it is imperative to note that key members of the commission, including Salomón Lerner and the late Carlos Iván Degregori, condemned the ethnic divide in Peru. In a post-CVR essay, Degregori wrote that Peru has a deep-rooted racism toward Indigenous groups and a "habit of repressing subaltern memories" (Degregori 2012, 178). Jelke Boesten (2014) also points to how it was racist "common sense" among the armed forces to see local Andean peasants as "Indios," and thereby violent and savage *terrucos* (terrorists), which facilitated violence against local populations and the sexual torture of young girls and women (24).

9. While prosecution and institutional reforms were encouraged in the report, they were not a requirement (United States Institute of Peace 2001).

10. The areas of reparation in Peru reflect how survivors demanded justice primarily in economic terms, as victims needed farm animals, adequate housing, or education for their children. Conversely, in Argentina, mothers of the disappeared denied compensation because it was a means for the state to evade criminal responsibility (Laplante and Theidon 2007, 243).

11. The Ministerio de la Mujer y Poblaciones Vulnerables (MIMDES, Ministry of Women and Social Development) oversaw the registry for displaced persons and the Defensoría del Pueblo (Ombudsman's Office) managed the registry of the disappeared.

12. A law approved in 2012 added victims of sexual violence, including sexual slavery, forced prostitution, and forced abortion. See Cabitza (2012).

13. The Reparations Council worked with municipalities, churches, regional governments, civil society organizations, and other institutions to open offices in affected regions and conducted workshops and public gatherings with local organizations and community leaders. To address challenges of accessibility and potential revictimization of survivors,

the Reparations Council adopted flexible guidelines in evaluating types of violations eligible for reparations.

14. While generally positively received, unfortunately, community members often conflated reparations projects designed to address economic and social needs of the community with existing national development programs. Moreover, implementation of programs has been mired down by a lack of communication across federal and local agencies (Correa 2013).

15. In 2018, I traveled to the city of Ayacucho with Graciela, Juan Pablo, and Nayely for Graciela to give her manifestation and finally be a registered victim of the violence. Graciela, Juan Pablo, Nayely, and I spent three full days getting the runaround in the city of Ayacucho in our quest to have Graciela give her manifestation. After traveling by foot, bus, and taxi and then waiting from twenty minutes to nearly two hours, five different government agencies redirected us elsewhere. It was not until I called a professional contact that an official at the CMAN office met with Graciela and gave her clear instructions on how to finalize her victim registration.

16. An improvised, short-term vision for the program was implemented for political reasons, which was criticized for the arbitrary nature of amounts and registry deadlines. The program was defined by Decree 051-2011-PCM to pay a lump sum of 10,000 soles (US$3,700) per victim, to prioritize the elderly, and to close registry on December 31, 2011. The amount and deadline were highly contested by victim and civil society organizations. In 2011, CMAN defined a payment of 36,000 soles (US$13,350) for all victims and decided to distribute 18,000 soles to the spouse and 4,500 soles to each child or parent and made the registry permanent. Nevertheless, a cabinet turnover led to the government rejecting most of CMAN's decisions and reinstating those under the García administration, except for criteria for prioritizing reparations. In January 2012, the Reparations Council accepted registering victims who had presented their application before December 2011 (Correa 2013), and in the summer of 2018, the CMAN office in Ayacucho accepted manifestations by victims to be registered.

17. The Ministry of Justice requested that CMAN interpret regulations so victims who suffered more than one violence or lost more than one family member would receive only one amount. In effect, if a mother lost two children in the war, she would be compensated for only one. The Humala administration also vetoed a law to include other categories of victims in the reparations program, which would override efforts to include various forms of sexual violence, as opposed to only rape. CMAN has largely rejected such efforts (Correa 2013).

18. As of 2010, a reported 146 women who were registered as victims of the violence passed away without the state addressing their rights to reparations (Servindi 2010).

19. Like Graciela's sentiments, throughout my time in Peru I have repeatedly heard individuals in Sacclaya and other campesino communities reflect a feeling of incapability and a desire that powerful outsiders capacitarnos (train us). I wondered if this perception resulted from internalizing the rhetoric of nongovernmental organizations and government agencies that continually sought to "empower" campesinos. Rather than

empowering individuals, the approach seemed to entrench already hierarchical systems in which campesinos were relegated in need of "saving" (see Cookson 2018).

20. Although not included in the PIR, the Ombudsman's Office defined a policy for locating and identifying human remains, collaborating with the Office of the Prosecutor, the Bureau of Forensic Medicine, the International Committee of the Red Cross, the Equipo Peruano de Antropología Forense, and other specialized organizations (Correa 2013). The above organizations created a Specialized Forensic Team (SFT) at the Bureau of Forensic Medicine. The SFT has recovered and returned many individual bodies to their families, yet much work remains.

21. This work was completed by the Ministerio Público (Public Ministry) through the Fiscalía Penal Supraprovincial de Huancavelica (Supraprovincial Criminal Prosecutor of Huancavelica) based in Ayacucho, the Dirección General de Búsqueda de Personas Desaparecidas de la Ministerio de Justicia y Derecho Humanos (General Directorate for the Search for Disappeared Persons of the Ministry of Justice and Human Rights), the Equipo Forense Especializado (the Specialized Forensic Team), the Dirección Regional de Salud (Regional Director of Health), the Comisión de Derechos Humanos (Commission on Human Rights), the Comité Internacional de la Cruz Roja (International Committee of the Red Cross), the Dirección Regional de Salud (Regional Directorate of Health), the Municipalidad de Oronccoy (Oronccoy Municipality), and, most importantly, the families of Oronccoy (Comité Internacional de la Cruz Roja 2019).

22. An extensive survey conducted in three regions of Peru examining how the proximity to violence is associated with remembering and forgetting found significant differences in the need to remember, with direct victims having lower agreement with this need than indirect victims and nonvictims (Espinosa et al. 2017). These results show that remembrance is painful and one must have some distancing from violence to value the recollection of traumatic events (Jara, Tejada, and Tovar 2007).

23. The program was directed at "individuals whose schooling was interrupted due to the violence, children of victims, and those forcibly recruited by self-defense committees" (Correa 2013, 7).

24. In 2012, CMAN and the Ministry of Education created a scholarship for victims' access to university education but limited the number of scholarships to fifty (of the 13,511 eligible children) and to people under the age of thirty, even though 92 percent of registered direct victims were thirty years old or older (Correa 2013). The Ombudsman's Office later recommended eliminating the restrictions, increasing the number of scholarships, and allowing eligible victims to pass on this right to their children, which the government later instated.

25. The proliferation of private institutions in Andahuaylas reflects an overall privatizing drive within the state. Beginning with Fujimori's administration, public education received less priority and the government authorized privately run universities and schools that worked for profit to fill the breach, with the backing of the World Bank. The quality of education has varied greatly, and profit-making universities have been entrenched in

scandal, leading to a supervisory body that has shown only modest improvements (Crabtree and Durand 2017).

26.   Shortly after I left Peru in 2006, Sumac Killa became pregnant. The father of her son, Robert, proved to be an abusive partner, which created chaos for the entire extended family. Sumac Killa lived in Lima for a short period to escape Robert's abuse. Fortunately, for Sumac Killa's safety, soon after she left for Lima, Robert moved to the Amazon, and by 2018, he rarely returned to Andahuaylas. Kennedy split his time between his paternal grandmother's house and Graciela's home where Sumac Killa lived.

27.   Overall poverty rates did decline during this time, moving from 52.2 percent in 2005 to 26.1 percent in 2013. Extreme poverty also reportedly dropped during this same period from 30.9 percent to 11.4 percent (World Bank 2018). The World Bank found that throughout Latin America, 130 million people in 2015 remained in poverty, particularly in remote areas and on the fringes of cities, despite their country's economic growth (*Economist* 2018). However, by 2014, overall economic growth stagnated, with a reported growth rate of 3.1 percent between 2014 and 2017, largely due to a drop in international commodity prices, particularly for copper (World Bank 2018). Moreover, the poverty rate in Peru rose for the first time in ten years in 2017, reflecting an unfortunate trend of rising poverty rates throughout South America. At the same time, family groups emerged in sectors that were previously excluded and poor in Peru, and there has been an appearance of what is sometimes referred to as "cholo capitalism" with internal migrants who are now businessmen (Crabtree and Durand 2017, 106). Such social mobility does not appear to be putting a dent in Peru's inequality, however. The push for privatization has resulted in a consolidation of a "new, more powerful, modern and better-organised elite with a presence throughout the country and with projection into the markets of surrounding countries" (106). For instance, in 1986 the fixed assets of the Twelve Apostles (dominant families) were worth an average of US$200 million, and by 2016 their fortune was listed as ten times more at US$2 billion (Crabtree and Durand 2017, 107). In addition, long-standing prejudices and separation between European-descended Limeño elites and those of mixed ancestry from the provinces impede coordination between emerging business organizations (Crabtree and Durand 2017, 119). Peru's most recent economic growth has partially been supported by remittances sent by emigrants (Van Vleet 2019).

28.   According to Richard Kernaghan (2009), in 2005 in Huallaga, "*Sendero* was very much alive" and Sendero was directing its violence toward the antinarcotics police, coca eradication teams, and anyone presumed to be an informer. Nevertheless, its numbers were dwindling, and it was not the menacing force it once was (258). Lingering Senderistas are under the leadership of the Quispe Palomino brothers (Aguirre 2018). The Counter-Terrorist Directorate captured one of the leaders of the Quispe Palomino brothers, Alex Pimentel Vidal, on August 12, 2018. Óscar Ramírez Durand was another leader of Sendero Luminoso that persisted past Abimael Guzmán's capture. He was captured in 1999, and in 2006 he was sentenced to twenty-four years in prison, which was changed to life imprisonment in 2018 when he was found guilty of the Tarata bombing in 1992 (Huaraca 2018).

29.   For a beautifully written exploration of how people experienced postwar violence

in El Salvador, see Moodie (2012). To examine causes of continued violence, see Zinecker (2007). For more information on postwar violence in Guatemala, see Smith and Offit (2010) as well as Kurtenbach (2014).

30. The military works closely with communities in the area to prevent their support of Senderistas, and the government tries to reorient coca farmers in VRAEM to cacao; however, coca is three times more profitable than cacao and markets are much more accessible. Moreover, the government has been cited as having their own hands in the drug trade (Houghton 2017).

31. From her research in rural Cajamarca, Tara Patricia Cookson (2016) describes issues of discrimination, absenteeism, staff shortages, and clinic closures during already limited hours in rural health clinics (1,194).

32. In 2010, Peru, a country roughly the size of South Africa, represented the world's largest producer of silver and ranked second for copper and zinc, third for tin, fourth for lead and molybdenum, and sixth for gold (Triscritti 2012). In 2011, 900 people blocked a road in the Department of Ancash in protest of the Antamina mine. Between 2006 and 2012, monthly conflicts tripled; over 2,400 people were injured and more than 200 were killed in clashes. When conflicts occurred, the Peruvian government declared a state of emergency that allows greater presence of riot police and military, limits civil liberties, and suspends freedom of assembly (Triscritti 2012). In 2015, 2,000 demonstrators took to the streets in Challhuahuacho (Cotabambas Province, Department of Apurímac) against a US$7.4-billion, Chinese-owned copper mine, Las Bambas. When four individuals were shot to death, a thirty-day state of emergency was declared, and troops were sent to "restore internal peace." This event followed a sixty-day state of emergency declared over protests of the Mexican-owned Tia Maria copper mine in the Islay Province of the Department of Arequipa (Pestano 2015). Other protests had taken place, halting progress of mining efforts in the Departments of Cajamarca and Puno (Ponce de Leon 2011). In all cases, protesters claimed the mines would ruin the environment and water supplies, as well as damage agriculture. Since 2002, security forces have killed 155 people in protest. In August of 2015, President Humala issued a decree that limited force by police, yet another previously passed law grants legal immunity to armed forces and police when acting in the line of duty, making the decree inoperable (Human Rights Watch 2019). The police units were also allowed to protect private installations of mining companies (Crabtree and Durand 2017).

33. The proposed mine near Andahuaylas is operated by Apurímac Ferrum, which is 100 percent owned by the Australian company Strike Resources. The projected development would consist of two open-pit iron ore mines yielding twenty million tons of iron ore a year for ten years (*Rumbo Minero* 2018). Although in the exploratory stage in 2011, more than five hundred mining concessions had been granted in the region (*Latin America Herald Tribune* 2018). The government responded to antimining protests with a heavy hand, declaring a state of emergency (Ponce de Leon 2011).

34. During the summer of 2018, various residents insisted that development of the Apurímac Ferrum mine was halted due to social protests and technical difficulties.

Nevertheless, in February of 2018, the mining magazine *Rumbo Minero* announced that Striking Resources planned to construct a railroad from Andahuaylas to Puerto San Juan de Marcona on the southern coast of Peru to transport the iron ore minerals (*Rumbo Minero* 2018).

35. To read more about how Peru's national identity is intimately tied to mining, the new narrative of modern and responsible mining, and relations to lived experiences in rural highland communities, see Himley (2014).

36. Exploitation of silver from the mine in Potosi, Bolivia, in the 1600s was only made possible through the mercury mined in Huancavelica. The Viceroy of Peru declared Huancavelica and Potosi to represent two primary sources in the advancement of Spain's economy (Whitaker 1941).

37. Contemporary mines promote a narrative of "modern and responsible" mining and community investment in agriculture, livestock, and education, as opposed to previous mining extractions throughout Peru. However, according to Matthew Himley (2014), community members from Condorjalca and Chacrapampa reported feeling further sociospatial marginalization because of the Barrick Gold Corporation Pierina mine, as well as greater social conflict within the community and other negative socioenvironmental consequences of large-scale mining.

38. Congress also approved the Ley de Canon (Canon Law) in 2001 to decentralize royalties, which detailed legislation governing gas royalties. In 2004, Congress amended the law to include legislation on mining royalties. To read more about the challenges of channeling tax revenues from extractive industries at the central government level to various levels of subnational administration (regional, provincial, and district), see Crabtree (2014).

39. Humala defended his stance, stating that campesino communities had been intermixed with Spanish colonizers and were integrated in domestic politics, making them merely "agrarian communities." His definition counters the United Nation's International Labour Organization Convention No. 169, which defines Indigenous populations by self-identity, traditional lifestyle, discrete culture, language, and social organization, and living in historical continuity in an area (Hoffman 2013). To read more about how Quechua-speaking peasants in Peru have been more wary of the Indigenous label than many of their South American neighbors, see Greene (2006).

40. When Humala's term was ending, five years after the legislation had been set, there were few instances of consultation with Indigenous groups in the Amazon. For instance, in 2018, Peru was striving to secure a thirty-year oil license in the infamous Amazonian block 192 that directly defies Kichwa, Quechua, Achuar, and Urarina land rights (see Albino 2017; Oxfam 2017).

41. Campesino assemblies in Huancabamba and Ayabaca protested the means in which mining companies obtained licenses, including inciting conflict and exchanging signatures for money, benefits, and development promises, and lack of consultation. In Carmen de la Frontera, 15,500 hectares were licensed to mining companies without recognition from local communities (Telesur 2018).

42. Within the Amazon, the state of Peru had given 65,800 hectares in concession to oil and gas companies and seven million to timber firms (Crabtree and Durand 2017).

43. For more information and audio recordings of interviews with Peruvians on the impacts of the CVR, see Martínez (2013).

44. Some projects that have failed to win consent include Tambogrande in Piura, Rio Blanco in Piura, Conga in Cajamarca, Tía María in Arequipa, and Santa Ana in Puno, among other, smaller mining operations. The dispute in Conga also resulted in political fallout, forcing Humala to fire two consecutive prime ministers: Salomón Lerner and Óscar Valdés (Crabtree and Durand 2017).

45. According to María Elena García (2005), while Peru's Indigenous social movements and ethnic politics differ from countries such as Bolivia and Ecuador due to the civil war, the Velasquez administration's focus on class relations, and other factors, complex cultural processes have fostered the construction of highland Indigenous citizenship and intercultural development in myriad ways. To read more about such differences and the demise and fragmentation of collective interests in Peru starting in the 1980s with roots in colonialism, also see Crabtree (2010).

46. Jaymie Patricia Heilman (2010) also discusses individuals in Carhuanca opposing road construction, citing that it would bring thieves that would steal their daughters, wives, animals, crops, and possessions, as well as bring hunger. The primary concern among the poorest Carhuanquinos was due to the road construction being done by unpaid labor, as they could not afford to be away from their fields or provide their own sustenance while away from home.

47. In December of 2007, Fujimori was convicted of ordering illegal search and seizure and was sentenced to six years in prison—a conviction Fujimori appealed but the Supreme Court upheld (Romero 2007). This sentence represented the first time an elected head of state had been extradited to their home country, tried, and convicted of human rights violations. In July of 2009, Fujimori was sentenced an additional seven and a half years in prison for embezzlement, wherein he was convicted of giving US$15 million from the country's treasury to Vladimiro Montesinos, the long-standing head of Peru's intelligence service, Servicio de Inteligencia Nacional (*BBC News* 2009a). In addition to serving as head of SIN—known to have instigated torture, disappearances, and murder—Montesinos was found guilty of bribing politicians, public figures, and military officers using government funds. For more information on the role of SIN in the war and the Vladivideos scandal, see Gorriti (1999). Two months later, in his fourth trial, Fujimori was found guilty of bribery, landing him an additional six years in prison (*BBC News* 2009b). The amount of money Fujimori had embezzled represented the seventh highest amount in the world for a head of government between 1984 and 2004 (Transparency International 2004). In December of 2017, when Fujimori was seventy-nine years old, Peru's president, Pedro Pablo Kuczynski, granted Fujimori a humanitarian pardon, which the Peruvian court overturned in October of 2018 (*BBC News* 2018a). In 2018, Congress passed a bill that would grant prisoners of a certain age the ability to serve the remainder of their sentence under electronic surveillance. In October of 2018, President Vizcarra

vetoed the bill. Also in 2018, a senior prosecutor ordered Fujimori and three health ministers to be indicted with connection to the forced sterilization of rural Indigenous women (Human Rights Watch 2019).

48. Following the incarceration of Alan García, who left office in 1990 with a 5 percent approval rating, he was elected in 2006 to serve his second term as president. García narrowly beat the former army officer Ollanta Humala (Webb 2009). In 2011, Ollanta Humala once again ran against Alan García, this time obtaining the overall majority of the votes, and served as president until 2016. In 2017, evidence emerged linking President Humala to egregious human rights violations in the early 1990s at the Madre Mía military base in the Alto Huallaga region. In 2016, Pedro Pablo Kuczynski was elected president and served only two years. Kuczynski resigned ahead of his second impeachment hearings as part of a corruption scandal. His firm was accused of taking money from Brazilian builder Odebrecht S.A., which was at the center of the Car Wash corruption scandal wherein hundreds of millions of bribes were doled out (Quigley 2018). Following Kuczynski's resignation, the first vice president, Martín Vizcarra, left his position as Peru's Ambassador to Canada in 2018 to serve as president. In 2019, previous president Alan García shot himself in the head after accusations related to the Odebrecht corruption scandal.

49. Interim president Martín Vizcarra was ousted with an impeachment vote for "moral incapacity" and replaced by Manuel Merino. Critics claimed this was a legislative coup, and massive protests broke out throughout the country. Merino resigned five days after taking office and was replaced by Francisco Sagasti (Taylor 2020).

50. Transparency International declared that the judiciary and Congress were the two most corrupt institutions in Peru, and interim president Martín Vizcarra vowed to tackle entrenched corruption. Alberto Fujimori's daughter Keiko Fujimori, who unsuccessfully ran for president in 2011 against Ollanta Humala and then again in 2016 against Pedro Pablo Kuczynski, was detained for her political party taking US$1.2 million in illegal contributions from Odebrecht S.A. (*BBC News* 2018b). In 2018, continued investigations revealed further corruption scandals that led to the resignation of the head of the Supreme Court, the firing of the justice minister and all seven members of the magistrate council, and the arrest of more than twenty judges (Tegel 2018).

51. Whereas the penal code of 2004 sought to impose penalties and improve training for judges and police to reduce discrimination against women and Indigenous peoples, as of 2016, the new code had yet to be fully implemented and was not applicable to Lima and Callao, where four out of ten Peruvians resided (Crabtree and Durand 2017).

52. According to Crabtree and Durand (2017) "golden cells" with luxury facilities became commonplace as prisoners planned crimes such as kidnappings using mobile phones while guards looked the other way.

53. In August of 2018, the National Criminal Chamber sentenced two retired military agents up to thirty years in prison for forced disappearances and the extrajudicial killings of fifty-three people in the Cabitos military base in Ayacucho in 1983. Later in the month, the remains of several bodies were exhumed and returned to family members (Human Rights Watch 2019).

54. During the CVR hearings, women who cared for children born of rape were applauded for their maternal love that obscures state responsibilities, paternal responsibilities, and persistent structural inequalities (Van Vleet 2019). Moreover, even though the CVR directly specified wartime sexual violence, of the forty-seven cases handed over to the Ministry of Public Prosecution by the CVR, only two were cases of sexual violence (Henríquez and Ewig 2013, 274).

55. In comparison, Argentina had a 90 percent conviction rate at a similar point postwar, while Peru had only 35 percent (Milton 2018).

Conclusion

1. Miguel La Serna documents conflicted sentiments toward hacendados. While hacendados were often feared and their use of power to exploit campesinos was readily apparent, it was somewhat to be expected. Indigenous tenants feared retaliation if they should protest, but at the same time some feared the Agrarian Reform would destroy a sense of internal order and security offered by their exploitative patrón. Moreover, while not expecting hacendados to labor alongside them, they did expect landlords to respect peasants' cultural practices and to keep a certain level of social distance (La Serna 2012, 122–24). As La Serna observes, while some hacendados clearly abused their position of power, villagers in Huaychaino "believed that their former estate owners had generally stayed within the parameters of the power pact," maintained order, respected Indigenous autonomy, and observed reciprocity (184).

2. Krista Van Vleet (2019) also notes that in Native Andean communities (in contrast to mestizo urban ones), political, social, and economic authority is more widely distributed between women and men (see also Allen 2002; Van Vleet 2008). Jelke Boesten (2006) points out that while women may prefer conciliation by parents, godparents, or community leaders, it is important to also note how economic dependency on the family unit can serve as reason for conciliation, as well as the practice of excluding Andean people from the national judicial system, which may deter women from seeking help from formal judicial institutions. Moreover, local class, ethnic, and gender hierarchies could disadvantage women (364).

3. Sexual violence and rape rank as the third most frequent crime in Peru (MIMDES 2008).

4. As previously mentioned, Graciela's daughter contended with domestic violence, and calls to local agencies and police departments proved to be ineffective. While conducting research in the Andahuaylas region, I found a distinct difference between the communal systems of justice regarding gender-based violence in Sacclaya versus what was available to mestiza women in the city. Middle- to upper-class mestiza women commonly lamented the inability to seek support for domestic violence or infidelity due to corrupt male lawyers and male-dominated state agencies, even those designed specifically to help women (see Kellett 2009). As a documentary made by the NGO Centro de Promoción y Desarrollo Poblacional suggests, existing social structures in rural areas of Ayacucho have

disappeared, while new structures are still evolving that sometimes sustain tensions or further conflict (Boesten 2010a).

5. I found a similar approach while living in Sacclaya. A woman told me that the community leaders whipped her along with her husband and his mistress when the community found him guilty of adultery because "when it rains on one, it rains on all."

6. Other-than-human entities are oftentimes active participants in public dialogue and political action. They are summoned in political dialogue and understood as active agents in change. This understanding questions the dominant Western ontology that dictates a nature–society dichotomy, as well as the relegation of politics to humans and the definition of *nature* as a purely scientific endeavor (see Salas Carreño 2020; de la Cadena 2015).

7. The term *idioms of distress*, as used in medical anthropology, stems from Mark Nichter's work in which he paid particular attention to culturally and socially mediated ways of expressing distress. Nichter was originally interested in the range of ways in which different members of a population express distress and the factors that influence such expressions. To read more about how psychiatric and anthropological research has continued to utilize this concept in the last thirty years, see Nichter (2010).

8. Cynthia Milton found through her analysis of survivors' performances that "memories were not consigned to the past but permeate the present and are actively lived" (Milton 2007, 19). She also found through an analysis of poems written by survivors that suffering is not limited to the past and that while some artists viewed children's poverty as a legacy of the war, other artists "place the violence within the context of a long historical struggle" (24).

9. Catherine Cole (2010) found that much of the meaning behind the Truth and Reconciliation Commission in South Africa was produced in lived embodied experiences (providing testimony, translating, reporting) as opposed to the final report's actual findings.

10. It should be noted that perhaps even successful truth commissions cannot realistically expect to do more than "narrow the range of permissible lies" (Ignatieff 1998, 174) or "provide momentary interventions in broader debates about the past" (Kent 2016 cited in Feldman 2018). This is especially true for Peru, as the CVR has no real political power to implement its own recommendations.

11. It is interesting to note that Anne Lambright (2015) found the novel to emphasize the "complexity of the indigenous experience" and privilege "indigenous modes of interpretation and proposals for resolution, while criticizing the suppression of Andean epistemologies by dominant national culture throughout Peruvian history" (112, 108).

REFERENCES

Abd, Rodrigo. 2013. "Biggest Exhumation Underway from Peru Conflict." *Omaha World Herald*, December 3, 2013. https://www.omaha.com/news/biggest-exhumation-underway-from-peru-conflict/article_6e1679e3-ec49-5b67-97a9-80200cb0cc2c.html.

Agüero, José Carlos. 2021. *The Surrendered: Reflections by a Son of Shining Path*. Translated and edited by Michael J. Lazzara and Charles F. Walker. Durham and London: Duke University Press.

Aguirre, Amef. 2018. "Capturan al operador de las redes sociales de los Quispe Palomino." *Perú 21*, August 17, 2018. https://peru21.pe/politica/vraem-capturan-operador-redes-sociales-quispe-palomino-421609.

Aláez García, A. 2001. "Duelo Andino: Sabiduría y Elaboración de la Muerte en los Rituales Mortuorios." *Chungará* 33 (2): 173–78.

Alarcón, Daniel. 2021. "Peru Processes the Death of Abimael Guzmán." *New Yorker*, September 19, 2021. https://www.newyorker.com/news/postscript/peru-processes-the-death-of-abimael-guzman.

Alayza, R. and M. Crisóstomo. 2007. *Sociedad Civil y Reconciliación: Diversas Miradas*. Lima: Instituto Bartolomé de las Casas.

Albino, Jorge Paucar. 2017. "La consulta previa debe generar confianza en la población indígena y estabilidad en las inversiones." *La Mula*, July 27, 2017. https://redaccion.lamula.pe/2017/07/27/consulta-previa-peru-pueblos-indigenas-ministerio-de-cultura-salvador-del-solar-ministro-canal-n-entrevista/jorgepaucar.

Albó, Xavier. 1991. "El Retorno del Indio." *Revista Andina* 9 (2): 299–345.

Alegría, Claribel. 1987. *They Won't Take Me Alive: Salvadorean Women in Struggle for National Liberation*. Translated by Amanda Hopkinson. London: Women's Press.

Allen, Catherine. 2002. *The Hold Life Has: Coca and Cultural Identity in an Andean Community*, 2nd ed. Washington, DC: Smithsonian Institution Press.

———. 2011. *Foxboy: Intimacy and Aesthetics in the Andes*. Austin: University of Texas Press.

Alvarado, Elvia. 1987. *Don't Be Afraid, Gringo: A Honduran Woman Speaks from the Heart*. Translated and edited by Medea Benjamin. San Francisco: Institute for Food Development Policy.

Amnesty International. 2004. *Peru: The Truth and Reconciliation Commission—A First Step towards a Country without Injustice*. AI Index: AMR 46/003/2004.

A'ness, Francine. 2004. "Resisting Amnesia: Yuyachkani, Performance, and the Postwar Reconstruction of Peru." *Theatre Journal* 56 (3): 395–414.

Ansión, Juan. 1989. *La Escuela en la Comunidad*. Lima: Food and Agriculture Organization.

Arguedas, José María. 1983. *Obras Completas*. Vol. 1. Lima: Editorial Horizonte.

Asad, Talal. 1973. *Anthropology and the Colonial Encounter*. New York: Humanities Press.

Babb, Florence E. 2012. "Theorizing Gender, Race and Cultural Tourism in Latin America: A View from Peru and Mexico." *Latin American Perspectives* 39 (6): 36–50.

Baer, R. D., S. C. Weller, J. G. de Alba Garcia, M. Glazer, R. Trotter, L. Pachter, and R. E. Klein. 2003. "A Cross-Cultural Approach to the Study of the Folk Illness Nervios." *Culture, Medicine, and Psychiatry* 27 (3): 315–37.

Baitzel, Sarah. 2018. "Parental Grief and Mourning in the Ancient Andes." *Journal of Archaeological Method and Theory* 25 (March): 178–201. https://doi.org/10.1007/s10816-017-9333-3.

Barre, Marie-Chantel. 1985. *Indeologías Indigenistas y Movimientos Indios*. 2nd ed. Mexico: Siglo Veintiuno Editores.

Barrig, Marruja. 1993. "Liderazgo Feminino y Violencia Política en el Perú de los 90." *Debates en Sociología* 18:96–97.

Barrios de Chungara, Domitila, Moema Viezzer, and Victoria Ortiz. 1978. *Let Me Speak!: Testimony of Domitila, a Woman of the Bolivian Mines*. New York: Monthly Review Press.

BBC News. 2006. "Conditional Release for Fujimori." May 18, 2006. http://news.bbc.co.uk/2/hi/americas/4994908.stm.

———. 2009a. "Fujimori Convicted of Corruption." July 20, 2009. http://news.bbc.co.uk/2/hi/americas/8160150.stm.

———. 2009b. "Fujimori Pleads Guilty to Bribery." September 28, 2009. http://news.bbc.co.uk/2/hi/americas/8279528.stm.

———. 2018a. "Peru Court Reverses Ex-President Alberto Fujimori's Pardon." October 3, 2018. https://www.bbc.com/news/world-latin-america-45738821.

———. 2018b. "Peru Opposition Leader Keiko Fujimori Arrested." October 11, 2018. https://www.bbc.com/news/world-latin-america-45819020.

Behar, Ruth. 2003. *Translated Woman: Crossing the Border with Esperanza's Story*. Tenth Anniversary ed. Boston: Beacon Press.

Berg, Ronald H. 1992. "Peasant Responses to Shining Path in Andahuaylas." In *Shining Path of Peru*, edited by D. S. Palmer, 83–104. New York: St. Martin's.

Beriain, David. 2014. "Los obreros de la cocaína." *El País Semanal*, January 22, 2014. https://elpais.com/elpais/2014/01/22/eps/1390408071_969586.html.

Beverley, John. 2004. *Testimonio: On the Politics of Truth*. Minneapolis: University of Minnesota Press.

Bickford, Louis. 2000. "Human Rights Archives and Research on Historical Memory: Argentina, Chile and Uruguay." *Latin American Research Review* 35 (2): 160–82.

Biehl, Joãl. 2013. *Vita: Life in a Zone of Social Abandonment*. Oakland: University of California Press.

Boesten, Jelke. 2006. "Pushing Back the Boundaries: Social Policy, Domestic Violence and Women's Organisations in Peru." *Journal of Latin American Studies* 38 (2): 355–78.

———. 2008. "Marrying Your Rapist: Domesticated War Crimes in Peru." In *Gendered Peace: Women's Struggles for Post-War Justice and Reconciliation*, edited by Donna Pankhurst, 205–27. New York: Routledge.

———. 2010a. "Analyzing Rape Regimes at the Interface of War and Peace in Peru." *International Journal of Transitional Justice* 4, no. 1 (March):110–29. https://doi. org/10.1093/ijtj/ijp029.

———. 2010b. "Revisiting 'Democracy in the Country and at Home' in Peru." *Democratization* 17 (2): 307–25. https://doi.org/10.1080/13510341003588732.

———. 2014. *Sexual Violence during War and Peace: Gender, Power, and Post-Conflict Justice in Peru*. New York: Palgrave Macmillan.

———. 2017. "Of Exceptions and Continuities: Theory and Methodology in Research on Conflict-Related Sexual Violence." *International Feminist Journal of Politics* 19 (4): 506–19.

Boesten, Jelke, and P. Wilding. 2015. "Transformative Gender Justice: Setting an Agenda." *Women's Studies International Forum* 51:75–80.

Boler, Megan. 1997. "The Risks of Empathy: Interrogating Multiculturalism's Gaze." *Cultural Studies* 11 (2): 253–73.

Bolin, I. 2006. *Growing Up in a Culture of Respect: Child Rearing in Highland Peru*. Austin: University of Texas Press.

Bourque, Susan C., and Kay B. Warren. 1989. "Democracy without Peace: The Cultural Politics of Terror in Peru." *Latin American Research Review* 24 (1): 7–34.

Brand, Ian. 2020. "Walter Benjamin on History, Collections, and Archives." New York Public Library, October 26, 2020. https://www.nypl.org/blog/2020/10/26/walter-benjamin-history-collections-and-archives.

Brush, Stephen B. 1977. *Mountain, Field, and Family: The Economy and Human Ecology of an Andean Valley*. Philadelphia: University of Pennsylvania Press.

Burt, Jo-Marie. 1998. "Unsettled Accounts: Militarization and Memory in Postwar Peru." *NACLA Report on the Americas* 32 (2): 35–41.

———. 2006. "'Quien habla es terrorista': The Political Use of Fear in Fujimori's Peru." *Latin American Research Review* 41 (3): 32–62.

———. 2007. *Political Violence and the Authoritarian State in Peru: Silencing Civil Society*. New York: Palgrave Macmillan.

Cabitza, Mattia. 2012. "Peru Widens Civil War Compensation for Victims of Sexual Violence." *Guardian*, June 28, 2012. http://www.guardian.co.uk/global-development/2012/jun/28/peru-civil-war-victims-sexual-violence.

Cachiguango, Luis Enrique, and Julián Pontón. 2010. *Yaku-Mama: La Crianza del Agua; La Música Ritual del Hatun Puncha—Inti Raymi en Kotama, Otavalo*. Quito: Ministerio de Cultura del Ecuador.

Campoamor, Leigh. 2016. "'Who Are You Calling Exploitative?': Defensive Motherhood, Child Labor, and Urban Poverty in Lima, Peru." *Journal of Latin American and Caribbean Anthropology* 21(1): 151–72.

Canessa, Andrew, ed. 2005. *Natives Making Nation: Gender, Indigeneity, and the State in the Andes*. Tucson: University of Arizona Press.

Cárdenas, N., M. Crisóstomo, E. Nyra, D. Portal, S. Ruiz, and T. Velázquez. 2005. *Noticias, Remesas y Recados de Manta Huancavelica*. Lima: DEMUS.

Center for Justice and Accountability. 2016. "Accomarca Massacre: Civilians Massacred by Peru's Military." Accessed December 5, 2018. https://cja.org/what-we-do/litigation/accomarca-massacre/.

Chanduví Jaña, Elsa. 2015. "Remains of Victims of Peru's Internal Conflict Returned to Family Members." *NotiSur*, August 28, 2015. Latin America Data Base, https://digitalrepository.unm.edu/notisur/14360.

Chauca, Edward. 2016. "Mental Illness in Peruvian Narratives of Violence after the Truth and Reconciliation Commission." *Latin American Research Review* 51 (2): 67–85.

Chávez de Paz, Denis. 1989. *Juventud y Terrorismo: Características Sociales de los Condenados por Terrorismo y Otros Delitos*. Lima: Instituto de Estudio Peruanos.

Chiappe, Mario, Moises Lemlij, and Luis Millones. 1985. *Alucinógenos y Shamanismo en el Perú Contemporáneo*. Lima: Editorial El Virrey.

Cole, Catherine. 2010. *Performing South Africa's Truth Commission: Stages of Transition*. Bloomington: Indiana University Press.

Comisión de la Verdad y Reconciliación (CVR). 2003. *Final Report*. Lima: Peru.

———. n.d. "Informe Final." Accessed June 10, 2018. https://www.cverdad.org.pe/lacomision/balance/index.php.

Comité Internacional de la Cruz Roja. 2019. "Los Desaparecidos de Perú que Descansan en las Alturas." August 30, 2019. https://www.icrc.org/es/document/los-desaparecidos-de-peru-que-descansan-en-las-alturas.

Cooke, Miriam. 1996. *Women and the War Story*. Berkeley: University of California Press.

Cookson, Tara Patricia. 2016. "Working for Inclusion? Conditional Cash Transfers, Rural Women, and the Reproduction of Inequality." *Antipode* 48 (5): 1,187–1,205.

———. 2018. *Unjust Conditions: Women's Work and the Hidden Cost of Cash Transfer Programs*. Oakland: University of California Press.

Coordinadora Nacional de Derechos Humanos. 1995. "Informe de la Coordinadora Nacional de Derechos Humanos Ante la Comisión Interamericana de Derechos Humanos." September 7, 1995. https://www.derechos.net/cnddhh/iachr1.htm.

Coral Cordero, Isabel. 1998. "Women in War: Impact and Responses." In *Shining and Other Paths: War and Society in Peru, 1980–1995*, edited by Steve J. Stern, 345–74. Durham, NC: Duke University Press.

Correa, Cristián. 2013. *Reparations in Peru: From Recommendations to Implementation*. International Center for Transitional Justice. www.ictj.org.

Crabtree, John. 2010. "Democracy without Parties? Some Lessons from Peru." *Journal of Latin American Studies* 42 (2): 357–82.

———. 2014. "Funding Local Government: Use (and Abuse) of Peru's Canon System." *Bulletin of Latin American Research* 33 (4): 452–67.

Crabtree, John, and Francisco Durand. 2017. *Peru: Elite Power and Political Capture*. London: Zed Books.

Crapanzano, Vinent. 1984. "Review: Life Histories." *American Anthropologist* 86(4):953–60.

Cruz, Rosayra Pablo, and Julie Schwietert Collazo. 2020. *The Book of Rosa: A Mother's Story of Separation at the Border*. San Francisco: HarperOne.

Das, Veena, Arthur Kleinman, Mamphela Ramphele, and Pamela Reynolds, editors. 2000. *Violence and Subjectivity*. Los Angeles: University of California Press.

Dauphinee, E. 2007. "The Politics of the Body in Pain: Reading the Ethics of Imagery." *Security Dialogue* 38:139–55.

Degregori, Carlos Iván. 1986. *"Sendero Luminoso": Parte I. Los Hondos y Mortals Desencuentros; Parte II. Lucha Armada y Utopía Autoritaria*. Lima: Instituto de Estudios Peruanos.

———. 1990. *Ayacucho 1969–1979: El Surgimiento de Sendero Luminoso*. Lima: Instituto de Estudios Peruanos.

———. 1991. "How Difficult It Is to Be God: Ideology and Political Violence in Sendero Luminoso." *Critique of Anthropology* 11 (3): 233–50.

———. 1998. "Harvesting Storms: Peasant *Rondas* and the Defeat of Sendero Luminoso in Ayachucho." In *Shining and Other Paths: War and Society in Peru, 1980–1995*, edited by Steve Stern, 128–57. Durham, NC: Duke University Press.

———. 2012. *How Difficult It Is to Be God: Shining Path's Politics of War in Peru, 1980–1999*. Edited by Steve J. Stern. Madison: University of Wisconsin Press.

de la Cadena, Marisol. 1996. "Las Mujeres son más Indias: Etnicidad y Género en una Comunidad de Cuzco." In *Detrás de la Puerta: Hombres y Mujeres en el Perú de Hoy*, edited by Patricia Ruiz Bravo, 181–202. Lima: Fond Editorial PUCP.

———. 1998. "From Race to Class: Insurgent Intellectuals de Provincia in Peru, 1910–1970." In *Shining and Other Paths: War and Society in Peru, 1980–1995*, edited by Steve Stern, 22–59. Durham, NC: Duke University Press.

———. 2010. "Indigenous Cosmopolitics in the Andes: Conceptual Reflections beyond 'Politics.'" *Cultural Anthropology* 25 (2): 334–70.

———. 2015. *Earth Beings: Ecologies of Practice across Andean Worlds*. Durham, NC: Duke University Press.

Del Pino, Ponciano. 1999. "Familia, Cultura, y 'Revolución.' Vida Cotidiana en Sendero Luminoso." In *Los Senderos Insólitos del Perú*, edited by Steve Stern, 161–91. Lima: Instituto de Estudios Peruanos and Universidad San Cristóbal de Huamanga.

Del Pino, Ponciano, and Eliana Otta Vildoso. 2019. "Extreme Violence in Museums of Memory: The Place of Memory in Peru." In *The Andean World*, edited by Linda J. Seligman and Kathleen S. Fine-Dare, 355–72. New York: Routledge.

DeLugan, Robin M. 2000. "*Indigenismo*: Interests, Motives, and Government Practices." Paper presented at Latin American Studies Association meeting in Miami, March 16–18, 2000.

de Soto, Hernando. 1989. *The Other Path: The Economic Answer to Terrorism*. New York: Harper and Row.

Drinot, Paulo. 2009. "For Whom the Eye Cries: Memory, Monumentality, and the Ontologies of Violence in Peru." *Journal of Latin America and Cultural Studies* 18 (1): 15–32. https://doi.org/10.1080/13569320902819745.

Economist. 2018. "A Warning on Poverty from Peru: A Setback on the Long Road to Poverty Eradication." May 10, 2018. https://www.economist.com/the-americas/2018/05/10/a-warning-on-poverty-from-peru.

———. 2021. "A Massacre Adds to Peru's Election Woes." May 29, 2021. https://www.economist.com/the-americas/2021/05/27/a-massacre-adds-to-perus-election-woes.

Einarsdóttir, J. 2004. *Tired of Weeping: Mother Love, Child Death, and Poverty in Guinea-Bissau.* Madison: University of Wisconsin Press.

El Comercio. 2018. "Ayacucho: Alcalde del Distrito de Oronccoy Fue Asesinado." February 28, 2018. https://elcomercio.pe/peru/ayacucho/ayacucho-alcalde-distrito-oronccoy-asesinado-noticia-500741.

El Peruano. n.d. "Ley No. 30457." Accessed November 13, 2018. https://busquedas.elperuano.pe/normaslegales/ley-de-creacion-del-distrito-de-oronccoy-en-la-provincia-de-ley-n-30457-1392946-1/.

Espinosa, Agustín, Darío Páez, Tesania Velázquez, Rosa María Cueto, Evelyn Seminario, Salvador Sandoval, Félix Reátegui, and Iris Jave. 2017. "Between Remembering and Forgetting the Years of Political Violence: Psychosocial Impact of the Truth and Reconciliation Commission in Peru." *Political Psychology* 38 (5): 849–66.

Favre, Henri. 1984. "Peru: Sendero Luminoso y Horizontes Ocultos." *Quehace* 31–32 (September–October): 25–35.

Feldman, Joseph P. 2018. "Yuyanapaq no entra: Ritual Dimensions of Post-Transitional Justice in Peru." *Journal of the Royal Anthropological Institute* 24, no. 3 (September): 589–606.

———. 2021. *Memories Before the State: Postwar Peru and the Place of Memory, Tolerance, and Social Inclusion.* New Jersey: Rutgers University Press.

Ferreira, Francisco. 2016. "De-demonizing the VRAEM: A Peruvian-Cocalero Area." *Substance Use & Misuse* 51 (1): 41–53.

Flores Galindo, Alberto. 2010. *In Search of an Inca: Identity and Utopia in the Andes.* New York: Cambridge University Press.

Fonseca, Claudia. 1986. "Orphanages, Foundlings, and Foster Mothers: The System of Child Circulation in a Brazilian Squatter Settlement." *Anthropological Quarterly* 59 (1): 15–27.

Frisancho Pineda, David. 1978. *Medicina indı́gena y popular.* Lima: Juan Mejı́a Baca.

Fuenzalida Vollmar, Fernando. 1970. *El Indio y el Poder en el Perú.* Lima: Instituto de Estudios Peruanos.

Gamarra, Jeffrey. 2000. "Conflict, Post-Conflict and Religion: Andean Responses to New Religious Movements." *Journal of Southern African Studies* 26 (2): 271–87.

———. 2002. "Las Dificultades de la Memoria, el Poder y la Reconciliación." In *Debates en Ciencias Sociales,* 1–37. Ayacucho: Instituto de Investigación de la Facultad de Ciencias Sociales, Universidad Nacional de San Cristóbal de Huamanga/Instituto y Promoción del Desarrollo y Paz de Ayacucho.

García, María Elena. 2005. *Making Indigenous Citizens: Identity, Development and Multicultural Activism in Peru.* Stanford, CA: Stanford University Press.

——. 2008. "Exceptional Others: Politicians, Rottweilers, and Alterity in the 2006 Presidential Elections." *Latin American and Caribbean Ethnic Studies* 3 (3): 253–70.

García, María Elena, and José Antonio Lucero. 2011. "Authenticating Indians and Movements: Interrogating Indigenous Authenticity, Social Movements and Field Work in Peru." In *Histories of Race and Racism: The Andes and Mesoamerica from Colonial Times to the Present*, edited by Laura Gotkowitz, 278–98. Durham, NC: Duke University Press.

Gavilán Sánchez, Lurgio. 2015. *When Rains Become Floods: A Child Soldier's Story*. Durham, NC: Duke University Press.

Getrich, Christina. 2019. *Border Brokers: Children of Mexican Immigrants Navigating U.S. Society, Laws and Politics*. Tucson: University of Arizona Press.

Goldstein, Donna M. 2009. "Perils of Witnessing and Ambivalence of Writing: Whiteness, Sexuality, and Violence in Rio de Janeiro Shantytowns." In *Women Fielding Danger: Negotiating Ethnographic Identities in Field Research*, edited by Marth K. Huggins and Marie-Louise Glebbeek, 227–49. Lanham, MD: Rowman and Littlefield.

González, Olga. 2011. *Unveiling Secrets of War in the Peruvian Andes*. Chicago: University of Chicago Press.

——. 2018. "Art Under Attack in Peru." North American Congress on Latin America, August 29, 2018. https://nacla.org/news/2018/08/29/art-under-attack-peru.

Gorbak, C., M. Lischetti, and C. Muñoz. 1962. "Batallas Rituals del Chiaraje y del Toqto de la Provincia de Kanas. Cusco, Peru." *Revista del Museo Nacional* 31:245–304.

Gorriti, Gustavo. 1999. *The Shining Path: A History of the Millenarian War in Peru*. Translated by Robin Kirk. Durham: University of North Carolina Press.

Graves, Christina, ed. 2001. *The Potato Treasure of the Andes: From Agriculture to Culture*. Lima: International Potato Center.

Greene, Shane. 2006. "Getting over the Andes: The Geo-Eco-Politics of Indigenous Movements in Peru's 21st Century Inca Empire." *Journal of Latin American Studies* 38 (2): 327–54.

Greenwood, Ashley. 2019. "Authority, Discourse and the Construction of Victimhood." *Social Identities* 25 (6): 746–58.

Guadalupe Martínez, Ana. 1992. *Las Cárceles Clandestinas de El Salvador*. San Salvador: UCA Editores.

Gugelberger, Georg, and Michael Kearney. 1991. "Voices for the Voiceless: Testimonial Literature in Latin America." *Latin American Perspectives* 18 (3): 3–14.

Guillerot, Julie. 2008. *Reparaciones en la Transición Peruana: ¿Dónde estamos y hacía donde vamos?* New York: International Center for Transitional Justice.

——. 2019. "Reparations in Peru: 15 Years of Delivering Redress." *Reparations, Responsibility, and Victimhood in Transitional Societies*. September 2019. https://reparations.qub.ac.uk/assets/uploads/Peru-Report-ENG-LR-2.pdf.

Gusterson, Hugh. 2007. "Anthropology and Militarism." *Annual Review of Anthropology* 36:155–75.

Halbwachs, Maurice. 1992. *On Collective Memory*. Chicago: University of Chicago Press.

Handelman, Howard. 1975. *Struggle in the Andes: Peasant Political Mobilization in Peru*. Austin: University of Texas Press.

Hayner, P. B. 2010. *Unspeakable Truths: Transitional Justice and the Challenge of Truth Commissions*. 2nd ed. Hoboken, NJ: Taylor & Francis.

Heilman, Jaymie Patricia. 2010. *Before the Shining Path: Politics in Rural Ayacucho, 1895–1980*. Stanford, CA: Stanford University Press.

Henríquez, Narda. 1996. "Gender Studies in Peru." *Women's Studies Quarterly* 24 (1/2): 365–78.

Henríquez, Narda, and Christina Ewig. 2013. "Integrating Gender into Human Security: Peru's Truth and Reconciliation Commission." In *Gender, Violence and Human Security*, edited by Aili Mari Tripp, Myra Marx Ferree, and Christina Ewig, 260–82. New York: NYU Press.

Himley, Matthew. 2014. "Mining History: Mobilizing the Past in Struggles over Mineral Extraction in Peru." *Geographical Review* 104 (2): 174–91.

Hinton, A. L. 2010. "Introduction: Toward an Anthropology of Transitional Justice." In *Transitional Justice: Global Mechanisms and Local Realities after Genocide and Mass Violence*, edited by A. L. Hinton, 1–22. New Brunswick, NJ: Rutgers University Press.

Hoffman, Benjamin. 2013. "Who Is Indigenous? Peruvian Minister Resigns after President Says That Quechua-Speaking Andean Campesinos Are Not Entitled to Prior Consultation." *Earth Rights* (blog), May 15, 2013. https://earthrights.org/blog/who-is-indigenous-peruvian-minister-resigns-after-president-says-that-quechua-speaking-andean-campesinos-are-not-entitled-to-prior-consultation/.

Hopkins, D. 1982. "Juego de Enemigos." *Allpanchis* 20:167–87.

Houghton, Lali. 2017. "Life in the VRAEM, Peru's 'Cocaine Valley.'" *Al Jazeera*, March 6, 2017. https://www.aljazeera.com/indepth/features/2017/03/life-vraem-peru-cocaine-valley-170302141426171.html.

Huaraca, Mario Mejía. 2018. "Cadena perpetua para toda la cúpula de Sendero Luminoso por Tarata." *El Comercio*, September 12, 2018. https://elcomercio.pe/politica/cadena-perpetua-cupula-sendero-luminoso-tarata-noticia-556606.

Huayhua, Margarita. 2014. "Racism and Social Interaction in a Southern Peruvian Combi." *Ethnic and Racial Studies* 37 (13): 2,399–417.

——. 2019. "Labeling and Linguistic Discrimination." In *The Andean World*, edited by Linda J. Seligman and Kathleen S. Fine-Dare, 418–38. New York: Routledge.

Human Rights Watch. 2001. "Human Rights World Report 2001: Peru." Accessed December 14, 2018. https://www.hrw.org/legacy/backgrounder/americas/peru-qna-1030.htm.

——. 2019. "World Report 2019: Peru Events of 2018." Accessed July 11, 2019. https://www.hrw.org/world-report/2019/country-chapters/peru.

Hyland, Sabine. 2016. *The Chankas and the Priest*. University Park: Pennsylvania State University Press.

Ignatieff, M. 1998. *The Warrior's Honor: Ethnic War and the Modern Conscience.* New York: Henry Holt.

INDEPA (Instituto Nacional de Desarrollo de Pueblos Andinos, Amazónicos y Afroperuanos). 2010. Mapa Etnolingüístico del Perú. Accessed December 7, 2018. http://sinia.minam.gob.pe/fuente-informacion/instituto-nacional-desarrollo-pueblos-andinos-amazonicos.

Instituto Nacional de Estadistica e Informatica. 2014. "Producción y empleo informal en el Perú." Accessed August 25, 2014. http://www.inei.gob.pe/media/MenuRecursivo/publicaciones_digitales/Est/Lib1154/index.html.

———. 2018. "Evolución de la Pobreza Monetaria, 2007–2017." Accessed December 13, 2018. https://www.inei.gob.pe/media/MenuRecursivo/publicaciones_digitales/Est/Lib1533/libro.pdf.

———. 2020. "Mapa de Pobreza Monetaria Distrital 2018." Accessed October 10, 2021. https://www.inei.gob.pe/media/MenuRecursivo/boletines/mapa-de-pobreza-25022020_ponencia.pdf.

Isbell, Billie Jean. 1978. *To Defend Ourselves: Ecology and Ritual in an Andean Village.* Prospect Heights, IL: Waveland Press.

———. 1992. "Shining Path and Peasant Responses in Rural Ayacucho." In *Shining Path of Peru,* edited by David Scott Palmer, 59–82. New York: St. Martin's Press.

———. 1997. "De Inmaduro o Duro: Lo Simbólico Feminio y los Esquemas Andinos de Género." In *Parentesco y Género en los Andes, Vol. 1: Más Allá del Silencio: Las Fronteras de Género en los Andes,* edited by Dense Y. Arnold, 253–300. La Paz: CIASE, ILCA,

———. 1998. "Violence in Peru: Performances and Dialogues." *American Anthropologist* 100 (2): 282–92.

Jara, L., M. Tejada, and C. Tovar. 2007. *Representaciones Populares y Reconciliación: Estudios Sobre Grupos Focales.* CEP 316. Lima: Instituto Bartolomé de las Casas.

Jara, Umberto. 2017. *Ojo Por Ojo: La Verdadera Historia del Grupo Colina.* Lima: Biblioteca Nacional del Peru, Planeta.

Jennings, Justin. 2019. "Drinking Together: Continuity and Change in the Andean World." In *The Andean World,* edited by Linda J. Seligman and Kathleen S. Fine-Dare, 128–42. New York: Routledge.

Jiménez, Edilberto. 2009. *Chungui: Violencia y Trazos de Memoria.* Lima: Instituto de Estudios Peruanos.

Kellett, Nicole. 2009. "Empowering Women: Microfinance, Development, and Relations of Inequality in the South Central Peruvian Highlands." PhD diss., University of New Mexico.

———. 2011. "Microfinance and Economic Inequality in the Peruvian Highlands." *Ethnology: An International Journal of Cultural and Social Anthropology* 50 (3): 1–22.

Kent, Lia. 2016. "After the Truth Commission: Gender and Citizenship in Timor-Leste." *Human Rights Review* 17:51–70.

Kernaghan, Richard. 2009. *Coca's Gone: Of Might and Right in the Huallaga Post-Boom.* Stanford, CA: Stanford University Press.

Kirk, Robin. 1993. *Grabado en Piedra: Las Mujeres de Sendero Luminoso*. Lima: Instituto de Estudios Peruanos.

Koc-Menard, Nathalie. 2015. "'We are a Marginal Community:' the Discourse of Marginality n the Theatre of War." *Latin American and Caribbean Ethnic Studies* 10(2):199–225.

Kovarik, Jacquelyn. 2018. "Why Don't We Talk about Peru's Forced Sterilization." *New Republic*, October 8, 2018. https://newrepublic.com/article/151599/dont-talk-perus-forced-sterilizations.

Kovats-Bernat, J. Christopher. 2002. "Negotiating Dangerous Fields: Pragmatic Strategies for Fieldwork amid Violence and Terror." *American Anthropologist* 104 (1): 208–22.

Krauss, Clifford. 2001. "Peru, Pressing Japan, Issues an Order for Fujimori's Arrest." *New York Times*, September 14, 2001. https://www.nytimes.com/2001/09/14/world/peru-pressing-japan-issues-an-order-for-fujimori-s-arrest.html.

Kurtenbach, Sabine. 2014. "Postwar Violence in Guatemala: A Mirror of the Relationship between Youth and Adult Society." *International Journal of Conflict and Violence* 8 (1): 120–33.

Lambright, Anne. 2015. *Andean Truths: Transitional Justice, Ethnicity and Cultural Production in Post-Shining Path Peru*. Liverpool: Liverpool University Press.

Laplante, Lisa J., and Kimberly Theidon. 2007. "Truth with Consequences: Justice and Reparations in Post-Truth Commission Peru." *Human Rights Quarterly* 29 (1): 228–50.

La Républica. 2003. "3 de noviembre de 1989 El Día que el Miedo se Acabó." August 16, 2003. https://larepublica.pe/archivo/345689-3-de-noviembre-de-1989-el-dia-que-el-miedo-se-acabo.

La Serna, Miguel. 2012. *The Corner of the Living: Ayacucho on the Eve of the Shining Path Insurgency*. Chapel Hill: University of North Carolina Press.

———. 2019. "Revolution and Violence." In *The Andean World*, edited by Linda J. Seligman and Kathleen S. Fine-Dare, 340–54. New York: Routledge.

Latin America Herald Tribune. 2018. "80 Injured in Peru Anti-mining Protests." Last updated December 3, 2018. http://www.laht.com/article.asp?CategoryId=14095&ArticleId=442709.

Lázaro, Juan. 1990. "Women and Political Violence in Contemporary Peru." *Dialectical Anthropology* 15:233–47.

Leinaweaver, Jessaca, B. 2005. "Mass Sterilizations and Child Circulation: Two Reproductive Responses to Poverty in Peru." *Anthropology News* 46 (1): 13–18.

———. 2008. *The Circulation of Children: Kinship, Adoption, and Morality in Andean Peru*. Durham, NC: Duke University Press.

LeVine, R. A. 1982. "Gusii Funerals: Meanings of Life and Death in an African Community." *Ethos* 10 (1): 26–65.

Liffman, Paul. 1977. "Vampires of the Andes." *Michigan Discussions in Anthropology* 2, no. 2 (Winter): 205–26.

Llamojha Mitma, Manuel, and Jaymie Patricia Heilman. 2016. *Now Peru Is Mine: The Life and Times of a Campesino Activist*. Durham, NC: Duke University Press.

Logan, Kathleen. 1997. "Personal Testimony: Latin American Women Telling Their Lives." *Latin American Research Review* 32 (1): 199–211.

Lucio, Óscar Colchado. 1997. *Rosa Cuchillo*. Madrid: Alfaguara.

Mallon, Florencia E. 1992. "Indian Communities, Political Cultures, and the State in Latin America, 1780–1990." Quincenenary Supplement: The Colonial and Post-Colonial Experience. *Journal of Latin American Studies* 24:35–53.

Manrique, Nelson. 1996. "The Two Faces of Fujimori's Rural Policy." *NACLA Report on the Americas* 30 (1): 39–43.

Martínez, Marta. 2013. "Peru's Painful Mirror." *openDemocracy*, December 12, 2013. https://www.opendemocracy.net/en/opensecurity/perus-painful-mirror/.

Mayers, Steven, and Jonathan Freedman, eds. 2019. *Solito, Solita: Crossing Borders with Youth Refugees from Central America*. Chicago: Haymarket Books.

McClintock, Cynthia. 1984. "Why Peasants Rebel: The Case of Peru's Sendero Luminoso." *World Politics* 37:48–84.

Menchú, Rigoberta, and Elisabeth Burgos-Debray. 1984. *I, Rigoberta Menchú: An Indian Woman in Guatemala*. New York: Verso.

Milton, Cynthia E. 2007. "At the Edge of the Peruvian Truth Commission: Alternative Paths to Recounting the Past." *Radical History Review* (Spring): 3–33. https://doi.org/10.1214/01636546-2006-025.

———. 2014. *Art from a Fractured Past: Memory and Truth-Telling in Post-Shining Path Peru*. Durham, NC: Duke University Press.

———. 2018. *Conflicted Memory: Military Cultural Interventions and the Human Rights Era in Peru*. Madison: University of Wisconsin Press.

MIMDES (Ministry of Women and Social Development). 2008. *Plan Nacional Contra la Violencia hacia la Mujer, 2009–2015*. Lima: MIMDES.

Minow, Martha. 1998. *Between Vengeance and Forgiveness: facing History after Genocide and Mass Violence*. Boston: Beacon Press.

Mitchell, William P. 1976. "Irrigation and Communities in the Central Peruvian Highlands." *American Anthropologist* 78:25–44.

———. 1979. "Inconsistencia de Status Social y Dimensiones de Rango en los Andes Centrales del Perú." *Estudios Andinos* 15:21–31.

———. 1991. "Some Are More Equal Than Others: Labor Supply, Reciprocity, and Redistribution in the Andes." *Research in Economic Anthropology* 13:191–219.

———. 1994. "Depeasantized Youth and Revolution: The Case of Peru." Paper presented at the symposium Conceptualizing Violence in Modern Society at the 93rd Annual Meeting of the American Anthropological Association, Atlanta, GA, November 1994.

Moodie, Ellen. 2012. *El Salvador in the Aftermath of Peace: Crime, Uncertainty and the Transition to Democracy*. Philadelphia: University of Pennsylvania Press.

Morote Best, Efraín. 1952. "El Degollador (Nakaq)." *Cusco: Tradición* 2 (4): 67–91.

Nichter, Mark. 2010. "Idioms of Distress Revisited." *Cultural Medical Psychiatry* 34:401–16.

Oliart, Patricia. 2003. *Territorio, Cultura e Historia: Materiales para la Renovación de la Enseñanza sobre la Sociedad Peruana.* Lima: IEP.

———. 2008. "Indigenous Women's Organizations and the Political Discourses of Indigenous Rights and Gender Equity in Peru." *Latin American and Caribbean Ethnic Studies* 3(3):291–308.

———. 2010. "Vida Universitaria y Masculinidades Mestizas." In *Políticas Educativas y la Cultura del Sistema Escolar en el Perú*, edited by Patricia Oliart, 185–244. Lima: Instituto de Estudios Peruanos.

———. 2019. "Education, Power, and Distinctions." *In The Andean World*, edited by Linda J. Seligmann and Kathleen S. Fine-Dare, 539–54. New York: Routledge.

Oliver, D. L. 1955. *A Solomon Island Society: Kinship and Leadership among the Siuai of Bougainville.* Cambridge, MA: Harvard University Press.

Oliver-Smith, Anthony. 1968. "The Pishtaco: Institutionalized Fear in Highland Peru." Paper delivered at the annual meetings of the Central States Anthropological Society in Detroit, Michigan, May 3, 1968.

Onofre Mamani, L. D. 2001. "Alma Imaña: Rituales Mortuorios Andinos en las Zonas Rurales Aymara de Puma Circunlacustre (Perú)." *Chungará* 33 (2): 235–44.

Orlove, Ben. 1994. "Sticks and Stones: Ritual Battles and Play in the Southern Peruvian Andes." In *Unruly Order: Violence, Power, and Cultural Identity in the High Provinces of Southern Peru*, edited by Deborah Poole, 133–64. Boulder, CO: Westview Press.

Oxfam. 2011. "Politics of Poverty." Accessed December 10, 2018. https://politicsofpoverty.oxfamamerica.org/2011/09/peru-congress-passes-precedent-setting-consultation-law/.

———. 2017. "Rights at Risk: The Fight for True Community Consultation Continues in Peru." Last updated August 8, 2017. https://politicsofpoverty.oxfamamerica.org/2017/08/rights-at-risk-the-fight-for-true-community-consultation-continues-in-peru.

Palmer, David Scott. 2007. "Terror in the Name of Mao: Revolution and Response in Peru." In *Democracy and Counterterrorism: Lessons from the Past*, edited by Robert J. Art and Louise Richardson, 195–220. Washington, DC: United States Institute of Peace Press.

Pedersen, Duncan. 2009. "Globalización, Salud y Sistemas Médicos Andinos." In *Medicina Tradicional Andina: Planteamientos y Aproximaciones*, edited by Ricardo Sanchez G. and Rodolfo Sánchez G., 47–62. Cuzco: Centro Bartolomé de las Casas/Centro de Medicina Andina.

Pedersen, Duncan, Hanna Kienzler, and Jeffrey Gamarra. 2010. "Llaki and Ñakary: Idioms of Distress and Suffering among the Highland Quechua in the Peruvian Andes." *Culture, Medicine, and Psychiatry*, 34 (2): 279–300.

Perez, Carmen. 1989. "La Marcha por la Paz." *Páginas* 100 (December): 181–83. http://lum.cultura.pe/cdi/sites/default/files/documento/pdf/100.%20Documentos.%20

Semana%20Social%20Surandino%20pr%C3%B2blematica%20y%20alternati-
vas_Parte2.pdf.

Perlman, Janice. 2010. *Favela: Four Decades of Living on the Edge in Rio de Janeiro.*
Oxford: Oxford University Press.

Pestano, Andrew V. 2015. "Peru Declares State of Emergency After Anti-mining Protest
Deaths." *United Press International.* Last updated September 30, 2015. https://www.
upi.com/Top_News/World-News/2015/09/30/Peru-declares-state-of-emergency-
after-anti-mining-protest-deaths/4581443620433/.

Petley, Julian. 2003. "War without Death: Responses to Distant Suffering." *Journal for
Crime, Conflict and the Media* 1:72–85.

Pike, John. 1992. "The Sendero File." FAS Intelligence Resource Program. Last updated
October 20, 2016. https://fas.org/irp/world/para/docs/sf2.htm.

Platt, T. 1986. "Mirrors and Maize: The Concept of Yanantin among the Macha of Bolivia."
In *Anthropological History of Andean Polities,* edited by J. Murra, N. Wachtel, and
J. Revel, 228–59. Cambridge: Cambridge University Press.

Ponce de Leon, Rafael. 2011. "Permanent Committee to Address Anti-mining Protests in
Andahuaylas." *BNAmericas,* November 16, 2011. http://www.bnamericas.com/news/
mining/permanent-committee-to-address-anti-mining-protests-in andahuaylas?idio
ma=I&tipoContenido=detalle&pagina=project&idContenido=956592.

Poole, Deborah, and Gerardo Rénique. 1991. "The New Chroniclers of Peru: U.S. Scholars and Their 'Shining Path' of Peasant Rebellion." *Bulletin of Latin American
Research* 10 (2): 133–91.

———. 1992. *Peru: Time of Fear.* London: Latin America Bureau (Monthly Review Press).

Portocarrero, Gonzalo. 2008. "Transgression as a Specific Form of Enjoyment in the Criollo World." *Theory and Event* 11 (3). https://www.doi.org/10.1353/tae.0.0022.

Portocarrero, Gonzalo, and Víctor Vich. 2012. "Cultural Studies in Peru: An Experience
from the Universidad Católica." *Cultural Studies* 26 (1): 141–52.

Quigley, John. 2018. "Peru's President Kuczynski Resigns Ahead of Impeachment Vote."
Bloomberg, March 21, 2018. https://www.bloomberg.com/news/articles/2018-03-21/
peruvian-president-kuczynski-resigns-ahead-of-impeachment-vote.

Radcliffe, Sarah A., Nina Laurie, and Robert Andolina. 2004. "The Transnationaliza-
tion of Gender and Reimagining Andean Indigenous Development." *Signs* 29
(2): 387–416.

Rendon, Silvio. 2019. "Capturing Correctly: A Reanalysis of the Indirect Capture-Recapture
Methods in the Peruvian Truth and Reconciliation Commission." *Research and Politics* 1–8.

Ritter, Jonathan. 2002. "Siren Songs: Ritual and Revolution in the Peruvian Andes." *British Journal of Ethnomusicology* 11 (1): 9–42.

Romero, Simon. 2007. "Peru's Ex-President Gets 6 Years for Illicit Search." *New
York Times,* December 12, 2007. https://www.nytimes.com/2007/12/12/world/
americas/12fujimori.html?ref=world.

Rousseau, Stéphanie, and Anahi Morales Hudon. 2015. "Path towards Autonomy in

Indigenous Women's Movements: Mexico, Peru and Bolivia." *Journal of Latin American Studies* 48:33–60.

Rubel, A. J., C. W. O'Neill, and R. Collado. 1984. *Susto: A Folk Illness*. Berkeley: University of California Press.

Rubio-Marín, Ruth, Claudia Paz y Paz Bailey, and Julie Guillerot. 2011. "Indigenous Peoples and Claims for Reparation: Tentative Steps in Peru and Guatemala." In *Identities in Transition: Challenges for Transitional Justice in Divided Societies*, edited by Paige Arthur, 17–53. Cambridge: Cambridge University Press.

Rueda, Carolina. 2015. "Memory, Trauma, and Phantasmagoria in Claudia Llosa's 'La teta asustada.'" *Hispania* 98 (3): 452–62.

Rumbo Minero. 2018. "Strike: Ferrocarril para Conectar el Sur y Costa del Perú Beneficiará a Apurímac Ferrum." Last modified December 3, 2018. http://www.rumbominero.com/noticias/mineria/strike-ferrocarril-para-conectar-el-sur-y-costa-del-peru-beneficiara-a-apurimac-ferrum/.

Saignes, Thierry. 1995. "Indian Migration and Social Change in Seventeen Century Carcas." In *Ethnicity, Markets, and Migration in the Andes: At the Crossroads of History and Anthropology*, edited by Brooke Larson and Olivia Harris with Enrique Tandeter, 167–95. Durham, NC: Duke University Press.

Salas Carreño, Guillermo. 2016. "Mining and the Living Materiality of Mountains in Andean Societies." *Journal of Material Culture* (December). https://doi.org/10.1177/1359183516679439.

———. 2020. "Indexicality and the Indigenization of Politics: Dancer-Pilgrims Protesting Mining Concessions in the Andes." *Journal of Latin American and Caribbean Anthropology* 25 (1): 7–27.

Salazar-Soler, Carmen. 1991. "El Pishtaku entre los Campesinos y los Mineros de Huancavelica." *Bulletin de L'Institut Francais d'Etudes Andines* 20 (1): 7–22.

Salomon, Frank. 2018. *At the Mountain's Altar: Anthropology of Religion in an Andean Community*. New York: Routledge.

Sanabria, Harry. 2016. *Anthropology of Latin America and the Caribbean*. New York: Routledge.

Sanders, T. G. 1984. "Peru's Population in the 1980s." *UFSI Rep.* 27 (December): 1–9.

Sarasota Herald Tribune. 1982. "255 Jail Inmates Freed in Assault." March 4, 1982. https://news.google.com/newspapers?nid=1755&dat=19820304&id=Gr4qAAAAIBAJ&sjid=HmgEAAAAIBAJ&pg=2752,1423715.

Scarritt, Arthur. 2012. "State of Discord: The Historic Reproduction of Racism in Highland Peru." *Postcolonial Studies* 15 (1): 23–44.

Seligman, Linda. 1995. *Between Reform and Revolution: Political Struggles in the Andes, 1969–1991*. Stanford, CA: Stanford University Press.

Servindi. 2010. "Perú: Seven Years after the Truth and Reconciliation Commission." Servindi, September 11, 2010. https://www.servindi.org/actualidad/31277.

Shweder, Richard, and Edward Bourne. 1984. "Does the Concept of the Person Vary Cross-Culturally?" In *Culture Theory: Essays on Mind, Self and Emotion*, edited by R. Shweder and Robert Le Vine, 158–99. Cambridge: Cambridge University Press.

Skar, Harold. 1982. *The Warm Valley People: Duality and Reform among the Quechua Indians of Highland Peru*. New York: Columbia University Press.

Slack, Jeremy. 2019. *Deported to Death: How Drug Violence Is Changing Migration on the U.S./Mexico Border*. Oakland: University of California Press.

Smith, Timothy J., and Thomas A. Offit. 2010. "Confronting Violence in Postwar Guatemala: An Introduction." *Journal of Latin American and Caribbean Anthropology* (April). https://www.doi.org/10.1111/j.1935-4940.2010.01060.x.

Spivak, Gayatri Chakravorty. 1988. "Can the Subaltern Speak?" In *Marxism and the Interpretation of Culture*, edited by Cary Nelson and Lawrence Grossbert, 271–313. Basingstoke, UK: Macmillan.

Starn, Orin. 1992. "Missing the Revolution: Anthropologists and the War in Peru." In *Rereading Anthropology*, edited by G. Marcus, 152–80. Durham, NC: Duke University Press.

———. 1994. "Rethinking the Politics of Anthropology: The Case of the Andes." *Current Anthropology* 35 (1): 13–38.

———. 1995a. "Maoism in the Andes: The Communist Party of Peru—Shining Path and the Refusal of History." *Journal of Latin American Studies* 27 (2): 399–421.

———. 1995b. "To Revolt against the Revolution: War and Resistance in Peru's Andes." *Current Anthropology* 10 (4): 547–80.

———. 1999. *Nightwatch: The Politics of Protest in the Andes*. Durham, NC: Duke University Press.

Starn, Orin, and Miguel La Serna. 2019. *The Shining Path: Love, Madness, and Revolution in the Andes*. New York: W. W. Norton.

Stepan, Alfred. 1978. *The State and Society: Peru in Comparative Perspective*. Princeton, NJ: Princeton University Press.

Stern, Steve J. 1982. *Peru's Indian Peoples and the Challenge of Spanish Conquest*. Madison: University of Wisconsin Press.

———. 1987. "Age of Andean Insurrection 1742–1782: A Reappraisal." In *Resistance, Rebellion, and Consciousness in the Andean Peasant World 18th to 20th Centuries*, edited by Steve Stern, 34–93. Madison: University of Wisconsin Press.

———, ed. 1998. *Shining and Other Paths: War and Society in Peru, 1980–1995*. Durham, NC: Duke University Press.

Strong, Simon. 1992. *Shining Path: The World's Deadliest Revolutionary Force*. London: HarperCollins.

Tait, Sue. 2008. "Pornographies of Violence? Internet Spectatorship on Body Horror." *Critical Studies in Media Communication* 25 (1): 91–111. https://doi/10.1080/15295030701851148.

Taylor, Adam. 2020. "Peru Had Three Presidents in One Week. Now It Has Four Months to Fix the System." *Washington Post*, November 20, 2020. https://www.washington-post.com/world/2020/11/20/peru-third-president-francisco-sagasti/.

Taylor, C. L., and M. C. Hudson, eds. 1972. *World Handbook of Political and Social Indicators*, 2nd ed. New Haven, CT: Yale University Press.

Tegel, Simeon. 2018, "Corruption Scandals Have Ensnarled 3 Peruvian Presidents." *Washington Post*, August 12, 2018. https://www.washingtonpost.com/world/the_americas/corruption-scandals-have-ensnared-3-peruvian-presidents-now-the-whole-political-system-could-change/2018/08/11/0cd43ab0-9a82-11e8-a8d8-9b4c13286d6b_story.html.

Telesur. 2018. "Campesino Communities in Peru in Their Struggle against Mining." Last updated July 16, 2018. https://www.telesurenglish.net/news/Campesino-Communities-in-Peru-in-Their-Struggle-Against-Mining-20180716-0016.html.

Theidon, Kimberly. 2003. "Disarming the Subject: Remembering the War and Imagining Citizenship in Peru." *Cultural Critique* 54:67–87.

———. 2004. *Entre Prójimos: El Conflicto Armado Interno y La Política de la Reconciliación en el Perú*. Lima: Instituto de Estudios Peruanos.

———. 2006. "Justice in Transition: The Micropolitics of Reconciliation in Postwar Peru." *Journal of Conflict Resolution* 50 (3): 433–57.

———. 2007. "Gender in Transition: Common Sense, Women and War." *Journal of Human Rights* 6:453–78.

———. 2010. "Histories of Innocence: Post-War Stories in Peru." In *Beyond the Toolkit: Rethinking the Paradigm of Transitional Justice*, edited by Rosalind Shaw, Lars Waldorf, and Pierre Hazan, 92–110. Palo Alto: Stanford University Press.

———. 2013. *Intimate Enemies: Violence and Reconciliation in Peru*. Philadelphia: University of Pennsylvania Press.

Thoma, Mark. 2006. "History of the Car Bomb: The Poor Man's Air Force." Last updated April 16, 2006. http://economistsview.typepad.com/economistsview/2006/04/history_of_the__1.html.

Transparency International. 2004. *Global Corruption Report*. Sterling, VA: Pluto Press.

Triscritti, Fiorella. 2012. "The Criminalization of Anti-mining Social Protest in Peru." *State of the Planet*, September 10, 2012. https://news.climate.columbia.edu/2012/09/10/peru-mining/.

Tula, María Elena, and Lynn Stephen. 1994. *Hear My Testimony: María Teresa Tula, Human Rights Activist of El Salvador*. Boston: South End Press.

Ulfe, María Eugenia. 2011. *Cajones de Memoria. La Historia Reciente del Perú a Través de los Retablos Andinos*. Lima: Fondo Editorial de Pontificia Universidad Católica del Perú.

Ulfe, María Eugenia, and Silvia Romeo. 2021. "Género y Violencia: Desmontando el Perfil de Victima del Informe Final de la Comisión de la Verdad y Reconciliación en Perú." In *Comisiones de la Verdad y Género en Países del Sur Global Miradas Decoloniales, Retrospectivas y Prospectiva*, edited by Diana Marcela Gómez Correal, Angélica Fabiola Bernal Olarte, Juliana González Villamizar, María Mónica Manjarrés Ramírez, Diana María Montealegue Mongrovejo, 161–204. Bogotá: Universidad de los Andes Colombia.

Ulfe, María Eugenia, Vera Lucía Ríos, and Mariana Ortega Breña. 2016. "Toxic Memories? The DINCOTE Museum in Lima, Peru." *Latin American Perspectives* 43(6):27–40.

United States Institute of Peace. 2001. "Truth Commission: Peru 01." Truth Commission Digital Collection. Last modified July 13, 2001. https://www.usip.org/publications/2001/07/truth-commission-peru-01.

van Dun, Mirella. 2009. *Cocaleros: Violence, Drugs and Social Mobilization in the Post-Conflict Upper Huallaga Valley, Peru.* Amsterdam: Rozenberg Publishers.

van Kessel, J. 2001. "El Ritual Mortuorio de los Aymara de Tarapacá Como Vivencia y Crianza de la Vida." *Chungará (Arica)* 33:221–34.

Van Vleet, Krista A. 2008. *Performing Kinship: Narrative, Gender, and the Intimacies of Power in the Andes.* Austin: University of Texas Press.

———. 2019. *Hierarchies of Care: Girls, Motherhood, and Inequality in Peru.* Urbana: University of Illinois Press.

Velasco, Juan. 1841–1844. *Historia del Reino de Quito en la América Meridional: La Historia Antigua 1841.* Quito: Imprenta del Gobierno por Suarez de Valdés. http://bibliotecadigital.aecid.es/bibliodig/es/consulta/registro.cmd?id=520.

Vincent, Susan. 2016. "Mobility of the Elderly in Peru: Life Course, Labour and the Rise of a Pensioner Economy in a Peruvian Peasant Community." *Critique of Anthropology* 36 (4): 380–96.

Waterston, Alisse. 2014. *My Father's Wars: Migration, Memory, and the Violence of a Century.* New York: Routledge.

Webb, Adam K. 2009. *A Path of Our Own: An Andean Village and Tomorrow's Economy of Values.* Wilmington, DE: Intercollegiate Studies Institute.

Webb, Richard, and Graciela Fernández Baca. 1990. *Almanaque Estadístocio: Perú en Numeros 1990.* Lima: Cuánto S.A.

Weismantel, Mary. 2001. *Cholas and Pishtacos.* Chicago: University of Chicago Press.

Whitaker, Arthur Preston. 1941. *The Huancavelica Mercury Mine: A Contribution to the History of the Bourbon Renaissance in the Spanish Empire*, Harvard Historical Monographs 16. Cambridge, MA: Harvard University Press.

Wibbelsman, Michelle. 2019. "Northern Andean Cosmology and Otavalan Hip Hop." In *The Andean World*, edited by Linda J. Seligman and Kathleen S. Fine-Dare, 128–42. New York: Routledge.

Wilson, Fiona. 2009. "Violence, Identity and (In)security: Experiencing the Maoist Insurgency in Peru." *IDS Bulletin* 40 (2): 54–61.

Wissler, Holly. 2009. "Grief-Singing and the Camera: The Challenges of Ethics of Documentary Production in an Indigenous Andean Community." *Ethnomusicology Forum* 18 (1): 37–53.

World Bank. 2018. "The World Bank in Peru." Last updated September 26, 2018. https://www.worldbank.org/en/country/peru/overview.

Yashar, Deborah. 1998. "Contesting Citizenship: Indigenous Movements and Democracy in Latin America." *Comparative Politics* 31(1): 23–42.

Yezer, Caroline. 2008. "Who Wants to Know? Rumors, Suspicions, and Opposition to Truth-telling in Ayacucho." *Latin American and Caribbean Ethnic Studies* 3(3):271–89.

———. 2013. "Del Machismo y el Machu-Qarismo: Derechos Humanos en un Ayacucho Desmilitarizado." In *Las Formas del Recuerdo: Etnografías de la Violencia Política en el Perú*, edited by Ponciano Del Pino and Caroline Yezer, 237–70. Lima: Instituto de Estudios Peruanos.

Yon, Ana J. 2014. "Sexuality, Social Inequalities, and Sexual Vulnerability among Low-Income Youth in the City of Ayacucho, Peru." PhD diss., Columbia University.

Zapata, Ivan Ramírez and Rogelio Scott-Insúa. 2019. "From Victims to Beneficiaries: Shaping Postconflict Subjects through State Reparations in Peru." *Latin American Perspectives* Issue 228 46(5):158–73.

Zinecker, Heidrun. 2007. "From Exodus to Exitus: Causes of Post-War Violence in El Salvador by Heidrun Zinecker." Peace Research Institute Frankfurt Reports No. 80. https://www.files.ethz.ch/isn/55174/prif80.pdf.

Zuidema, Tom. 1990. *Inca Civilization in Cuzco*. Austin: University of Texas Press.

INDEX

Abd, Rodrigo, 195
abduction, 10, 131, 187, 205, 213
Accomarca maassacre, 98, 248n18
ADEVRA, 179
Africans, 6, 257n7
Agrarian Reform, 50–52, 54–55, 221, 246n6, 265n1
Agüero, José Carlos, 54, 198
Allen, Catherine J., 38
alpacas, 36–37
Amazon: coffee cultivation, 122, 125; genocide, 185; mining and oil, 208; Indigenous peoples, 131; violence, 131
amnesia, 13
amnesty law, 147–48
Andahuaylas: Agrarian Reform, 246n6; anti-mining protests, 209; climate, 94–95; Quechua, 150; revolution, 247n9; schools, 113–14; water, 180
Andeanism, 32, 242n5
Andes: communal labor, 242; family networks, 162–63; identity, 230; mining and oil, 208; mud-brick houses, 157; reciprocal exchange, 224; settlement patterns, 139; state-funded schools, 199; temporality, 227; vertical ties, 220
animals: overview, 35–38; dangerous, 81; NGOs and, 153; resettlement and, 163–65; social relations and, 224–25; theft of, 67–68, 212; torture of, 249n1. *See also specific animals*
Apurímac, 10, 51, 66, 246n7

Apurímac Ferrum Company, 209, 261–62
Apurímac River Valley, 66–67, 73
apus, 93, 95, 224, 240n40
Argentina, 257n10
Arguedas, José María, 6
Army Intelligence Service (SIE), 131
artists, 11–12, 239n33
Asháninka, 131–32, 157, 185, 207
assassinations, 9, 51, 56, 58, 67, 247n11, 248n20
Atahualpa, 6
Atahualpa, Juan Santos, 236n12
Ayacucho: Agrarian Reform, 51; CVR report, 188; death tolls, 56, 247n13; poverty, 246n7; terrorism, 183; victims, 10
ayllus, 50, 218–19, 246n5
ayni, 31–32, 218, 230

Bailey, Claudia Paz y Paz, 184
Barnet, Miguel, 240n42
Barrios Altos massacre, 148
Barrios de Chungara, Domitila, 241n44
Behar, Ruth, 16
Belaúnde Terry, Fernando, 50, 56
Bella Vista, 139–40
Berg, Ronald, 54
Beverley, John, 19, 241
Boesten, Jelke: conciliation, 265n2; gendered violence, 79–80, 98–99, 105, 221, 222, 257n8; war and rupture, 228
Bolivia, 205, 211
Bourque, Susan C., 56

www.ingramcontent.com/pod-product-compliance
Lightning Source LLC
Chambersburg PA
CBHW020829270326
41928CB00006B/468